THE FOREMOST GUIDE
TO
UNCLE SAM
COLLECTIBLES

Gerald E. Czulewicz Sr.

COLLECTOR BOOKS
A Division of Schroeder Publishing Co., Inc.

The current values in this book should be used only as a guide. They are not intended to set prices, which vary from one section of the country to another. Auction prices as well as dealer prices vary greatly and are affected by condition as well as demand. Neither the Author nor the Publisher assumes responsibility for any losses that might be incurred as a result of consulting this guide.

Searching for a Publisher?

We are always looking for knowledgable people considered to be experts within their fields. If you feel that there is a real need for a book on your collectible subject and have a large comprehensive collection, contact Collector Books.

Cover design: Beth Summers
Book design: Joyce Cherry

Dedication

I would like to dedicate this publication to all patriotic Americans who truly know and understand what an opportunity it is to be an American, and to all of my fellow collectors, dealers, and historians who have shared with me, similar pathways in their own individual pursuits; and to all the men and women of the U. S. Armed Forces; past, present, and future.

On a more personal note, this book is most specifically dedicated in honor and remembrance of my father, Stephen Raymond Czulewicz, who departed from us much too young and much too soon; to my mother, Julia Gutowski Czulewicz, whom I love so dearly for all that she has been to me as a mother and a friend; and to my wife, Barbara Jean, who is most deserving of all the love and recognition I could possibly give her.

Acknowledgments

Over the past 35 years of collecting and researching Uncle Sam and other Patriotic Americana, I have had the opportunity to experience some of the most fun-fulled times and places, and have developed everlasting friendships and acquaintanceship with a countless number of very special and truly supportive people. Most all of them came to know and understand my pursuit and continued for years to contact me whenever they had something to add to my collection, from little tidbits of information to major acquisitions. They all have my equal heart-felt thanks for helping me complete this first and *Foremost Reference Guide to Uncle Sam Collectibles.*

Before I begin to befittingly acknowledge so many, I first would like to begin to express my gratitude and appreciation to Patricia Lee Porter for her six years of assisting me in cataloging items and compiling reference material in the process of writing this book. As my secretary, assistant, and friend, she truly put her heart into giving me her professional best. As for the testing of my memory regarding the multitude of others that I will always be grateful to, without order of preference, I would like to say thank you to the following:

My oldest brother, David Czulewicz, who has always been an inspiration to me and was partly responsible for my initial interest in pursuing Uncle Sam material;

Gerald E. Czulewicz II, Minneapolis, MN
Sue Huffaker-Czulewicz, Minneapolis, MN
Margot Czulewicz, Minneapolis, MN
Timothy Kamholz, Erie, PA
Joyce Regenauer, North St. Paul, MN
William Sablon, Elizabeth City, NC
Charles Jackson, Elgin, IL
Louis Caropreso, Lee, MA
William White, Erie, PA
John and Gene Anderson, River Forest, IL
L. Don Andrews, Sioux Falls, SD
Little Jimmy Engle, Mound, MN
Jean & Bud Frantzen, Rockford, IL
Jack Rohr, M.D., Rolling Meadows, IL
Angelo Pastor, Rolling Meadows, IL
Gordon & Betty Fraser, Eden Prairie, MN
Raymond Veloff, Middleton, WI
Al & Gene Grzegorzewski, Harbor Creek, PA
Robert & Vi Gunn, Olathe, KS
Willard Gordon, Fallbrook, CA
Truett Lawson, Stillwater, MN
Everett Raymond Kinstler, New York, NY
Neil Lanigan, Philadelphia, PA
Jim & Betsy Flanigan, Ypsilanti, MI
Wad & Caroline Miller, Two Harbors, MN
Cornell Norby, Newport Beach, CA
Gary & Karlene Ophaug, Edina, MN
Raymond Steele, Great Falls, MT
Demetrios Anthony Nikolaou, Minneapolis, MN
Victor & Dorothy Stein, Wayzata, MN
Donald Stolz, Excelsior, MN
Terry Vose, Boston, MA
William Vose, Boston, MA
William Weschler, Washington DC
Jerry Kranz, Bayport, MN
James Bailey, Minneapolis, MN
Richard Gurley, Bethel, MN
Joseph Camardo, Palmetto, FL
Wayne & Lucy Ebeling, Isanti, MN
Daniel Clinton Hynes, Chicago, IL
Stan & Sue Slocum, Edina, MN
Fred Krach, Downers Grove, IL
Lynn Luber, Wayzata, MN
Steve Lamazow, M.D., Montclair, NJ
William Krais, South Lee, MA
Timothy Lawrence, Washington DC
Blair (Buzz) Merwin, Maple Grove, MN
Thomas H. Murphy, Minneapolis, MN
Mike & Betty Nickol, Bremen, IN

James Peterson; Minneapolis, MN
Jerry Goroski, Great Falls, MT
Ronald Streit, Princeton, MN
Chuck & Karen Steele, Stacy, MN
Carl Williams, M.D., Fort Smith, AR
Frank's Antiques, Hilliard, FL
Steve Gronowski, Barrington Hills, IL
Dunbars Gallery, Milford, ME
Betty G. Williams, Worthington, OH
Mary Mady, Coon Rapids, MN
Marcia Flicker, Oak Grove, MN
Doreen Douvier, Anoka, MN
Dan Innotti, Bloomfield Hills, MI
Rosalie Stolinski, Toms River, NJ
Sylvia O'Malley, Oshkosh, WI
Thomas Czulewicz, Virginia Beach, VA
Francis Czulewicz, Claysville, PA
Joseph Marusik, Minneapolis, MN
Clement Conger, Washington, DC
Nancy Druckman, New York, NY
Peter Rathbone, New York, NY
Ed & Rena Coen, Minneapolis, MN
John Lang, Atty., Minneapolis, MN
James Lang, Mound, MN
Cordula Soeffker, Minneapolis, MN
Edwin & Helen Page, Erie, PA
John Vanco, Erie, PA
Donald L. Evans, Madison, WI
Paul Flick, Minneapolis, MN
Terry Peyer, Brooklyn Center, MN
Margot Neilsen, Palm Desert, CA
U.S. Army Recruiting Station, Duluth, MN
Shoney's Restaurant, Gaffney, SC
Lynn & Gertie Tupper, Minneapolis, MN
George Theofiles, New Freedom, PA
Peter Todd, Trenton, NE
William Masuda, Richmond, VA
Daniel Zivko, Kirtland, OH
Rick Davis, Deer Lake, MN
Koehler Brothers Antiques, Lafayette, IN
Mary Anderson, Minneapolis, MN
Michael Wodnick, St. Paul, MN
Lee's Antiques, Erie, PA
Poor Richard's Antiques, Bethel, MN
Charles Hudgins, St. Paul, MN
Blue Dolphin Antiques, Lincolnville, ME
James McNaughton (deceased), Palm Springs, CA
Sascha Brastoff (deceased), West Los Angeles, CA
Sam Chernoff (deceased), St. Louis Park, MN

Contents

To The Reader

I truly hope that this book will help to make you aware of the great variety of Uncle Sam items that are out there, readily available to add to your existing collection or to inspire many of you to begin a specific collection of Uncle Sam. For those of you who go to garage sales and flea markets as well as those who frequent the finest shows and antique shops in the country, after you have read this book I believe you will begin to notice and recognize Uncle Sam objects as you never have before. There is no doubt in my mind that the use of the image of Uncle Sam will continue for many generations to come. Therefore there is an ongoing "new" collectible market to look forward to as well as the existing market for the old or antique Uncle Sam collectibles. Other than the fun and profit you can experience by way of collecting Uncle Sam items, you will also gain a vast knowledge of American history.

Preface

Every collector, historian, antique dealer, art dealer, if not simply everyone, most likely has experienced a passion for one specific area or subject in the pursuit of their hobby or profession. In my particular case, I was confronted with this experience at the very early age of 13. Rambling through the local library while doing research for a school paper, I was sidetracked by some very interesting and somewhat rare early images of Uncle Sam.

These images so deeply stirred my interests to where I immediately began to search for additional images and information on Uncle Sam.

That momentary distraction in the library was the beginning of a 35-year pursuit of the knowledge and understanding of just exactly where Uncle Sam truly fit into American history and into the minds of most Americans. In the early years of my research, I unexpectedly experienced the passionate desire of possession and became one of the most intense collectors anyone could ever imagine.

I soon came to accept the fact that there was nothing wrong with this type of passion as long as it had a sense of direction and an eventual moment of fruition. Hence, to be totally honest, this book has that very special meaning for me. It represents the moment of fruition which also includes the opportunity I have always wanted, to be able to share all of the knowledge and information with as broad a cross section of Americans that I could possibly reach. I have come to believe that, other than the American eagle, there is no single image entering into more different areas of collecting than does Uncle Sam. Therefore, I hope collectors and historians of specific areas of interest find some truth in how I believe the information and reference material contained in this volume does, in fact, have an application to practically everyone.

I sincerely believe I have put forth my best effort to compile the most accurate and complete information source that I possibly could on this subject. There have been many areas of personal debate and uncertainty to deal with in relation to exact periods of time, authenticity, and price.

Just like all of the historians and collectors, published or not, who have preceded me, and from whom I have acquired a great amount of my knowledge and information, I may in some way, shape, or form, be found to be in error. If this should be the case, I do apologize for whatever misinformation that could lead to this conclusion. Setting this possibility aside, I simply hope you, the reader or user of this reference guide, will get at least a fraction of the enjoyment I have experienced in the process of finally bringing this information to you.

Introduction

From the very beginning of my pursuit of information on the subject of Uncle Sam, one of the most constantly confusing and somewhat controversial issues was, in fact, just exactly who is Uncle Sam? Most previously published sources reflect upon the story of Sam Wilson of Troy, New York. During the war of 1812 and for many years thereafter, Samuel Wilson was a meat packer and a purveyor of goods to the U. S. Army. Crates prepared for shipment and delivery to U. S. Army troops were required to be stamped "U S." Direct recipients of these goods from Sam Wilson eventually began to refer to Mr. Wilson as Uncle Sam since his initials in that context were on his goods. However, one of the confusing aspects of Uncle Sam's true identity extends from the different illustrated images symbolically representative of Uncle Sam in early political cartoons. The other being the existence of, or as some might believe, the preexistence of Brother Jonathan either being the original Uncle Sam or having held the equally symbolic position, that of an Uncle Sam. To many, this may be a moot point, but to those collectors and historians who have a need to know, I hope to bring some additional clarity through my opinion on these two areas in question.

Political cartoonists of the late eighteenth and early nineteenth centuries depicted Brother Jonathan as one of the original "Yankee Doodles." "Yankee" was a name used by the Massachusetts Indians in reference to the early English colonists as early as the 1750s during the French and Indians wars. "Doodle" or a "Doodler" was a jack-of-all-trades that would travel throughout the colonies offering a variety of services. Brother Jonathan was also referred to as "Yankee Jonathan." The early cartoonists chose to utilize Brother Jonathan symbolically as a political upstart and issue maker during this period of trying times between the colonists and Great Britain. It is also often suggested that Brother Jonathan was the younger brother of, or possibly the son of, Great Britain's politically satirical "John Bull." Whereas the strength of the character of "John Bull" representing Great Britain continued to be utilized by political cartoonists to this present day, Brother Jonathan fell somewhat by the wayside in the mid-nineteenth century mainly because of his lack of character and the necessary degree of dignity to properly symbolically represent a country and its people that had a much greater sense of dignity and pride, that being the United States of America.

Though I am, without question, accepting the existence of Brother Jonathan and that he in fact symbolically existed prior to Uncle Sam, I simply want to differentiate between the two characters and their individual identities. Brother Jonathan was periodically illustrated wearing red-and-white striped pants, a tailcoat, and a tophat, but he was also depicted in a variety of other clothing, some of which had no reflection whatsoever on what is the accepted image and attire of Uncle Sam. Most importantly is to simply establish the fact that the two had existed together during the same period of time. One of the best images I have personally discovered illustrating their individual identities is a fine hand-colored impression of

☞ **Plate 1. Uncle Sam with La Grippe – Broadside**
Hand-colored impression of the lithograph published by Henry R. Robinson, circa 1838. Size: 17½″ x 25½″. Condition: Very Good.

the lithograph published by Henry R. Robinson (Plate 1) in approximately 1838. This cartoon depicts Uncle Sam ailing, wearing a robe made up of the American flag and a red nightcap with the word "Liberty" on the headband. This broadside deals with Andrew Jackson's involvement with the collapse of the Bank of the United States. In this cartoon Secretary of State Martin Van Buren is dressed and referred to as "Aunt Mattie," George Washington's head breaks and falls from the pedestal, and the eagle mentions flying to Texas to avoid starvation. While Uncle Sam is seated in his "woe," Brother Jonathan is outside the window discussing Uncle Sam's condition with Dr. Biddle in hopes that he may come up with a remedy. In this cartoon Uncle Sam is clearly representing the United States government and Brother Jonathan, on the outside, is clearly representing the "people." It should be noted that this 1838 image, as well as several others discovered to exist shortly before and after, is ample proof that the cartoonist Frank H.T. Bellow did not create the first published image of Uncle Sam. His did not appear until 1852.

In addition to this particular cartoon of 1838, several other cartoons illustrating the various attires of Brother Jonathan, from as late as 1859 (Plates 2, 3, 4), are herein included. However, Thomas Nast, one of the greatest and most prolific political cartoonists of all time, continued to illustrate Uncle Sam and/or Brother Jonathan as "Yankee Doodle" confusingly clothed similar to how he, during the same period of time, clothed his illustrations of Uncle Sam. A set of four full-color stone lithographs by Thomas Nast (Plates 5, 6, 7, 8) from the early 1870s clearly depict Yankee Doodle in this attire. An additional image (Plate 9) of Uncle Sam by Mr. Nast, from a September 1872 issue of *Harper's Weekly* shows the similarity in attire to that of Brother Jonathan, the two notable differences being the absence of a feather in Uncle Sam's hat and the addition of a goatee to Uncle Sam's chin.

In relationship to Uncle Sam's goatee there are a variety of stories accounting for when and why Uncle Sam began wearing a goatee. The actuality of his being a symbolic cartoon character, the illustrators or cartoonists from this period of time are obviously most responsible for the addition of the goatee. The reason I chose to believe they began to illustrate Uncle Sam with the goatee is based on the story of Abraham Lincoln as a senator running for office of President of the United States as a clean-shaven, beardless politician. During this period of time, in many circles it was somewhat considered that you could not trust a clean shaven, beardless gentleman, let alone a politician. The story is that Mr. Lincoln, during his campaign for the presidency had received a letter from a young 12- or 13-year-old girl who had pointed out to Senator Lincoln that if he would like to increase his chances of being successful in the election that he should grow a beard. This letter, or the story of it, became public knowledge during this time. Senator Lincoln, being graciously thankful for this young girl's advice, grew a beard. Also, during the Lincoln-Douglas debate it was stated by Mr. Douglas of Mr. Lincoln, "How can anyone trust a fair-faced man?" Because of the popularity, or publicity created by the Lincoln-Douglas debate and the fact that Lincoln had shortly thereafter grown his beard, it seemed that most all of the political cartoonists of this time began to likewise grow a beard on Uncle Sam.

Trying to establish the actual individual identities of Uncle Sam, Yankee Doodle, and Brother Jonathan does, for me, have a very significant purpose. I'm attempting to do this as simplistically as I possibly can, sparing the reader the quantity of in depth historic data surrounding this issue. However, to any collector or historian, myself included, it is very necessary information. How would one know if a folk art wood carving, whirligig, weathervane, or primitive painting was depicting Uncle Sam or Brother Jonathan. If it were an advertisement or early broadside without descriptive copy identifying the subjects, once again how would you distinguish the difference. Only the artist from that period of time would, in fact, know who he/she was depicting. Being that the images of Uncle Sam, Yankee Doodle, and Brother Jonathan could only be acquired by being exposed to the multitude of

THE WAR IN EUROPE.

JOHN BULL. "What! fighting again! I suppose I must thrash some of the Fellows."

🖙 **Plate 2. Brother Jonathan**

variations created by the cartoonists and illustrators published in the illustrated periodicals of the early to mid-nineteenth century, I believe that the end product or work of art of any artist during this time, whether an academic, itinerate, or folk artist, would have been directly influenced by those published images.

In my early years of collecting, I myself had fallen victim to my own ignorance on this subject. Many pieces that I had acquired as "Uncle Sam" related items were in fact not Uncle Sam. In some instances, they weren't even Brother Jonathan or Yankee Doodle. Sometimes that passion that I had for new acquisitions led me into a temporary state of undisciplined wishful thinking. I hope

Plate 3. Brother Jonathan

to at least reduce the odds of your having to experience similar situations of disappointment. This publication may not contain the absolute best examples of what exists in every category of the imagery of Uncle Sam. However, I feel certain that it must be considered the most concise attempt at doing so, to date. I have tried to include examples in practically every area imaginable, in one form or another, for collectors and historians alike.

Included in this text you will also find a section of artists' biographies, artists who I have discovered or who had commonly been known to have created images of Uncle Sam. In most instances these are brief biographical sketches to help the reader with the placement of time and place of an Uncle Sam item inscribed

by or attributed to one of these artists. I truly hope you find this section helpful in your personal pursuit for additional information for whatever specific area your collecting interests may be.

Though I have often been referred to as a "serious collector," I never particularly cared for the use of the word "serious." In my 35 years of collecting Uncle Sam related items and material I have had the good fortune to meet some of the most wonderful people from every walk of life and profession imaginable. I had some of the greatest times, and will continue to have some of the happiest memories because of them. It's these people and these memories that make collecting anything a worthwhile pursuit.

Plate 4. Brother Jonathan

Set of four colored chromolithographs by Thomas Nast, published in 1876 by *Harper's Weekly* as a supplement titled, "Nast's Almanac." Extremely Rare & Desirable.

Plate 5. Number One
Yankee Doodle riding a pony in front of a hat-tossing crowd. 10" x 8". Condition: Excellent. **$250.00 – 300.00.**

Plate 6. Number Two
Yankee Doodle on a pony in front of an arch labeled, "United States." 10" x 8". Condition: Excellent. **$250.00 – 300.00.**

Plate 7. Number Three "Yankee Doodle"
Seated with his feet resting on a pillar, smoking. Above the door behind him is a sign saying, "White House." 10" x 8". Condition: Excellent. **$250.00 – 300.00.**

Plate 8. Number Four "Yankee Doodle"
A paper marked, "English Rule" in the waste-basket. 10" x 8". Condition: Excellent. **$250.00 – 300.00.**

☞ **Plate 9. September 28, 1872**
"News from Vermont & Maine."
Artist: Thomas Nast. **$20.00 –
25.00.**

Dolls and Figurines

The full dimensional imagery of Uncle Sam dolls and figurines was without question originally influenced by the illustrated images of Uncle Sam by a great variety of artists and illustrators of the nineteenth century. Each of these artists had their own individual concept of how Uncle Sam should be illustrated to best comply with the political by-line or storyline— everything from how he was clothed to his facial expressions. These artists influenced the variety of different images utilized by doll and figurine makers, whether mass-produced or in the primitive or folk art sense.

This category of Uncle Sam collectibles has the greatest potential for new discoveries because of the great number of national, as well as regional and local manufacturers who produced in some instances limited quantities of dolls or figurines for a specific occasion or event. The Uncle Sam dolls or figurines can be found made of the finest bisque, porcelain, composition, wood, plaster, papier maché, metal, and other materials.

☜ **Plate 10. Uncle Sam Doll**
Uncle Sam with bisque head, exceptionally fine flesh tones, grayish blond hair and goatee, molded eyebrows, and glass eyes; blue felt jacket with tails, red and white striped tousers, dark blue vest with white stars, white laced shirt and red bow tie, gray velvet hat with dark blue band with thirteen white stars, black boots. Bisque head bears the incised mark "S 1." This doll was made by Schlaggenwald under the manufacturing firm of Haas & Czjzek, in 1892, to be sold at the 1892 – 93 Columbian Exposition. Overall height with hat: 14½". Condition: Excellent. **$2,500.00 – 3,000.00.**

Plate 11. Composition Doll
Uncle Sam with cotton clothing of red, white, and blue. Composition head, stuffed cloth arms, legs, and torso. 12". Circa 1892. Condition: Excellent. **$250.00 – 275.00.**

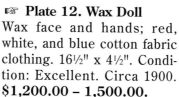

Plate 12. Wax Doll
Wax face and hands; red, white, and blue cotton fabric clothing. 16½" x 4½". Condition: Excellent. Circa 1900. **$1,200.00 – 1,500.00.**

Plate 13. Plastic and Rubber Doll
Moveable arms, hands, feet, legs, and head. Red and white striped pants, blue jacket, white shirt, and red bow tie, on a black plastic stand. Made in Hong Kong by Fun World Inc., 1107 Broadway, New York. 7¾". Condition: Excellent. Circa 1948. **$60.00 – 75.00.**

🐚 **Plate 14. Papier Maché Figure**
Striped pants, blue coat, red vest, blue hat with stars band, on a blue base. Unger Doll and Toy Co., Unger's Cell-U-Pon Toys, Milwaukee, WI. 12". Condition: Very Good. Circa 1890 – 1893. **$250.00 – 300.00.**

☝ **Plate 15. Figurine (Bisque)**
Blue jacket, gray top hat, and red striped pants on a yellow toned base. Embossed "Uncle Sam on base." 8¼" x 3". Condition: Excellent. Circa 1870. **$300.00 – 350.00.**

☞ **Plate 16. Brownie Doll**
Uncle Sam Brownie doll (Palmer Cox) from the 1893 Columbian Exposition. Red and white striped pants and blue tails, striped top hat, holding a blue flag with six stars in the form of the Dipper, painted face. 6½". Circa 1892 – 1893. Condition: Good. **$65.00 – 85.00.**

🦚 **Plate 17. Celluloid Doll**
Full figure of Uncle Sam. 7" x 2¼". Condition: Excellent. Circa 1915 – 1918. **$200.00 – 250.00.**

☞ **Plate 18. Carnival Figurine**
Plaster statue of Uncle Sam rolling up his sleeves, blue base. Three-quarter dimensional. 15¼" x 4¾". Condition: Very Good. Circa 1940. **$90.00 – 115.00.**

☞ **Plate 19. Carnival Figurine**
Plaster statue of Uncle Sam rolling up his sleeves, blue base. Full-dimensional. 15¼" x 4¾". Condition: Very good. Circa 1940. **$115.00 – 130.00.**

👆 **Plate 20. Plastic Doll – Whirligig**
Red and white striped pants, blue jacket, red vest, stars and stripes top hat. Doll's arms swing, holding paper paddles. 14⅞". Condition: Very good. Circa 1942. **$75.00 – 85.00.**

👆 **Plate 21. Flag Holder – Figurine**
Plaster statue with left hand holding a flag pole bearing the American Flag and right hand dropped at his side holding his top hat. Full-color, red, white, and blue and flesh tone paint. 28" x 8½" diameter. Condition: Very Good. Circa 1930. **$500.00 – 600.00.**

👆 **Plate 22. Pewter Santa**
Santa wearing Uncle Sam uniform, holding a striped bag. "History of Santa, Civil War, 1st/500 1660-p, Ltd Ed. Duncan Royal, Copyright 1983" stamped on the bottom. Original label. One of 12 in History of Santa Collection. 2⅞" x 1⅛". Condition: Excellent. **$45.00 – 60.00.**

15

☝ **Plate 23. Figurine – Clay**
Full-color solid fired clay Santa Claus wearing simulated Uncle Sam suit and top hat with basket of toys on back. Maker and artist unknown. 4¾" x 2¾". Condition: Excellent. Circa 1992. **$30.00 – 45.00.**

☝ **Plate 24. Uncle Sam Gnome**
Typical Tom Clark gnome wearing a dark blue Uncle Sam type hat with three white stars. Full-color molded composition. Artist: Tom Clark Studios. 6½" x 4½". Condition: Excellent. Circa 1985. **$35.00 – 50.00.**

🐾 **Plate 25. Circus Clown**
Composition head, arms, and legs, cloth body. Original costume. Made for the Shrine Circus in 1944. 18" tall. Condition: Excellent. **$350.00 – 400.00.**

📖 Plate 26. Display Item
Uncle Sam jointed cardboard figure, ¾ life-size, full color. Artist and maker unknown. 55" x 15¼". Circa 1944. Condition: Excellent. **$135.00 – 150.00.**

☞ Plate 27. Marionette – Puppet
Window display item. Composition and wood jointed figure of a young Uncle Sam dressed in a metallic threaded red, white, and blue Uncle Sam suit with red, white, and blue metallic threaded and sequined top hat and metallic speckled shoes. Maker: Macy & Company. Overall dimensions: 36" tall. Condition: Very Good. Circa 1944. **$150.00 – 200.00.**

☞ Plate 28. Bicentennial Stuffed Doll
Uncle Sam with red and white striped pants, blue coat, and red and white striped hat with blue top and brim. Fake fur hair and felt eyes, official Bicentennial ribbon sewn to chest of Uncle Sam. 63" tall. Condition: Very good. Circa 1976. **$200.00 – 250.00.**

↤ **Plate 29. Elephant and Donkey Stuffed Dolls**
The Republican elephant and the Democratic donkey, dressed in Uncle Sam attire. 1976 Bicentennial stuffed animals. Manufactured by Animal Fair Inc., Chanhassen, Minnesota. Each 27" tall. Condition: Very good. Circa 1976. **$150.00 – 200.00.**

Banks

The most rare and most desirable Uncle Sam bank is the 1886 Shepherd cast-iron bank. Hence, this is also the most heavily copied or reproduced bank of all the Uncle Sam banks. The "Book of Knowledge" Uncle Sam bank, being a true replica of the original has become more desirable in recent years because of its quality and its limited production. Beware of the faking and aging of the heavily mass produced "Taiwan" and "Hong Kong" reproductions of this bank. If you have the slightest doubt in the process of purchasing one of these banks consult with a knowledgeable toy bank dealer or collector before making a final purchase.

Other Uncle Sam banks of cast iron, tin, porcelain, pottery, plastics, and other materials can be found in a variety of design concepts and price ranges.

Regarding original paint, rust, chips, cracks, or the like, condition will most affect the value of the bank.

↤ **Plate 30. Original Metal Uncle Sam Bank — Cast Iron**
Pat., June 8, 1886, by Shepherd. Full figure of Uncle Sam, a blue umbrella in his left hand, which fits into a hole on the base of the bank. A red suitcase by his right foot is labeled,"U. S." Red base of the bank pictures the American eagle with a blue banner reading, "Uncle Sam" above it. On either side of the base is marked, "bank." A keyed opening is in the rear of the base, the bottom of the base has twenty-four ¼" holes. Put a coin in his hand, push the button behind him, and the suitcase opens to receive the coin, as his mouth opens and his goatee wobbles. 11" x 4¾" x 3⅞". Condition: Very good. **$4,500.00 – 6,500.00.**

☞ **Plate 31. Cast Iron Bank**

Reproduction of Plate 30 with the following differences: Uncle Sam's feet are closer together, straighter, with the right foot further forward, yet not quite even with the left. The umbrella is green and does not fit into a hole in the base. The eagle on the front of the base is painted gold, the banner red with gold lettering. The bottom of the base does not contain the ¼" holes, and the opening to remove the money is on the bottom. The bottom is marked, "Taiwan." Push button on base to drop the coin. The removal slot on the bottom makes this bank slightly higher, otherwise the measurements are identical. Circa 1974 to present. Condition: Very good. **$15.00 – 20.00.**

☝ **Plate 32. "Book of knowledge" Cast Iron Bank**

Almost identical to the original 1886 cast iron bank, except the background of the banner on the base of this bank is blue, the eagle is not solid gold, it contains some red, and the underside of the base is marked, "Reproduced from original in collection of the Book of Knowledge. Made in U. S. A." in the casting. The coin is dropped by pushing button on base. 11" x 4¾" x 3⅞". Condition: Excellent. Pat., Feb. 2, 1932. **$500.00 – 600.00.** *Note: This bank has been rapidly increasing in value in recent years.

☞ **Plate 33. Plastic Bank**

Image and function are the same as the original 1886 cast iron version. Uncle Sam is red, white, and blue with a gray hat with blue band containing gold stars. The umbrella is blue and affixed to his leg. The top and bottom of this bank are green, the center red with a gold eagle and gold banner. The lettering of "bank" on either side is gold. The coin removal hole is a twist-off. Made in Hong Kong. 8¾" x 2" x 4¼" x 3⁵⁄₁₆". Circa 1952. Condition: Excellent. **$30.00 – 40.00.**

☞ **Plate 35.**
Cast Iron Mechanical Bank
"Uncle Bugs." American Legends Uncle Bugs. Produced exclusively for Warner Brothers, This "Original" cast iron mechanical bank was manufactured in mainland China. Bank mechanism works in the same manner as the 1886 "Shepherd" Uncle Sam Bank. 10". 1994. **$150.00 – 200.00**

*Note: This bank may rapidly increase in value because of its limited production and its originality. It's not a reproduction.

👆 **Plate 34. Cast Iron Mechanical Bank**
Uncle Sam in wooden barrel and an Arab with Arab Oil coin receiving barrel between them. Full-color baked paint. Manufactured by John Wright Company. *Note: Only 250 of these banks were produced. Production was stopped for political reasons. Becoming very scarce. Copyright 1975 Wright Cat. No 22-350. 11". Condition: Excellent. **$1,200.00 – 1,500.00.**

👆 **Plate 36.**
"Dairy Cream Bottle Bank"
Glass cream bottle with lock-on stainless steel top with coin-drop slot. Bottle decorated with red, white and blue Uncle Sam waving banner in front of American flag. Half-pint bottle. 4½" high. Manufactured for the Whiterock State Bank of Minnesota. Circa 1954. **$35.00 – 45.00.**

👆 **Plate 37. Tin Hat Bank**
Red, white, and blue metal Uncle Sam hat. Manufactured by Chein. 3¼" x 3¼" x 4⅛". Circa 1952. Condition: Excellent. **$50.00 – 60.00.**

☜ **Plate 38. Ceramic Bank**
Red, white, and blue bust figure of Uncle Sam holding a banner by Geo. Z Lifton. 882 incised on bottom. 7" x 4¾". Condition: Excellent. Circa 1941. **$50.00 – 60.00.**

☞ **Plate 39. Ceramic Bank**
Uncle Sam with his hands grasping his lapels. Red, white, and blue with a gray vest. "Made in Japan – Santa Claus Programs – Imported" on label on bottom. Coin slot in the top of his hat. 6¼" x 4¾" x 2¾". Condition: Excellent. Circa 1955. **$50.00 – 60.00.**

☞ **Plate 40. Pottery Bank**
Uncle Sam with top hat. Olive green. 4½". Circa 1908. Maker unknown. No marks. **$75.00 – 85.00.**

☝ **Plate 41.**
Semiporcelain Bank
White with gold hatband. 4⅛" x 3¼" x 3¼". Condition: Excellent. Spanish American War era, 1898. **$125.00 – 150.00.**

☞**Plate 42. Cash Register Bank**
Uncle Sam's Register Bank, Three Coin Durable Toy and Novelty Company, Madison Avenue, Cleveland, Ohio. Patent applied for 1-42. To open, press here at 00-00. No lettering or labels on either side. On the back is a set of instructions for the bank in faded gold letters. The bottom left has a deposit for paper bills. 5⅞" x 4½" x 5⅛". Circa 1942. Condition: Very good. **$60.00 – 70.00.**

☞**Plate 43. Cash Register Bank**
Identical to Plate 42 with the following exceptions: only the base of the bank is black, the balance is natural tin, lettering on the back is in black. Patent applied for 4-40. Condition: Very good. **$60.00 – 70.00.**

☞**Plate 44. Cash Register Bank**
Uncle Sam's Dime Bank with eagle in gold on the top. Bottom marked, "Durable Toy & Novel, Office, New York City, Factory, Cleveland." Dollar and cents counters. 4½" x 3⅜". Circa 1942. Condition: Very good. **$40.00 – 50.00.**

☞**Plate 45. Cash Register Bank**
Uncle Sam's Nickel Bank with eagle in gold on the top. Bottom marked, "Durable Toy & Novel." Dollar and cents counters. 4½" x 3⅜". Circa 1942. Condition: Very good. **$40.00 – 50.00.**

Toys and Games

The earliest toys or games utilizing the image of Uncle Sam were originally found in the form of folk art. Eventually manufacturers produced a wide variety of tin and wooden toys and graphically illustrated board games and puzzles to instill a sense of patriotism into the minds and hearts of children as well as adults during trying times. From the post Civil War years and the Reconstruction, through the Spanish American War period, and World War II and the Korean War, a new market was continuously being created for Uncle Sam in this area. I personally have found it most interesting how "patriotism" could so playfully be embedded into a child's growth and learning process by way of a toy or game. What's become of this process?

Condition is most important in relationship to prices in this category.

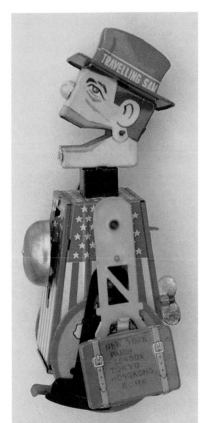

Plate 46. Traveling Sam
Tin wind up toy with bell. Manufactured by: "54" Company, made in Japan. Copyright: 1952. 6⅞". Condition: Excellent. **$375.00 – 450.00.**

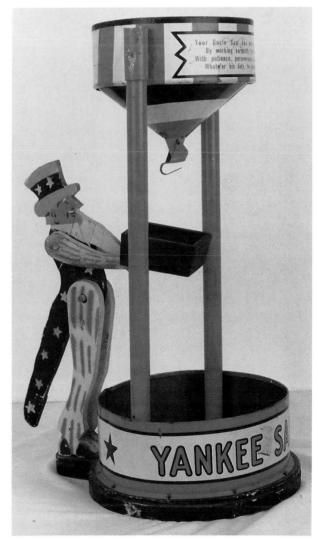

Plate 47. "Yankee Sand Mill"
Wood and metal. 17½" x 11". Condition: Excellent. Circa 1944. **$400.00 – 450.00.**

🐦 **Plate 48. Bicycle Act**
Fully colored red, white, and blue tin mechanical Uncle Sam on bicycle riding on wire suspended on rocking base with wood posts, metal eagles on top. By American Flyer Toy Company. 20½" x 17" x 3". Circa 1915. Condition: Excellent. **$600.00 – 700.00.**

👆 **Plate 49. Paint Set**
"Uncle Sam's Paint Set" by the Master Toy Co., New York, No. 45. Complete set with 16 paints, brush, water tray, and four pictures to paint. Each picture measures 3⅛" x 5¼". Set measures 8½" x 5¼". Circa 1942. Condition: Very good. **$90.00 – 110.00.**

☞ **Plate 50. Paint Set — The American Brilliant Paints**
Box of eight different watercolors. Manufactured by the
American Crayon Company, Sandusky, Ohio. 4⅝" x 5⅞" x
⅜". Condition: Very good. Copyright 1943. **$60.00 – 70.00.**

☜┓ **Plate 51. United States Map Puzzle**
A full-color chromo-lithographic puzzle. Front is map of the
United States of America, reverse is the United States Capi-
tal Building with 36 flags of allied countries. Manufactured
by Milton Bradley Co. Springfield, Mass. Copyright 1914.
Box: 8" x 9¾" x 1½". Very rare. Condition: Very good.
$350.00 – 450.00.

☞ **Plate 52. Jigsaw Puzzle**
"Dissected Map of the United States." Puzzle size:
9¾" x 14¼". Full-color chromo-lithograph on paper
mounted on wood. Box size: 11¾" x 10¼" x ⅞".
Made By Milton Bradley Co., Springfield, MA, USA.
Condition: Very good. Circa 1890. **$450.00 –
500.00.**

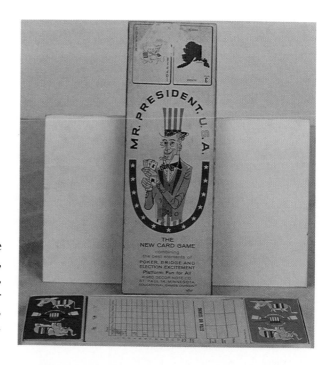

🐚 **Plate 53. Board Game**
"Uncle Sam's Mail" made by Milton Bradley Co., Springfield, MA., USA. Serial No. 4053. 16¼" x 15" x 1¼". Condition: Very Good. Circa 1910. **$500.00 – 600.00.**

☞ **Plate 54. Card Game**
"Mr. President, U. S. A. "The New Card Game combining the best elements of Poker, Bridge, and election excitement." 1960 Decor Note Co., St. Paul 14, Minnesota, Educational Games Division. Contains two decks of cards, score sheets, and instructions. 11" x 4". Condition: Very good. **$35.00 – 45.00.**

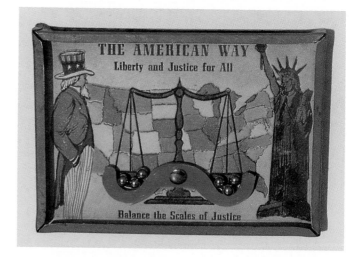

✍ **Plate 56. Balance Game**
Glass enclosed, tin framed game of skill. "The American Way Liberty and Justice For All." Six chrome-plated steel balls are to be maneuvered to "Balance the Scales of Justice." 3½" x 5" x ½". Manufacturer unknown. Circa 1940. **$100.00 – 125.00.**

✍ **Plate 55. Board Game**
"Game of Politics" by Parker Brothers, Inc. 17" x 19¾". Circa 1950. Condition: Excellent. **$70.00 – 80.00.**

☝ **Plate 57. Cribbage Board**
Wood. Image of Uncle Sam carved with "U.S.," 1876, for the centennial of the Declaration of Independence. 10⅜" x 3⅛". Condition: Excellent. Dated on the back, 1876. **$600.00 – 700.00.**

☞**Plate 58. "Uncle Sam at the Fair"**
Patented, August 20, 1889, for the World's Fair–Columbian Exposition, the B & B Mfg. Co., Norwalk, Ohio. Paper label on the back, numbered "1" thru "10" with "easy to learn when you get instructions." C. G. Kenyon, General Agent. 6¼" x 3½" x ½" thick. Condition: Very good. **$1,000.00 – 1,200.00.**

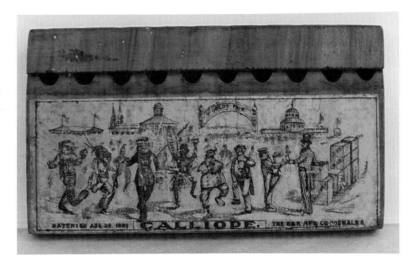

☜ **Plate 59. Uncle Sam Drum**
Metal drum with leather skin, rope binders, and wood rims. Circa 1914. 10⅞" in diameter. Condition: Very good. **$200.00 – 225.00.**

✎ **Plate 60. Gambling Device — Punch Board**
110 punch-punch board with caption "Uncle Sam wants you to win!" Manufactured by World Wide, Inc., New York, New York. 3½" x 2⅛" x ½". Condition: Very good. Circa 1942. **$35.00 – 45.00.**

☞ **Plate 61. Columbian Exposition Pocket Knife**
Full color lithograph of Uncle Sam on one side, American flag and Miss Liberty on the reverse of knife. 2⅞" x ¾". Condition: Very good. Circa 1893. **$300.00 – 350.00.**

✎ **Plate 62. Drummer**
Tin key-wind toy manufactured by "A.B.C." Made in Japan. Circa 1953. 8½" x 3½". Condition: Very good. **$375.00 – 425.00.**

☞ **Plate 63. Tin Wind-up Clown**
J. Chein & Co., made in U. S. A. Wind and clown walks on his hands. 5" x 2". Circa 1950. Condition: Excellent. **$40.00 – 45.00.**

☞ **Plate 64. Playing Cards**
James Montgomery Flaggs "I want You" deck of cards. 3½" x 2¼". Condition: Very good, deck is complete with two Jokers (Boxed). Copyright 1953. **$12.00 – 15.00.**

☝ **Plate 65. Newsboy**
Tin key-wind toy manufactured by "T.K." Toys. Made in Japan. Design Pat. No. 92209. 5⅞" x 4½". Original issue, 1953, has plastic head, all other aspects identical to later issue. Condition: Excellent. **$500.00 – 550.00.** 1965 reissue. Condition: Excellent with original box. **$100.00 – 125.00.**

☝ **Plate 66. Windsock (nylon)**
Manufactured for Hallmark Cards, Inc., Kansas City, USA, made in China. Circa 1993. 36" x 23". Condition: Excellent. **$15.00 – 20.00.**

Penny Arcade Machines

The two most noted Uncle Sam Arcade machines, here included, are among the rarest and most expensive of all manufactured Uncle Sam items ever produced. The 'Caille' Uncle Sam strength tester has been reproduced with an electric, as opposed to mechanical, strength indicator dial with lights. Other than the electrical aspect of this reproduction, the overall physical appearance and dimensions of this machine are identical to the original. It is available at approximately 10% to 15% of the value of the original 1908 "Caille" Uncle Sam strength tester described in this section.

Plate 67. Uncle Sam's Strength Tester
"Shake with Uncle Sam." Cast metal bust of Uncle Sam mounted on oak columnated cabinet with cast iron paw feet. Cast iron marque extends from two shoulder brackets and arches over Uncle Sam's head. The squeezing of Uncle Sam's extended right hand will indicate your strength on round dial in the center of Uncle Sam's chest. Originally a one cent strength tester. Original paint. Original arch was either cast bronze or cast iron with gilted raised letters against a deep red field. Condition: Very good. Manufactured by Caille Company. Circa 1908. Overall 77". **$25,000.00 – 30,000.00.**

Plate 68. Uncle Sam's Strength Tester
"Shake with your Uncle Sam." Cast metal bust of Uncle Sam mounted on tapered oak cabinet resting on cast iron base with four extending serpentine feet. The squeezing of Uncle Sam's extended right hand will indicate your strength on round dial in the center of Uncle Sam's chest. Originally a one cent strength tester. Condition: Very good (restored). Manufactured by Howard Company. Circa 1904. Overall height: 66". **$15,000.00 – 18,000.00.**

*Note: Strength testers, like all other penny arcade machines, received an excessive amount of abuse by virtue of exposure to and use by thousands of people each year. Therefore, it is most likely that most every strength testing machine received an overhaul including repainting. The likelihood of finding a strength testing machine with its original paint is next to none.

Postcards

Postcards are one of the most unique of all Uncle Sam collectibles. Unlike most other items, postcards were being kept and collected immediately during the period of time in which they were produced, purchased, and mailed to family and friends. Many recipients of postcards would put them into scrapbooks and photo albums and would continue to collect them throughout most of their lives. This process, of course, helped to preserve them to where you can find Uncle Sam postcards from the mid 1890s through the early 1920s in near-mint condition. Raphael Tuck and Tabor Prang produced some of the finest full-color chromo-lithographic postcards with Uncle Sam images during this period. These cards in particular are most desirable and will bring the highest prices. Along with the various seasons greeting and holiday postcards, political campaign and military wartime postcards with Uncle Sam images are extremely sought after.

All postcards are 5½" x 3½" and are in excellent condition, unless otherwise specified.

☝ **Plate 69. "Fourth of July Greetings"**
Raphael Tuck & Sons. **$60.00 – 70.00.**

☝ **Plate 70. "Independence Day"**
Series No. 109, Art Publications to their Majesties the King and Queen. Raphael Tuck & Sons. **$75.00 – 85.00.**

☞ **Plate 71. "4th of July"**
Spelled out in firecrackers. Raphael Tuck & Sons.
$100.00 – 110.00.

☞ **Plate 72. "4th of July"**
Spelled out in firecrackers. Raphael Tuck & Sons.
$100.00 – 110.00.

✍ **Plate 73.**
"Hurrah for the Fourth of July"
Raphael Tuck & Sons. 3½" x 5½".
$45.00 – 50.00.

👆 **Plate 74. "By the Grace of God Free and Independent"**
Copyright 1907 artist: Fred C. Lounsbury. 3½" x 5½". **$40.00 – 45.00.**

👆 **Plate 75. "Hurrah! For the Fourth of July Hurrah!"**
Stone lithograph, embossed. "Post Card" in 14 languages on the back. **$65.00 – 75.00.**

👆 **Plate 76. "Hurrah! For the Fourth of July Hurrah!"**
Stone lithograph, embossed. "Post Card" in 14 languages on the back. **$50.00 – 60.00.**

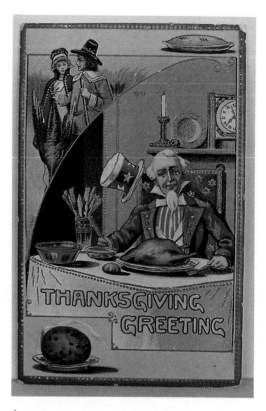

☞ **Plate 77. "For A Merry 4th"**
American Post Card, "Independence Day,"
Series No. 122, Subject No. 2317. Published by
the Ullman Manufacturing Co., New York.
$50.00 – 60.00.

☞ **Plate 78. "Thanksgiving Greeting"**
Made in Germany. **$35.00 – 40.00.**

☞ **Plate 79. "Thanksgiving Day
Ruler of the Day." $40.00 –
45.00.**

☞ **Plate 80. "Wishing you a Happy
Thanksgiving." $45.00 – 50.00.**

☝ **Plate 81.** "Gee! But I wish I was growed up." **$35.00 – 45.00.**

☝ **Plate 82.**
"Brothers Still – Tis God's Will"
Copyright 1907 by Fred C. Lounsbury.
Uncle Sam shaking hands with an Irish
Lad. **25.00 – 30.00.**

☝ **Plate 83.** "Uncle Sam Suffragee"
$45.00 – 55.00.

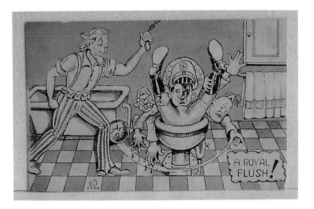

☝ **Plate 84.** "A Royal Flush!"
Black & white cartoon illustration. Artist: unknown.
3½" x 5½". Copyright: D.R. & Co. 1943. **$30.00 –
40.00.**

☞ **Plate 85. "Sammy"**
Portion of a song on top with Uncle Sam tipping his hat to Ms. Canada. Copyright 1905 – A. J. **$40.00 – 50.00.**

☞ **Plate 86. "That's Uncle Sam and maybe I'm not proud of him"**
Illustrated Postal Card and No. Co., New York. Date hand written, July 2, 1917. **$20.00 – 25.00.**

☞ **Plate 87. No message on front**
Bust of Uncle Sam pictured with the story of Samuel Wilson on the back. 1966 Yankee Colour Corp., Southboro, MA. Art by Bam Sawler. **$15.00 – 25.00.**

Plate 88. "Hands Across the Sea"
"Here's to you Uncle Sam — may your shadow never grow less." **$18.00 – 24.00.**

Plate 89. "Here's to you Uncle Sam. May your shadow never grow less. Same to you John. Hands Across the Sea"
Uncle Sam extending his hand across the ocean to John Bull. Leather postcard. Copyright 1907. Cancelled with a flag postal cancellation. 5⅛" x 3⅛". Condition: Excellent. **$50.00 – 60.00.**

Plate 90. "When this gentleman takes off his coat – he means business"
Illustrated Postal Card & No. Co., New York. **$20.00 – 25.00.**

☞ **Plate 91. "Somebody is going to get what they've been looking for P. D. Q."** $25.00 – 30.00.

☞ **Plate 92. "Uncle Sam Says: The peace of a nation is its greatest asset"** By H. Boente. $25.00 – 30.00.

☞ **Plate 94. "Adolf's Going Places!"** Black & white cartoon illustration. Artist: Unknown. 3½" x 5½". Copyright: D. R. & Co. 1943. **$30.00 – 40.00.**

☞ **Plate 93. "Our Uncle, He Can't be Beaten!"** Hand dated, October 13, 1917. **$25.00 – 30.00.**

☝ **Plate 95. "Thanksgiving Rivals"**
P.R., Postmark November, 1910. Condition:
Very good. **$25.00 – 30.00.**

☝ **Plate 96. "Thanksgiving Greetings"**
P. Sanders, New York. **$35.00 – 45.00.**

☝ **Plate 97. "I See A Bad Finish For You Rats"**
Black & white cartoon illustration. Artist:
Unknown. 3½" x 5½". Copyright: D. R. Co. 1943.
$30.00 – 40.00.

☞ **Plate 98.**
"Wishing you a Happy Thanksgiving"
Postmarked 1910. **$20.00 – 25.00.**

☞ **Plate 100. "Uncle Sam and Columbia"**
Postmarked October 12, 1909. 3½" x 5½". **$40.00 – 50.00.**

☞ **Plate 99. "Uncle Sam"**
Copyright 1907, Ullman Mfg. Co., New
York. Art by B. Wall. **$18.00 – 21.00.**

☞ **Plate 102.**
"Presidential Campaign 1908 G.O.P. at Bat"
Copyright 1908 by I Grollman, Chi. G.O.P. elephant at
bat with Theodore Roosevelt. William J. Bryan as
catcher. 3½" x 5½". **$100.00 – 115.00.**

☞ **Plate 101. "Presidential Fight—1908 Democracy Knocked Out"**
Copyright 1908 by I Grollman, Chicago. William J.
Bryan beside the donkey, Theodore Roosevelt with a
hand on the elephant. 3½" x 5½". **$100.00 –
115.00.**

Greeting Cards

Just a few examples of greeting cards utilizing Uncle Sam imagery are included in this text. Greeting cards as opposed to postcards have not experienced the decline of their usage yet are becoming collectible among a variety of paper collectors and dealers. Images notably depicting the period of time in which the greeting card was produced will add to its value.

Plate 103. "Greetings at Christmas"
4¾" x 5". Condition: Very good. **$8.00 – 10.00.**

Plate 104. "We're Rootin for you SOLDIER!"
The American Flag rises as the card is opened. Made in the U. S. A. 5⅛" x 4⅛". Condition: Excellent. **$6.00 – 9.00.**

Plate 105. Cover: "I Want You"
Inside message, "To Get Well! (Hope it's Soon)." Hallmark. 6¼" x 4¼". Condition: Excellent. **$5.00 – 8.00.**

Books, Comics, Pamphlets, and Calendars

A variety of applications of Uncle Sam's name or image have been utilized on the embossed cover or dust jacket of many hardbound books from as early as the 1870s. The graphic quality, as well as the design concept can create varying individual interests to the collector.

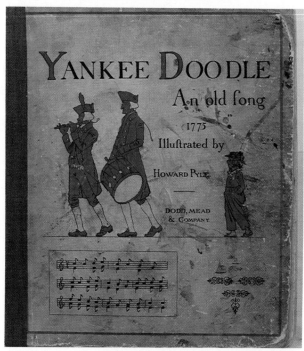

Plate 106. Yankee Doodle. An Old Song
"1775." Illustrated by Howard Pyle. Dodd, Mead and Company. Copyright 1881. Condition: Good. **$300.00 – 400.00.**

Plate 107. Yankee Doodle an Old Friend in a New Dress
Pictured by Howard Pyle. Printed by Dodd, Mead and Company, No. 755 Broadway, New York. Copyright 1881 by Dodd, Mead and Company, page 25. "Old Uncle Sam come then to change some pancakes and some onions." Sam Wilson pictured as a purveyor of goods, being referred to as Uncle Sam. This is one of the best illustrated books (Plate 106) to emphasize the true story of how Uncle Sam came into being.

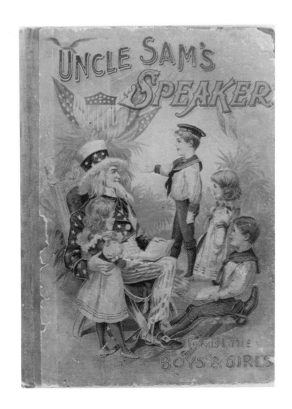

☞ Plate 108. The United States of the World
Copyright 1902 by Wm. M. Goldwaite. Press of the Henry O. Shepard Co., Chicago. 9⅞" x 6¾". Condition: Very good. **$65.00 – 75.00.**

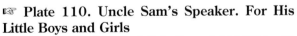

☜ Plate 109. Uncle Sam's Story Book
By Wilhelmina Harper. Illustrated by Grace Paull. Uncle Sam on jacket, not on book's cover. Copyright 1944, Jr. Literary Guild, New York and David McKay Co., Philadelphia. 8¼" x 7½". Condition: Very good. **$35.00 – 45.00.**

☞ Plate 110. Uncle Sam's Speaker. For His Little Boys and Girls
By Florence Underwood Colt. Copyright 1899 by K. T. Boland. 9⅝" x 6¾". Condition: Very good. **$75.00 – 90.00.**

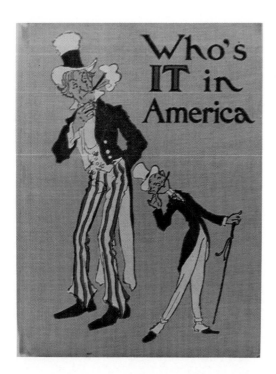

☞ **Plate 111. Who's It In America**
By Charles E. Merriman. 7" x 5⅛". Copyright 1918.
Condition: Very Good. **$40.00 – 50.00.**

☞ **Plate 112. Uncle Sam in the Eyes of His Family**
By John Erskine. Copyright 1930, 1st edition. Press of
Braurworth & Co., Brooklyn. 8" x 5½". Condition:
Excellent. **$30.00 – 35.00.**

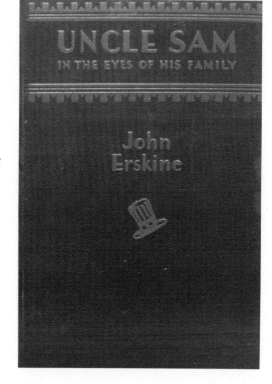

☞ **Plate 113. Nicodemus Helps Uncle Sam**
Copyright 1943. Written and illustrated by Inez
Hogan (African-American author and illustrator).
Distributed by E. P. Dutton & Co., Inc., New York.
Black, red, and blue stone lithographs, full-page car-
toons w/several black Uncle Sams. Pages are not
numbered. Page size: 7¼" x 5". Book: 7½" x 5⅝".
Condition: Excellent. Illustration No. 26 "Nicodemus
bought a war stamp." **$75.00 – 100.00.**

☞ **Plate 114. Indiana, Intellectually She Rolls Her Own**
Copyright 1924 by George H. Doran Company. Copyright 1923 by International Magazine Company, Indiana. Illustrated by John T. McCutcheon. Image on jacket, cover, and page 15 identical. "Your Indianian of Today, pure northerner on one side and one hundred percent southerner on the other, is the most typical American in the whole democracy." 7½" x 5". Condition: Excellent. **$50.00 – 60.00.**

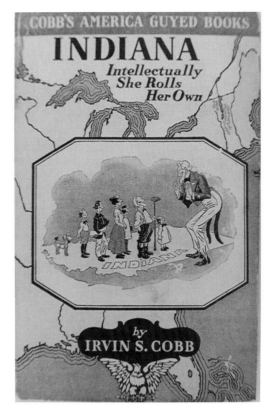

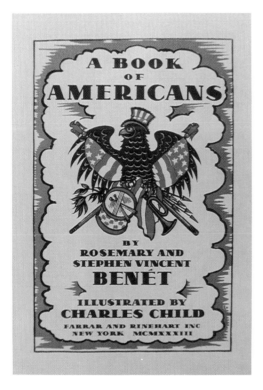

✎ **Plate 115. A Book of Americans**
By Rosemary and Stephen Vincent Benet. Copyright 1933, National Process Co., Inc., New York. Uncle Sam in red, white, and blue, seated, on page 115. 8⅞" x 5⅞". Condition: Very good. **$20.00 – 25.00.**

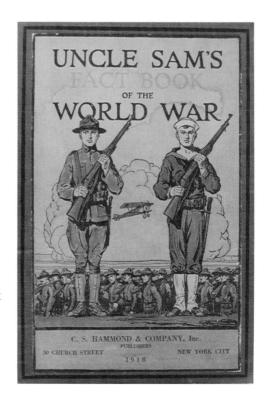

☞ **Plate 116. Uncle Sam's Fact Book of the World War**
C. S. Hammond & Company, Inc. – Publishers. Copyright 1918. 8½" x 6¼". Condition: Excellent. **$60.00 – 70.00.**

✒ **Plate 117. You, Too, Can be an Aviation Cadet**
"Ask-Class 44-E – War Eagle Field." 11¼" x 8⅝".
Condition: Excellent. **$75.00 – 85.00.**

Comic Books

Comic books pick on everybody, why not Uncle Sam? Yet, when utilized in the properly historic context the subliminal influence to the reader can and should be educational as well as entertaining.

☞ **Plate 118. Comic Book (Cover Illustration)**
Volume 1, Number 1. Published by Marvel Comics Group, New York, NY. Artists: ink by H. Trimpe, J. Romita, B. Smith; colored by Phil Rachelson. 1976. 13¼" x 10". Condition: Very good.
$30.00 – 40.00.

☞ **Plate 119. Remember Pearl Harbor**
"Battle of the Pacific." A thrilling graphic picture story. Four color. Published 1942. Copyright S & S. 10½" x 6½". Condition: Excellent. **$350.00 – 425.00.**

Pamphlets

Pamphlets, brochures, and catalogs utilizing Uncle Sam have been published in great numbers by the United States government as well as by numerous corporations and organizations for a variety of informative or educational purposes. The graphic quality of the art work as well as the content will reflect prices. Condition and period of time are most important.

☜ **Plate 120. The ABC of the USA Army and Navy**
Vol. 1 – Price 15 cents, Presto Publ. Co., Hamilton, OH. Copyright 1917. Military illustrations with cover only in color. 6⅜" x 3⅜". Condition: Excellent. **$20.00 – 25.00.**

☜ **Plate 121. Know Your Government**
Copyright 1953 by Osborne Co., Clifton, NJ.
9" x 6". Condition: Excellent. **$20.00 – 25.00.**

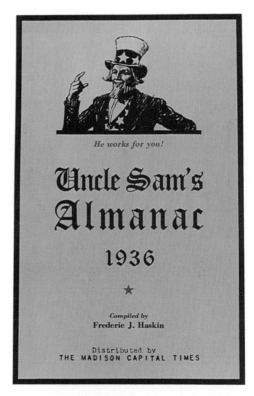

☞ **Plate 122. Uncle Sam's Almanac 1936**
"He works for you!" Compiled by Frederic J. Haskin.
$25.00 – 30.00.

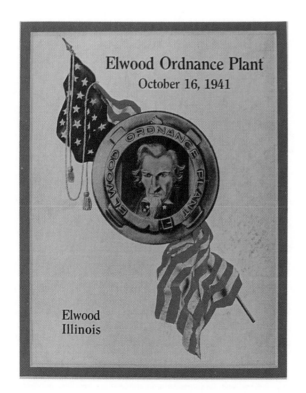

☜ **Plate 123. Elwood Ordnance Plant, Elwood, Illinois**
October 16, 1941. 7" x 5½". Condition: Excellent. **$40.00 –
50.00.**

✍ **Plate 124. "When you sell for Uncle Sam"**
Wheelwright Made (W) right Index. Folded card.
11" x 8½", folded. Condition: Excellent. **$15.00 –
20.00.**

✍ **Plate 125. Wet or Dry?**
A brief, candid examination of Moot Question in American Life, by Francis D. Nichol.
Pacific Press Publishing Assn., Mountain
View, California. Copyright 1932 by Review
& Herald Publishing Assn. Black and white
illustrations. **$15.00 – 20.00.**

Calendars

From the 1890s on through to the present day, calendars utilizing the image of Uncle Sam have been published
on a regular basis. The calendars produced during the war years are most desirable. Condition is most important.
Images by more notable illustrators are more desirable and will reflect higher prices.

☞ **Plate 126. The days of 1918**
Small calendar pasted to the bottom of a drawing of a young
Uncle Sam holding a banner which reads, "Merry Christmas." Red, white, and blue striped strings are punched into
the top for hanging. 12½" x 9½". Condition: Excellent.
$40.00 – 60.00.

🕮 **Plate 127. Pin-up Calendar**
Printed by Brown & Bigelow, St. Paul, MN, USA.
Artist: Floyd R. Munson. January 1944. 13¼" x
9". Condition: Very good. **$40.00 – 50.00.**

☝ **Plate 128. August, 1898**
"I've used these colors over a hundred years, they'll
stand forever." Uncle Sam has just painted the American flag. F. W. Devoe & C. T. Raynolds Co. 12½" x
9½". Condition: Very good. **$75.00 – 100.00.**

🕮 **Plate 129. Calendar Print**
Full color illustration. Artist: Dean Cornwell. 22½" x
20½". Copyright: American Legion, Indianapolis, Ind.
1952. **$100.00 – 125.00.**

Scrapbooks

Most all of the scrapbooks utilizing the image of Uncle Sam on the cover were produced during World War I and World War II. There purpose, more than likely was to be used for the accumulation of photographs and news clippings of family and friends involved in the war effort. The condition of the cover is most important. The contents obviously will vary and sometimes will contain some very interesting war time paper ephemera.

☞ **Plate 130. Scrapbook**
Green and Gold simulated leather embossed with Uncle Sam, behind a ship's wheel. 11½" x 15¼". Condition: Excellent. Circa 1945. **$60.00 – 75.00.**

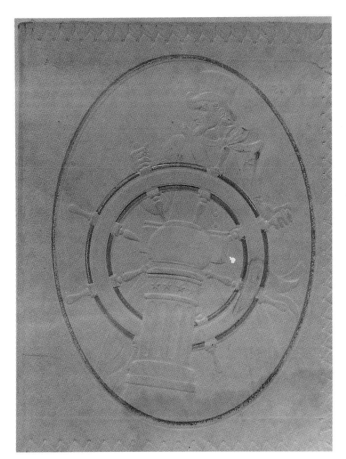

🕮 **Plate 131. Stationery Portfolio**
For paper and envelopes. Off-white simulated leather embossed with Uncle Sam, behind a ship's wheel. The black interior holds paper on the right with two pouches on the left marked, "envelopes." 11½" x 9". Condition: Good. **$75.00 – 95.00.**

Pottery, Porcelain, and Glassware

From as early as the 1850s manufacturers of pottery, porcelain, and glassware have used the image of Uncle Sam in the production of utilitarian as well as decorative items. Vases, gravy boats, butter dishes, cookie jars, salt & pepper shakers, figurines, and so on are among the many objects you can expect to find in your collecting pursuits.

From the exceptionally fine and rare to the simplistically inexpensive, the collector can discover wonderful pieces practically anywhere in a wide variety of price ranges. "Excellent condition" in this category is most important.

Plate 132. Gravy Boat
Union porcelain works (Green Point) Brooklyn, NY Fine porcelain gravy boat with Uncle Sam and John Bull reclining on the top of a boat. 7½" x 3½", 5⅛" high. Condition: Very good. Circa 1868. **$1,200.00 – 1,500.00.**

Plate 133. Covered Dish
Opalescent milk glass with Uncle Sam seated between the smokestacks of the ship U.S.S. Olympia. The bottom of the boat has an eagle on the bow with port holes and guns on the sides. 6½" x 3" x 4⅝". Condition: Excellent. Ca. 1898. **$125.00 – 140.00.**

☝ **Plate 134. Creamer**
Uncle Sam's face influenced by image of Abraham Lincoln. Ridgway Sterling Pottery, Lawley, England, est. 1792. 3¼" x 2¼". Condition: Excellent. Circa 1909. **$90.00 – 110.00.**

☝ **Plate 135. Pitcher**
Made in England by Royal Winton, Grimwades. Painted. 11½" x 7¾". Condition: Excellent. Circa 1920. **$175.00 – 195.00.**

☝ **Plate 136. Pitcher**
Uncle Sam's face influenced by image of Abraham Lincoln. Ridgway Sterling Pottery, Lawley, England, est. 1792. 11¼" x 7". Circa 1909. Condition: Excellent. **$175.00 – 195.00.**

☝ **Plate 137. Creamer**
Made in England by Royal Winton. Smaller version of plate 135. 4¾" x 3¼". Condition: Excellent. Circa 1920. **$90.00 – 110.00.**

🐚 **Plate 138. Royal Doulton Dewars White Label Bottle.**
One of the finest images of Uncle Sam ever produced in quality porcelain or ceramic. Marked on the bottom: Royal Doulton, England, the Lion standing on the crown, Dewars White Label whisky and Rd No 504,944. Marked on the back, 1907. High-glazed porcelain with a dark brown base and dark brown top fading to a light brownish gold center. 7¼" x 6½" x 2¾". Condition: Excellent. **$550.00 – 600.00.**

☞ **Plate 139. Shot Glasses and Stir Sticks**
Blown glass Uncle Sam top hats with blown glass stir sticks (set of six). Maker: Unknown. Circa 1918. Hats – 2" x 2¼". Each stir stick – 5¼". Condition: Excellent. Set: **$125.00 – 150.00.**

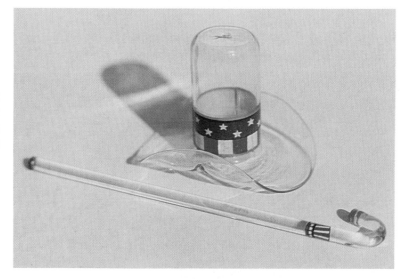

🐚 **Plate 140. Coffee Mugs**
Pair of clay pottery Frankoma coffee cups or mugs. One all in red with white throughout inside, the other all in blue, inside and out. Manufactured by Frankoma Pottery, 1976, Series No. 600. Dimensions: 4" x 4". Condition: Excellent. Each **$25.00 – 30.00.**

Plate 141. Cookie Jar
Uncle Sam's hat. Maker: Unmarked. Date 1973.
Ref/Lindberg. Photo courtesy of Fred & Joyce
Roerig. **$200.00 – 300.00.**

☞ **Plate 142. Cookie Jar**
Uncle Sam bear. Metlox, Calif, USA. Photo courtesy
of Fred & Joyce Roerig. **$400.00 – 500.00.**

Plate 143. Serving Plate
Semiporcelain plate with 24K gold plated scalloped
edge. 11¼" x ¾" deep. Manufacturer: unknown (no
marks). Circa 1950. **$35.00 – 50.00.**

Plate 144. Salt and Pepper Shakers
Hand-painted ceramic. Circa 1920. 2½" x 1½". Condition: Very good. **$75.00 – 95.00.**

☞ Plate 146. Salt and Pepper Shaker Set
Clay pottery figurine. Marked: "J. A. M." Dated: 1976. Each 4½" x 2⅝".
Condition: Excellent. **$35.00 – 45.00.**

☞ Plate 145. Salt Shaker
One of pair. Hand-painted
ceramic. Circa 1920. 2⅛" x
1½". Condition: Excellent.
$35.00 – 40.00.

☞ Plate 147. Vase
Glazed ceramic. Marked: "McCoy." 7½" x 4½". Condition: Excellent. **$75.00 – 85.00.**

☞ **Plate 148. Planter**
Off-white semiporcelain bust. Maker: Unknown. Circa 1915. 6" x 4¼". Condition: Excellent. **$100.00 – 120.00.**

☜ **Plate 149. Planter**
Molded poly-ceramic top hat planter. Manufactured by Ruben's Originals. Copyright 1974. 4½" x 4½". Condition: Excellent. **$15.00 – 20.00.**

☞ **Plate 150. Vase**
Plastic composition. Stars contain rhinestones. Circa 1952/53. Pride of New York City, Product of Japan on a triangular label on the bottom. 5⅛" x 4" x 4½". Condition: Excellent. **$65.00 – 85.00.**

Clothing and Textiles

Sorry to say that I do not have representation of any quilts or coverlets in this category. They do exist yet are very difficult to find and you can expect to pay premium prices for them. Uncle Sam suits can be found from various periods of time, as early as the 1850s. Silk or cotton scarves commemorating expositions, world fairs, and the various wars are most desirable. Embroidered handkerchiefs and napkins with images of Uncle Sam were also made up until the Korean War. Many one-of-a-kind items can be found in this category. The period of time and condition are most important in relationship to price.

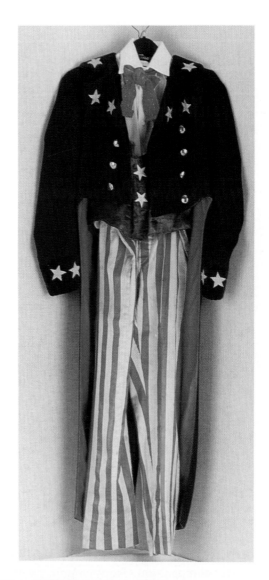

☞ **Plate 151. Uncle Sam Sculpture**
Life-size sculpture of Uncle Sam, hand sculpted in clay composition wearing the original suit used by James Montgomery Flagg in 1917 for the original artwork for the first issue "I Want You" poster. Artist: Gerald Czulewicz. Date: 1991. Condition: Excellent. Sculpture only: **$2,500.00 – 3,000.00.**

☞ **Plate 152. Uncle Sam Suit**
Original Uncle Sam suit used by Thomas Nast for his model while with Harper's Publishing Company in New York. From the Thomas Nast Estate. Condition: Very good. Circa 1870. **$20,000.00+.**

Plate 153. Uncle Sam Suit and Top Hat
Worn by James Montgomery Flagg while using himself as a model for the original painting of the first "I Want You" poster. This original suit was also used by Mr. Flagg while producing the very first "I Want You" images for the July 6th 1916, and Feb. 15, 1917, *Leslie's* Magazine cover art. He continued to use this suit and top hat for all of his Uncle Sam images. From the James Montgomery Flagg estate. Circa 1916. Condition: Very good. **$30,000.00+.**

Plate 154. Handkerchief
"Remember the Maine." Silk, blue on white. 18½" x 19". Spanish-American War era. Circa 1898. Condition: Excellent. **$250.00 – 300.00.**

☜❧ **Plate 155. Bookmark (silk)**
"United We Stand–Welcome Home." 8¼" x
1⅜". Spanish-American War era–1898. Condition: Excellent. **$50.00 – 60.00.**

☞ **Plate 156. Pennant (cloth)**
"Welcome Home" W.W.I. Uncle
Sam amid the stars with his arms
around two military personnel,
"Well Done My Boys." 25¾" x
10¾". Circa 1919. Condition:
Excellent. **$90.00 – 115.00.**

☜❧ **Plate 157. Pillow**
Purple, with the U. S. flag forming a pocket
on the bottom half. 14" x 10". Condition:
Excellent. Circa 1918. **$50.00 – 70.00.**

Plate 158. Pillow
"God Bless America" cross-stitched in different colors. Trimmed in crocheted lace. 13" x 17". Circa 1930. Condition: Excellent. **$125.00 – 150.00.**

Plate 159. Linen Cloth
Embroidery work measures 3½" x 5". Cloth measures 18½" x 13¾". Condition: Very good. Circa 1940. **$20.00 – 25.00.**

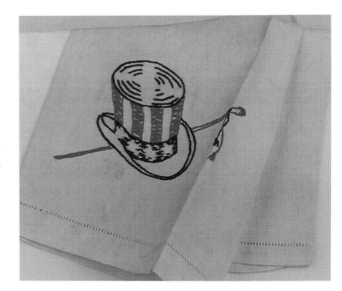

Plate 160. Linen Scarf
"Washing up Certificate." Gray, black, and blue scarf made to resemble a dollar bill. "This certifies that there is on deposit in the Treasury of the United States of America One Fast Buck." Signed by John Doe, Treasurer of the Kitchen and Uncle Sam, Secretary of the Kitchen. 15⅝" x 27¼". Circa 1960. Condition: Excellent. **$10.00 – 15.00.**

Advertising Trade Cards

What is attractive about the nineteenth century trade cards is the quality of the full-color stone lithography, especially for the size of the cards. Because of what the advertising collectible market has been doing in recent years, I can only see trade cards becoming much more sought after, much scarcer, and accordingly, much more expensive. As in postcards or sports cards, condition is most important. The value of these cards will vary depending upon what the product is as well as what the overall image includes.

☞ **Plate 161. "Highest Gold Medal Awarded, Hub Gore Makers Elastic for Shoes"**
"Uncle Sam, the wonderful Edison Talking Automation at World's Fair, delivering 40,000 speeches during the Exhibition, about Highest Award, Gold Medal, Hub Gore. 3⅝" x 6". Columbian Exposition 1893. Condition: Very good. **$35.00 – 45.00.**

☞ **Plate 162. "They Return"**
From Dives, Pomery & Steward. J & P Coats Best Six Cord. Uncle Sam pictured with a Scotsman. 2½" x 3⅞". Circa 1876. Condition: Very good. **$35.00 – 45.00.**

☞ **Plate 163. Ladies Pocket Calendar Trade Card of 1879** Uncle Sam handing out Clark's thread to women of international origin. 1879 calendar (verso) 2⅝" x 4⅜". Condition: Excellent. **$40.00 – 50.00.**

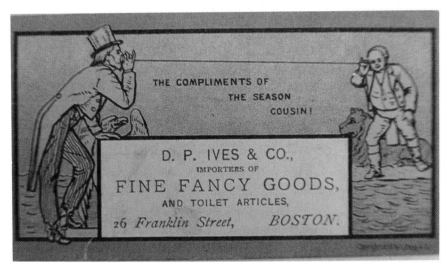

🖃 **Plate 164. "The Compliments of the Season Cousin"** D. P. Ives & Co., Importers of fine fancy goods and toilet articles, Boston. Copyright 1878. 2¼" x 4⅛". Condition: Excellent. **$30.00 – 40.00.**

☞ **Plate 165. "Frank Miller's Blacking"** J. Ottmann Lith., Puck Building, New York. 3½" x 5¼". Condition: Excellent. Copyright 1882. **$65.00 – 75.00.**

☝ **Plate 166. "Tis the National Food and the Food for International Quarrels"**
Minced Codfish, Henry Mayo & Co., Boston. 1892. Lithographer: Louis Prang. 4½" x 3". Condition: Excellent. **$50.00 – 60.00.**

☝ **Plate 167. Brother Jonathan**
Standing among sale items. 1876 (Philadelphia) Centennial Exposition. Artist: Thomas Nast. Condition: Excellent. **$65.00 – 80.00.**

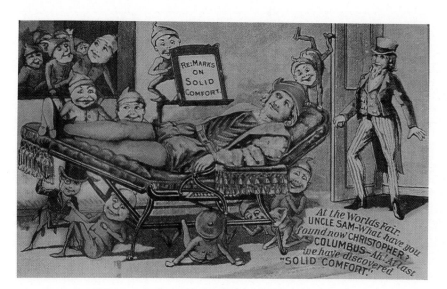

☜ **Plate 168. Re: Marks on Solid Comfort, at the World's Fair**
Uncle Sam: "What have you found now Christopher Columbus?" "Ah! At last we have discovered Solid Comfort." Lithographer: Louis Prang, 1893. Marks Adjustable Folding Chair Co., Ltd., New York. Bigelow Lith. Co., Springfield, Mass. Advertising on back. 3½" x 5⅜". Condition: Excellent. **$50.00 – 60.00.**

☞ **Plate 169. "Uncle Sam Supplying the World with Berry Bros. Architectural Finishes"** Calvert Lith., Co., Detroit. Advertising on back. 3½" x 5⅝". Circa 1880. Condition: Excellent. **$40.00 – 45.00.**

☜ **Plate 170. "Frank Miller's Improved French Blacking"** Black and white image. Advertising on back. 3⅛" x 4¾". Circa 1878. Condition: Excellent. **$75.00 – 85.00.**

☞ **Plate 171. 1776 – 1876** Rare card of Uncle Sam with Britannia. 3⅛" x 5⅛". 1876 (Philadelphia) Centennial Exposition. Condition: Very good. **$75.00 – 100.00.**

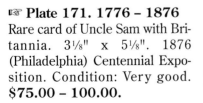

☞ **Plate 172.**
"A thing of worth is a joy forever"
B. T. Babbitt's Soap Powder. "Buffo"
lower right. Advertising on back. 3⅝" x
5". Circa 1877. Condition: Excellent.
$35.00 – 45.00.

☜ **Plate 173. "Light Oil"**
Uncle Sam and Miss Liberty
endorsing "White Rose Stove
Gasoline." National Refining
Co., Cleveland. Advertising on
back. 3¼" x 6". Circa 1882.
Condition: Excellent. **$40.00
– 50.00.**

☞ **Plate 174.**
"Uncle Sam's Harness Oil"
C. Drake, Rushord, MN. Advertis-
ing on back. 3" x 5". Circa 1878.
Condition: Excellent. **$35.00 –
45.00.**

☞ **Plate 175. "Uncle Sam Supplying the World with Berry Bros. Hard Oil Finish"**
Calvert Litho. Co., Detroit. Circa 1878 3½" x 5⅝". Condition: Excellent. **$20.00 – 25.00.**

☞ **Plate 176. "Use Hygienic Kalsomine"**
Rubber Paint Co., Chicago. Milwaukee Litho. & Engr. Co. Advertisement on back. 1893 Columbian Exposition. 5½" x 3¾". Condition: Excellent. **$35.00 – 45.00.**

King Flours showed how quick-rising its product was, with boy being lifted by rising flour.

☜ **Plate 177. King's Flour Ad**
"King Flours showed how quick-rising its product was, with boy being lifted by rising flour." King's Flour logo in upper left corner. 5⅜" x 3⅛". Circa 1903. Condition: Excellent. **$25.00 – 30.00.**

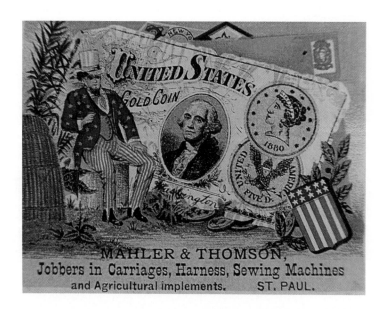

Plate 178. Trade Card
Full-color stone lithograph. Mahler & Thompson Jobbers in carriages, harnesses, sewing machines, and agricultural implements. St. Paul. Circa: 1890. 2¾" x 3½". Condition: Very good. **$25.00 – 30.00.**

Plate 179. "Long Life and Happiness"
"Now exhibit elegant styles of silks, cloaks, suits, and fur lined garments. Child dressed in oversized Uncle Sam attire. Mandel Bro's. 6" x 4½". Condition: Very good. **$40.00 – 45.00.**

Advertising Items

One of the most active areas of Uncle Sam collectibles falls in this category. Hundreds, if not thousands, of manufacturers and merchants have utilized the image of Uncle Sam in the process of advertising their products. From the mid-nineteenth century to this present day you will find one-, two-, and three-dimensional objects. From early lithographic broadsides of the 1840s to present day magazine advertisements and posters, Uncle Sam is constantly chosen as a spokesperson for one product or another. Trade signs, coffee and tobacco containers, candy containers, and a number of other three-dimensional advertising items of the late nineteenth and early twentieth century are most desirable. The quality of the imagery of Uncle Sam, the actual product the period of time, and the condition are important indicators in relationship to prices.

Plate 180. Stand-up Display Sign
"Nationally Advertised – Sold Here Furnished by *Good Housekeeping* magazine." Full-color stone lithograph cut out mounted on hard cardboard. Copyright "N. A. A. R." New York. Nation Easel, patented Dec. 1912. 36" x 16". Condition: Very Good. **$700.00 – 900.00.**

Plate 181. "Harmony Chewing Tobacco"
Daniel Scotten & Co., Detroit, Michigan. Full-color stone lithograph. The Calvert Lith. Co., Detroit. Copyright 1879. 10⅝" x 13⅜". Condition: Excellent. **$1,200.00 – 1,500.00.**

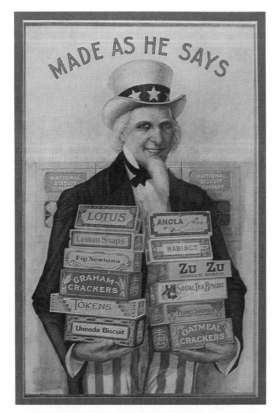

☞ **Plate 182. "Made as he says"**
National Biscuit Company. August 10, 1918. 10" x 6½". Condition: Excellent. **$50.00 – 60.00.**

☞ **Plate 183. "The Big Tin"**
"The Best Tobacco Value." Union Leader Tobacco collapsible display box (very rare). Circa 1916. 18½" x 17½". Condition: Excellent. **$3,000.00 – 3,200.00.**

☞ **Plate 184. "My Hat's Off To The Quality Of…"**
"Union Leader, Biggest and Best Tobacco Value." "10 cent tin." Inside cover of *Lorillards Magazine*. Circa 1918. Red, white, blue, and yellow. 10¾" x 7½". Condition: Excellent. **$45.00 – 60.00.**

Plate 185. Tobacco Tin
"Union Leader Redi Cut Tobacco." Back reads, "Genuine 'Union Leader' Redi-cut," Specially prepared for pipe and cigarette. Hinged top, metal container in red, white, and blue. 1⅝ ounces tobacco. Labels on both sides and across the top, Series 01917, U.S. Inter. Rev. J. Adams, with picture of Adams. Uncle Sam on the front. 4¾" x 3". Circa 1917. Condition: Very good. **$60.00 – 70.00.**

Plate 186. Tobacco Tin
Round metal Tin with cover. Union Leader–Redi Cut Tobacco. Federal Tin Co., Baltimore. 6⅛" x 5". Circa 1915. Condition: Very good. **$90.00 – 115.00.**

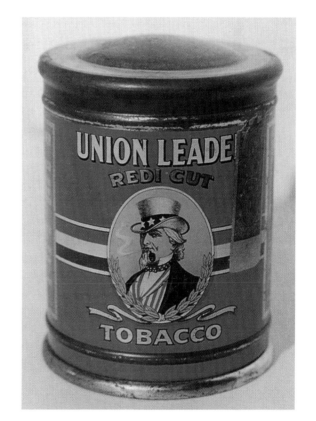

Plate 187. "American Brands, Inc."
Summary of Annual Stockholders Meeting. May 6, 1976. Artist: E. N. Blue. 8½" x 6½". Condition: Excellent. **$10.00 – 12.00.**

⇛ **Plate 188. Union Leader Sign**
Enameled tin. 11" x 9⅛". Condition:
Excellent. Circa 1917. **$75.00 – 90.00.**
*Beware of smaller reproduction.

☞ **Plate 189. Match Holder**
Unitus Uncle Sam Cigars, advertising match holder,
wall hanging relief plaque. Molded plaster, hand
painted. Circa 1918. 6½" diameter. Condition: Very
good. **$350.00 – 400.00.**

⇛ **Plate 190. Snuff Box**
Machine press-wood relief carved image of Uncle
Sam offering snuff to John Bull. All birch bark,
including hinges. Circa 1876. "Tag En Pris!" on the
top, "Tack godt snus" across the bottom. Grapes,
vines, and leaves are carved around the sides. 2¾" x
1¼" x ⅞". Condition: Excellent. **$600.00 – 700.00**

☞ **Plate 191. Cigar Box**
"Uncle Sam's Hot Shot." Name and design registered. Circa 1918. 1⅞" x 11" x 7⅜". Condition: Excellent. **$100.00 – 125.00.**

Plate 192. Advertising Sign
"Protect Your Hands with 'Yankee Doodle' Gloves and Mittens." Printed on heavy composition cardboard. 14½" x 20". Manufacturer: Galena Glove & Mitten Co. Dubuque Iowa. Circa 1940. Condition: Excellent. **$70.00 – 90.00.**

☞ **Plate 193. Cigar Box Label**
"Uncle Sam, Smoke Uncle Sam Cigars." 7" x 10". Circa 1920. **$300.00 – 350.00.**

Plate 194. "Preparedness"
Cream of Wheat. Artist: Galen J. Perrett. Full-color print. 11½" x 9½". Copyright 1917. Condition: Excellent. **$50.00 – 60.00.**

Plate 195. "Well You're Helping Some!"
Cream of Wheat. Artist: Galen J. Perrett. Full-color print. 13¾" x 9". Copyright 1915. Condition: Excellent. **$50.00 – 60.00.**

Plate 196. "An International Agreement"
Shredded Wheat — Associated Sunday Magazines, Inc., April 16, 1905. The Natural Food Company, Niagara Falls, New York, Toronto, Canada, London, England. Full-color print. 14" x 11". Condition: Good. **$65.00 – 85.00.**

☞ **Plate 197. Stand-Up Premium Card**
Cut-out of Uncle Sam holding a sign which reads, "Sold by all good grocers." Wheatlet Breakfast Food. Stand-up advertisement, in full-color lithography. 6⅝" x 3½". Circa 1890. Condition: Very good. **$65.00 – 75.00.**

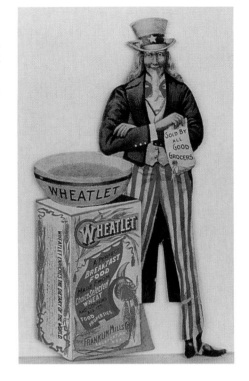

〰 **Plate 198. Cereal**
Uncle Sam Cereal. "A Natural Laxative, toasted whole grain wheat flakes sprinkled with crispy whole flaxseed. High in Fiber•Low in Sodium•No Added Sugar." "Since 1908." U. S. Mills, Inc., Omaha, Nebraska 68111. 8⅝" x 6½". Condition: Excellent. **$2.00 – 4.00.**

☞ **Plate 199. Zippo Lighter**
"Uncle Sam Cereal. A Natural Laxative." "Thanks John McGowan." Bradford Zippo, Pat. No. on bottom. 2¼" x 1½" x ½". Circa 1952. Condition: Excellent. **$35.00 – 45.00.**

Plate 200. "Your First Duty to Your Country — Buy War Bonds"
Swift — Food Purveyor to the USA. 13⅞" x 10¼". Circa 1942. Condition: Very good. **$15.00 – 20.00.**

☞ **Plate 201. Candy Cylinder**
Fanny Farmer. Cylinder is Uncle Sam with wooden arms. His hat, which is labeled "Fanny Farmer," pulls off. Patent D-120-460. Circa 1944. 10⅝" x 3". Condition: Very good. **$85.00 – 100.00.**

Plate 202. "Are YOU Eating Right?"
Durkee's Vegetable Oleomargarine. Free gifts for Durkee coupons, recipes using Durkee products. When sheet is folded, Uncle Sam is pictured, in color on the front. Folded size with image of Uncle Sam, 4⅜" x 2⅜". Condition: Very good. **$15.00 – 20.00.**

☞ **Plate 203. Doan's Directory of the United States**
A 1910 pamphlet, Foster-Milbur Co, Buffalo. "Peace &
Plenty." 8" x 5⅞". Condition: Very good. **$75.00 –
85.00.**

☜ **Plate 204. Cloth Flour Sack**
Manufactured by Belgrade Flour Mill Co., Belgrade,
MN. Circa 1941. 36" x 18". Condition: Excellent.
$100.00 – 125.00.

☞ **Plate 205. America Flour**
"The Talk of the Hour." Jas Wilson & Co., Rochester
NY Northwestern Miller. Copyright 1903. 14⅞" x 10½".
Condition: Excellent. **$100.00 – 125.00.**

77

Plate 206. Coffee Can
Universal Blend Coffee. E. B. Millar & Co., Chicago. Importers and Roasters of Strictly Fine Coffees. Metal can with the paper label covering all but the cover. 7" x 4¼" in diameter. Circa 1870. Condition: Good. **$200.00 – 250.00.**

☞ **Plate 207. Uncle Sam Brand Yakima Valley Apples**
Wapato, WA. "Contents one bushel by volume." Green background. 9" x 11". Circa 1918. Condition: Excellent. **$40.00 – 50.00.**

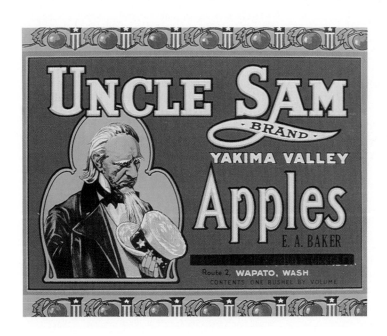

Plate 208. Uncle Sam Brand Yakima Valley Apples
Wapato, WA. "Contents one bushel by volume." Red background. 9" x 11". Circa 1918. Condition: Excellent. **$40.00 – 50.00.**

Plate 209. Uncle Sam Brand Yakima Valley Apples.
Wapato, WA. "Contents 40 lbs. net, one bushel." Blue background. 9" x 11" Circa 1918. Condition: Excellent. **$40.00 – 50.00.**

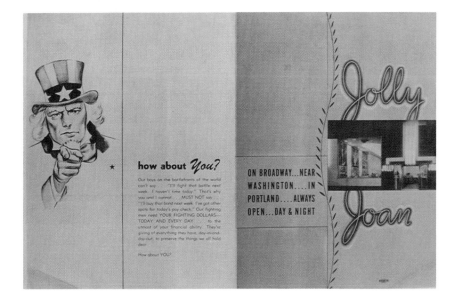

Plate 210. Menu
"Jolly Joan on Broadway, Near Washington, in Portland, Always Open Day & Night." The back cover pictures Uncle Sam saying, "How about you?" and goes on to ask the customer to buy bonds. L.I.P & BA Printing Co. Portland, Oregon. Circa 1941–42. 11" x 8½" folded. Condition: Excellent. **$10.00 – 15.00.**

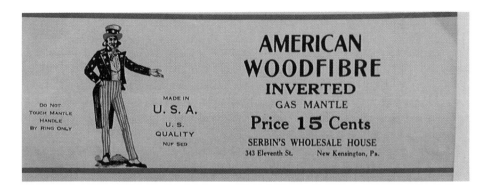

Plate 211. Advertising Label
"American Woodfibre" inverted gas mantel paper label. 3" x 6½". Manufacturer: Serbin's Wholesale House, New Kensington, PA. Circa 1920. Condition: Excellent. **$8.00 – 12.00.**

☜ **Plate 212. Van Camp's Pork and Beans**
Woman's Home Companion, June, 1914. 4¾" x 4½". Condition:
Excellent. **$8.00 – 10.00.**

☝ **Plate 213. Metal Sign**
"Buy OshKosh B' Gosh Union Made Overalls. J. F. Geraghty & Co.,
Rosemount, Minn." Patented May 14, 1918. The Kemper-Thomas Co.,
Cin. O. 14" x 29¾". Condition: Very Good. **$900.00 – 1,200.00.**

☞ **Plate 214. Store Display**
Cardboard cut-out of Uncle Sam with sleeves rolled up
holding sign "OshKosh B' Gosh. The world's best overall – Union made." 1942. 45" x 27". Condition: Very
good. **$750.00 – 1,000.00.**

☞ **Plate 215. OshKosh B' Gosh Time Book**
Artist: James Stuart. Green in color. 6⅛" x 3⅜".
Condition: Very good. **$35.00 – 45.00.**

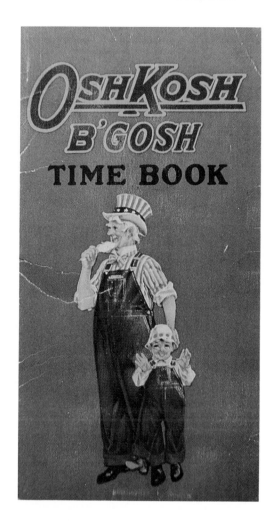

☝ **Plate 216. Popel – Giller Co., Inc., Warsau, IL**
Two-fold brochure for various types of liquor. July 17,
1917, typed on back page. 9⅜" x 5½" folded. Condition: Very good. **$100.00 – 120.00.**

☞ **Plate 217. Victor Brzezinski Poster**
Chromo lithographic print (full color). Compliments of Victor Brzezinski choice wines,
liquors, beers, cigars. 742 Burnet Avenue,
Syracuse, NY. Circa 1905. 20" x 15". Condition: Excellent. **$500.00 – 600.00.**

🕮 **Plate 218. "Old Overhot Rye"**
Its flavor a national delight." *Life* Magazine, December 8, 1910. 11" x 9". Condition: Excellent. **$12.00 – 15.00.**

☞ **Plate 219. Beer Bottle**
Uncle Sam Beer, Glencoe Brewing Company, Glencoe, Minnesota. 14 fluid ounces. Amber bottle with two paper labels, "Uncle Sam Bottle Beer." 9¼". Circa 1918. Condition: Excellent. **$125.00 – 150.00.**

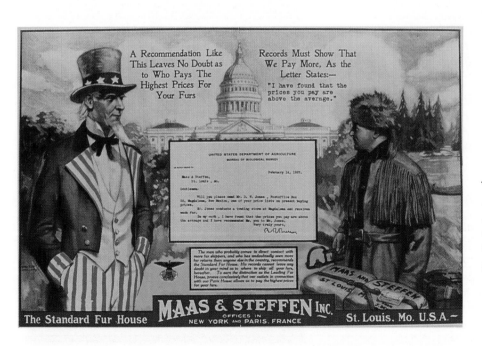

🕮 **Plate 220. Display Sign**
Artist: Walter Omison. Fur Advertisement for Maas & Stiffen, Inc., St. Louis. 12" x 18". Circa 1920. Condition: Very good. **$175.00 – 200.00.**

☞ **Plate 221. Jigsaw Puzzle**
The "Hush Puppies" Hound Dog dressed as Uncle Sam. Copyright 1976. Wolverine World-Wide, Inc., Rockford, Michigan. 19" x 12¾". Condition: Excellent. **$15.00 – 20.00.**

✍ **Plate 222. Metal Sign**
Baked enamel with chain hanger. "Statement Jan. 1, 1921, Capital, Reserve, Surplus, Assets." 12⅛" x 13⅛". Condition: Good. **$2,400.00 – 2,700.00.**

☞ **Plate 223. Store Display**
"For distinguished paint service." Full-color stone lithograph. Circa 1918. Dutch Boy Paints, USA. Artist: unknown. 48⅜" x 25⅜". Condition: Very good. **$1,200.00 – 1,500.00.**

✆ Plate 224. Wood Soap Box
Andrew Jergens & Co., Cincinnati. Glued on paper label on one side with Uncle Sam holding soap and an umbrella. 10⅝" x 15" x 9⅜". Circa 1870. Condition: Label, good; Box, very good. **$300.00 – 350.00.**

☞ **Plate 225. "Fairbanks – Gold Dust Washing Powder"**
Stone lithograph on paper on hardboard. Copyright by the Morgan Lithograph Company, Cleveland, Ohio. This image says it all! 13" x 26". Circa 1900. Condition: Very good. $6,000.00–6,500.00.

✆ Plate 226. Hotel Week Ad – Window Display
"National Hotel Week Sponsored by the American Hotel Association. June 2 – 8, 1942. Come on, folks, it's all yours! Travel-America Year. Hotels. An Asset to the Community. A Service to the Nation." Artist: Antonio Petruccelli. 16" x 22". Condition: Excellent. **$225.00 – 250.00.**

☞ **Plate 227.**
"United States. Defense Bonds and Stamps"
"This poster contributed by Gruen Watches." Circa 1941.
Industries Cooperation Series. 20¼" x 15¼". Condition:
Excellent. **$100.00 – 125.00.**

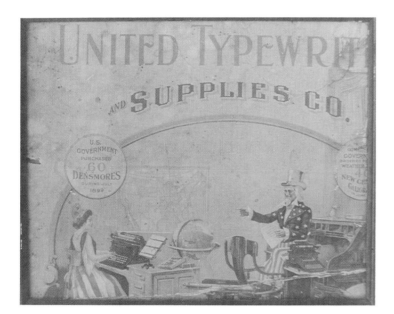

Plate 228.
United Typewriter and Supplies Company
8" x 10". Condition: Good. **$70.00 – 90.00.**

☞ **Plate 229. Score Card**
"Uncle Sam's Choice." D & M
Sporting Goods. Copyright 1913.
The Drape-Maynard Co., Plymouth,
N.H. 6⅛" x 3½", folded. Condition:
Excellent. **$75.00 – 100.00.**

☞ **Plate 230. Felt Banner**
"New York Yankees."
Bound in gold felt. 8" x 26".
Circa 1940. Condition: Very
good. **$60.00 – 75.00.**

☞ **Plate 231. Mug**
1984 Los Angeles Olympic Games mug with Sam, the
Olympic Eagle. Designed and decorated by Papel, Official Licensee, 1980 L.A. Olympic Committee. 3⅜" x 5".
Condition: Excellent. **$10.00 – 12.00.**

☞ **Plate 232. Stuffed Eagle**
Sam the Olympic Eagle. "Go for the Gold"
on a red vest. 7½". Los Angeles, 1984
Olympics. Condition: Excellent. **$25.00
– 35.00.**

☞ **Plate 233. Seat Cushion**
Official Rectangular Inflatable Cushion. Los Angeles 1984 Olympics. Pictures Olympic Eagle wearing Uncle Sam's hat and carrying the American Flag and Miss Liberty's torch. Manufactured by Moochie's under license. Copyright 1980 L.A.O. O.C. Exclusive Distributor: American Spectator, Inc. Condition: Excellent. **$20.00 – 25.00.**

✎ **Plate 234. "Greyhound presents a great new super-coach!"**
1939 magazine advertisement. 13½" x 21½". Condition: Excellent. **$25.00 – 35.00.**

☞ **Plate 235. Pontiac Silver Streak**
"Here's the Inside Story of the 1938 Pontiac Silver Streak, America's Finest Low-Priced Car." Inside folds show various views of the car. 1937, Copyright: The National Process Company, Inc. 20¼" x 12⅞", full size. Condition: Excellent. **$60.00 – 70.00.**

❧ **Plate 236. Continental Motors**
"The World's Greatest Truck Owner." Black and off white magazine advertisement. Circa 1917. 14" x 11". Condition: Excellent. **$15.00 – 20.00.**

☞ **Plate 237. Advertisement for Travel**
Bus Ride Magazine, October, 1975. Image 4¾" x 4¼". Page size 11" x 8½". Condition: Excellent. **$5.00 – 8.00.**

❧ **Plate 238. "The National Pen"**
1939 magazine advertisement. L. E. Waterman Co., New York. 10" x 7". Condition: Very good. **$15.00 – 20.00.**

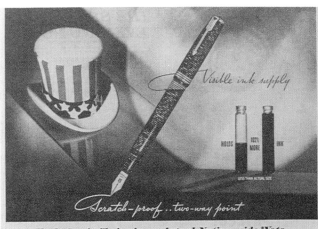

☞ **Plate 239. Parker Pen Company**
"Uncle Sam's choice in an actual nation-wide vote." The miracle pen — it carries all 48 states. Black and off-white magazine advertisement. Circa 1942. 14" x 11". Condition: Excellent. **$15.00 – 20.00.**

✎ **Plate 240. Parfait Glass**
Uncle Sam's Firecracker in blue and white with Uncle Sam's face with eleven cities printed in white on the back, Boston, Pasadena, Houston, Buffalo, Syracuse, Detroit, Minneapolis, Lincoln, Des Moines Knoxville, and Davenport. 10" x 3½" diameter at the lip, 3" diameter at base. Circa 1954. Condition: Excellent. **$10.00 – 15.00.**

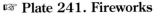

☞ **Plate 241. Fireworks**
1976 Independence Celebration Fountain, BC-232. Hexagon shaped cardboard box. Manufactured by Black Cat, Inc., Made in China. 6" x 5¼" x 4". Condition: Excellent. **$6.00 – 10.00.**

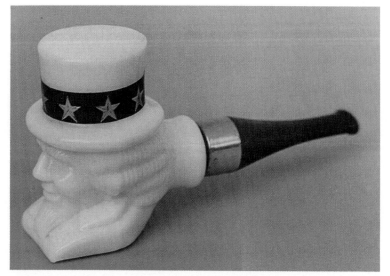

🖙 **Plate 242. Avon After-Shave Bottle**
Milk glass Uncle Sam in the form of a pipe.
The cap section of the pipe is blue plastic,
banded in gold. Uncle Sam's face serves as the
bottle. 3½" x 6¼". Circa 1976. Condition:
Excellent. **$15.00 – 18.00.**

☝ **Plate 243. Ashtray**
Triangular in shape. "I Want You" pose on
the bottom in blue. "Fyfe 'N Drum Needs
You. De Kalb, Ill. 815-758-1776." 3½" edges.
Condition: Excellent. Circa 1975. **$3.00 –
6.00.**

🖙 **Plate 244. "Register the Baby's Birth"**
Published by the U.S. Census Bureau.
Unsigned. 8¾" x 6". Copyright 1941. Condition:
Excellent. **$30.00 – 35.00.**

☞ **Plate 245. "Gem Damaskeene Razor"**
"Khaki Service Outfit." *Life* Magazine, December 5, 1918. 10" x 5½". Condition: Excellent.
$8.00 – 10.00.

☞ **Plate 246. Corning Glass Works**
Sergeant Snorkel in "I Want You" pose. Artist:
Mort Walker. 34" x 20⅞". Circa 1958. Condition:
Excellent. **$50.00 – 60.00.**

☞ **Plate 247. "I Want You to Keep this Package Moving"**
(Thanks, REA EXPRESS). Official Government Shipment
sticker. 5¼" x 3⅞". Circa 1960. Condition: Excellent. **$5.00 –
7.00.**

✒ **Plate 248. Magazine Ad**
"What you as a woman should know about the draft."
Ad for *Family Circle* Magazine. *Look* Magazine, June
25, 1968. 13" x 10½". Condition: Very good. **$8.00 –
12.00.**

☞ **Plate 249. La-z-boy Chair Ad**
"La-Z-Boy Wants You to Relax." Variation after
J. M. Flagg. 11¾" x 10½". Circa 1960. Condi-
tion: Excellent. **$10.00 – 15.00.**

Plate 250. "I Invite You to Attend 'America' "
"The Most Spectacular Musical Celebration in Our
Nation's History." A Project of the Great Miami
Chamber of Commerce in cooperation with the City
of Miami and the Miami Beach Tourist Development
Authority. Celebrate with us. American Revolution
Bicentennial, 1776 – 1976. 9" x 8", open. Condition:
Excellent. **$5.00 – 8.00.**

☞ **Plate 251. "Com'on In Join Our Red, White & Blue Party."**
"We want to do Business with You." 15½" x 9¼". Circa 1972. Condition: Excellent. **$15.00 – 20.00.**

☜ **Plate 252. United States Savings Bonds**
"We want you to stay with us to get a free U. S. Savings Bond." Uncle Sam in "I Want You" pose above U. S. Savings Bond. Advertising print, full color. Circa 1952. 9" x 4½". Condition: Excellent. **$12.00 – 15.00.**

☞ **Plate 253. Matchbook**
"Today's Army wants to join you. See your army recruiter, over 300 matchless opportunities guaranteed in writing before you enlist." "I Want You" illustration on the cover. Universal Match, Chicago. 2" x 3". Circa 1952. Condition: Very good. **$2.00 – 4.00.**

Plate 254. Matchbook Cover
"Beware of counterfeits. Know your money." The United States Secret Service Treasury Department. Made in the U. S. A. by the Diamond Match Co., N. Y. C. 4¼" x 1½". Circa 1948. Condition: Excellent. **$3.00 – 5.00.**

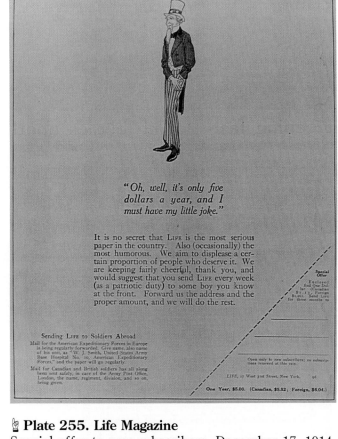

☞ **Plate 255. Life Magazine**
Special offer to new subscribers. December 17, 1914. Artist: A. D. Blashfield. 11" x 9". Condition: Excellent. **$10.00 – 12.00.**

≈ **Plate 256. Life Magazine**
Subscription offer. May 11, 1916. Artist: William Walker. 11" x 9". Condition: Excellent. **$10.00 – 12.00.**

☞ **Plate 257. Life Magazine**
Subscription offer. July 6, 1916. Artist: William Walker. 11" x 9". Condition: Excellent. **$10.00 – 12.00.**

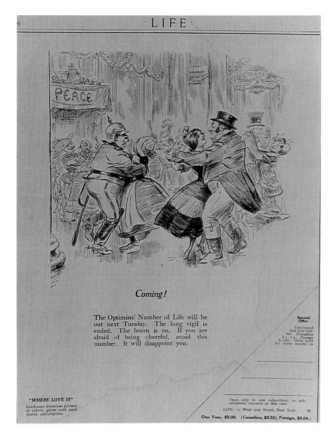

🖙 **Plate 258. Life Magazine**
Subscription offer. May 24, 1917. 11" x 9". Condition: Excellent. **$8.00 – 10.00.**

☞ **Plate 259. Budweiser**
"This Bud's For You." Mounted on red cardboard. 9" x 7". Circa 1976. Condition: Excellent. **$10.00 – 15.00.**

Plate 260. Liquor Bottle
Democratic National Commemorative. 1776 – 1976.
Campaign "76." Ezra Brooks. 80 Proof, 101 Months
Old ⅘ quart. Kentucky Straight Bourbon Whiskey.
Bottled by Ezra Brooks Distilling Co., Frankfort, KY.
Genuine Heritage China. Copyright 1976 R. H-60.
Ezra Brooks Liquor Bottle 185. 9¼" x 8½" x 3". Condi-
tion: Excellent. **$40.00 – 50.00.**

Cartoon Characters as Uncle Sam

This is an area of Uncle Sam collectibles that deals with noted cartoon characters dressed, in one form or another as Uncle Sam. Children, as well as adults, can have fun in this category of collecting. There always is, and always
will be, a patriotic event or other occasion where cartoon characters will be dressed as Uncle Sam. This is truly an
area of opportunity for the young, future collector to pursue.

☞ **Plate 261. Stuffed Garfield**
Label, "Garfield Uncle Sam," No. 31-0309, R. Dakin &
Co., San Francisco, Product of Korea. Copyright 1978
and 1981, United Feature Syndicate. 8" x 7". Condition: Excellent. **$30.00 – 35.00.**

☞ **Plate 262. Mickey Mouse Purse**
Fully beaded image of Mickey Mouse. Purse is brown leather trimmed with ¼" beadwork. Manufactured by Walt Disney Productions. Circa 1960. 8½" x 9½" x 3". Condition: Very good. **$100.00 – 125.00.**

🖎 **Plate 263. Painting on Velvet**
Uncle Scrooge in Uncle Sam's hat. "Quack!" 18" x 12". Condition: Very good. **$75.00 – 95.00.**

☞ **Plate 264. Bugs Bunny (hard rubber)**
Bugs Bunny's arms, legs, and head move; his right index finger is pointing, and his left palm is open and extended. Copyright 1975 Warner Bros. Inc. R. Dakin & Co., San Francisco, CA. Product of Hong Kong. 8⅝" x 3½" x 3". Condition: Excellent. **$25.00 – 35.00.**

Posters

Another of the extremely active categories of Uncle Sam collectibles is that of Posters. Illustrated posters depicting Uncle Sam in one form or another have been sought after and collected for the past 40 or 50 years. Some of the finest American and European artists and illustrators have had their creations reproduced in some of the best quality lithographic processes applied to the printing of posters. As far as World War I and World War II posters are concerned, I believe that Uncle Sam was utilized more effectively, than any other image. I cannot imagine any poster more widely known than that of James Montgomery Flagg's image of Uncle Sam on his 1917 "I Want You" poster. Dozens of other Uncle Sam posters by numerous noted artists are sought after by poster collectors, some of which can fetch prices equal to, if not more than, Flagg's most noted poster.

Condition in this category is extremely important. Try to acquire the finest condition possible in the posters that you seek to purchase.

☞ **Plate 265. "I Want You for the U. S. Army"**
"Nearest Recruiting Station." Most famous of all recruiting posters. First issued as a poster in 1917 by the Leslie Judge Publishers. James Montgomery Flagg's image for this poster was originally used as a *Leslie* magazine cover on July 6, 1916. The origional caption being "what are you doing for preparedness." "I Want You" with this image was first used on the *Leslie* cover on Feb 15, 1917. 40" x 30". Condition: Very good to fine. **$1,500.00 – 1,800.00.**

🕱 **Plate 266. "I Want You for the U. S. Army"**
"Enlist Now." Leslie-Judge Co., 1941. Artist: James Montgomery Flagg. Condition: Very good to fine. 40" x 28". **$500.00 – 600.00.**

☞ **Plate 267. "Side by Side – Britannia"**
"Britain's Day, December 7th 1918. Mass Meeting." Artist: James Montgomery Flagg. Condition: Very good to fine. 34" x 24". **$1,000.00 – 1,200.00.**

☞ **Plate 268. "Some Backing!"**
"The Empire State Needs Soldiers. Join the New York State Guard." 42" x 30". Artist: James Montgomery Flagg. Circa 1917. Condition: Very good to fine. **$1,200.00 – 1,500.00.**

☞ **Plate 269. "Help him to help U. S."**
"Help the Horse to Save the Soldier. The American RED STAR Animal Relief National Headquarters, Albany, N. Y." 33" x 23". Circa 1918. Artist: James Montgomery Flagg. Condition: Very good to fine. **$600.00 – 800.00.**

✎ **Plate 270. "I am telling you"**
"On June 28th I expect you to enlist in the army of war savers to back up any army of fighters. W.S.S. Enlistment." Artist: James Montgomery Flagg. 30" x 20". Circa 1917 – 1918. **$300.00 – 400.00.**

☞ **Plate 271.**
"Hold on to Uncle Sam's Insurance"
33" x 23". Circa 1918. Artist: James Montgomery Flagg. **$300.00 – 350.00.**

✎ **Plate 272. "Boys and Girls!"**
"You can help your Uncle Sam win the War. Save your quarters. Buy War Savings Stamps." Full-color stone lithograph. W.S.S. poster issued by U.S. Government with the Torch of Liberty Seal. 30" x 20". Circa 1917. Artist: James Montgomery Flagg. Condition: Very good to fine. **$400.00 – 450.00.**

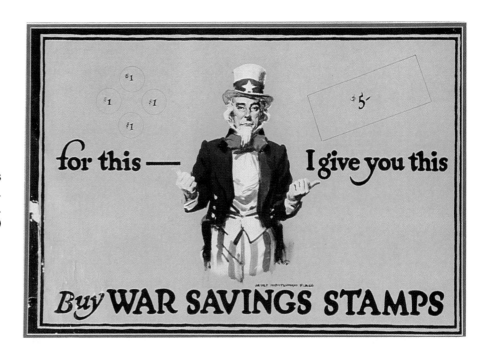

☞ **Plate 273.**
"For This – I Give You This"
"$5.00 for $4.00. Buy War Savings Stamps." 20" x 30". Circa 1917. Artist: James Montgomery Flagg. Condition: Very good. **$300.00 – 350.00.**

☞ **Plate 275. "Help China!"**
"China is Helping Us. United China Relief." 42" x 28". Circa 1938. Artist: James Montgomery Flagg. Condition: Very good. **$350.00 – 400.00.**

☜ **Plate 274. "Beware the Wrath of a Patient Man!"**
"Keep your War Savings Pledge." 30" x 20". Circa 1918. Artist: James Montgomery Flagg. Condition: Very good to fine. **$300.00 – 400.00.**

☞ Plate 277. "Your Forests — Your Fault — Your Loss!"
20" x 12". Circa 1934. Artist: James Montgomery Flagg. Condition: Very good. **$200.00 – 225.00.**

✐ **Plate 276. "Jap…You're Next!"**
"We'll Finish the job!" 42" x 30". Circa 1941. Artist: James Montgomery Flagg. Condition: Very good. **$800.00 – 900.00.**

✐ **Plate 278. "Your Red Cross Needs You!"**
21" x 14". Circa 1943. Artist: James Montgomery Flagg. Condition: Very good. **$250.00 – 300.00.**

☞ **Plate 279. "I WANT YOU — FDR"**
"Stay and Finish the Job! Independent Voters Committee of the Arts and Sciences for Roosevelt." 24" x 18". Circa 1939. Artist: James Montgomery Flagg. Condition: Very good. **$400.00 – 500.00.**

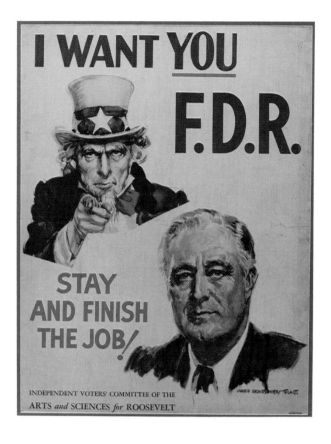

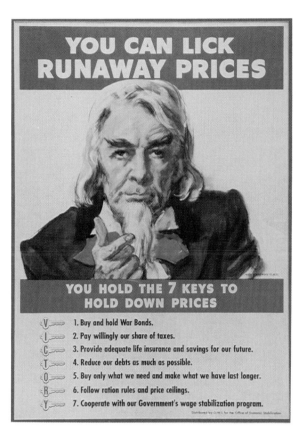

☜ **Plate 280. "You Can Lick Runaway Prices"**
"You Hold the 7 Keys to Hold Down Prices." 24" x 18". Circa 1950. Artist: James Montgomery Flagg. Condition: Very good to fine. **$100.00 – 125.00.**

☞ **Plate 281. "Appreciate America"**
"Everybody Pull Together! Buy United States War Bonds and Savings Stamps." 22" x 16". Circa 1943. Artist: James Montgomery Flagg. Condition: Very good to fine. **$250.00 – 300.00.**

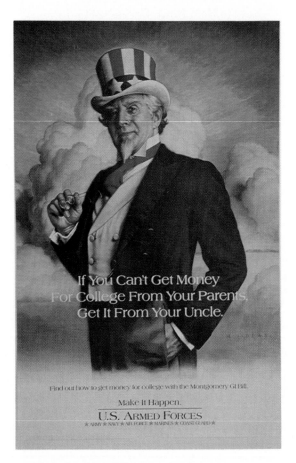

Plate 282. "I Want You"
"To Vote on Nov. 6 for Korean Bonus. In 1918 the famous artist, James Montgomery Flagg, painted this historical recruiting poster, known to every doughboy of WWI, and now in the permanent collection of the Smithsonian Institution. In order to use it once again in a great cause, *The American Legion Magazine* obtained permission to reproduce it from Mr. Flagg and the Smithsonian. The words, 'To vote on Nov. 6' have been substituted for the original, for the U. S. Army, Enlist Now.' " 13½" x 10". 1952. **$125.00 – 150.00.**

Plate 283. "I Want you For U. S. Army"
"Nearest Recruiting Station" 40" x 30". Circa 1953. Artist: James Montgomery Flagg. Condition: Good. **$100.00 – 125.00.**

Plate 284. "Recruiting Poster"
"If You Can't Get Money For College From Your Parents, Get It From Your Uncle." The most recently issued U. S. Army Forces Recruiting Poster. Artist: M. J. Deas. Copyright 1994. 36 x 24". Condition: Excellent. **$15.00 – 20.00.**

☝ **Plate 285. "I Want You for the U. S. Army"**
Metal with image on both sides. Fully baked enamel with wood frame. 37½" x 25½". Circa 1952. Artist: James Montgomery Flagg. Condition: Very good to fine. **$250.00 – 300.00.**

☝ **Plate 286. Very rare poster of Uncle Sam, John Bull, Miss Liberty, and Britannia**
"A Union in the Interest of Humanity — Civilization, Freedom and Peace for all time." 38" x 27". Circa 1900. Condition: Very good. **$1,200.00 – 1,500.00.**

🖐 **Plate 287. War Bond Poster**
"Shall we be more tender with our dollars than with the lives of our sons. Buy a United States Government Bond of the 2nd Liberty Loan of 1917." Artist: Dan Sayre Groesbeck. 20" x 30". Condition: Very good. **$300.00 – 350.00.**

☞ **Plate 288. "Free to learn...and free to benefit from our learning"**
"Americanism Appreciation Month. Sponsored by the American Legion and the American Legion Auxiliary". Magill-Weinsheimer Co. Circa 1940. Condition: Excellent. **$200.00 – 250.00.**

 Plate 289.
"America Lets Us Worship as We Wish"
"Attend the church of your choice. American Appreciation Month sponsored by the American Legion and the American Legion Auxiliary." Magill-Weinsheimer Co. Circa 1940. Condition: Excellent. **$200.00 – 250.00.**

☞ **Plate 290.**
"America Lets Us Choose Our Own Leaders"
"Do your part — you will benefit. American Appreciation month sponsored by the American Legion and the American Legion Auxiliary." Magill-Weinsheimer Co. Circa 1940. Condition: Excellent. **$200.00 – 250.00.**

Plate 291. "Reward for Honest Effort"
"In the U. S. A. you make your own success formula. Americanism Appreciation Month sponsored by the American Legion and the American Legion Auxiliary." Magill-Weinsheimer Co. Circa 1940. Condition: Excellent. **$200.00 – 250.00.**

Plate 292. "Shall we be more tender with our dollars than with the lives of our sons."
"MacCadoo, Secretary of Treasury." Stone litho., IL Litho. Co., Chicago. 20" x 30". Circa 1917. Condition: Very good. Artist: Dan Sayre Groesbeck. **$300.00 – 350.00.**

Plate 293. "I'm Counting on You!"
"Don't Discuss: Troop Movements • Ship Sailings • War Equipment." U. S. Government Printing, Circa 1943. Artist: Leon Helguera. 28" x 20". Condition: Excellent. **$150.00 – 175.00.**

☞ **Plate 294. "No Third Term!"**
"Democrats for Wilkie." Artist: Howard Scott. 14" x 24". Circa 1939. Condition: Very good. **$400.00 – 450.00.**

☞ **Plate 295. "Cost of Living in Two Wars"**
"Keep up the good work. Keep down living costs. Pay no more than ceiling prices." U. S. Government Printing, 1944. Condition: Excellent. **$100.00 – 125.00.**

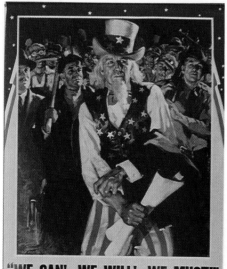

☞ **Plate 296. "WE CAN! WE WILL! WE MUST!"**
"All effort. All production. All possessions. Brain power. Horse power. Muscle power. Will power. Everything cheerfully channeled in one drive to one goal — VICTORY! Let's work harder at our jobs and do them better." J. B. Simpson, Inc., 30 N. Dearborn St., Chicago, ILL. Brown & Bigelow, St. Paul, Minnesota. Artist: J. W. Schlaikjer. Talio-Chrome process. 39½" x 19". Circa 1942. Condition: Excellent. **$125.00 – 150.00.**

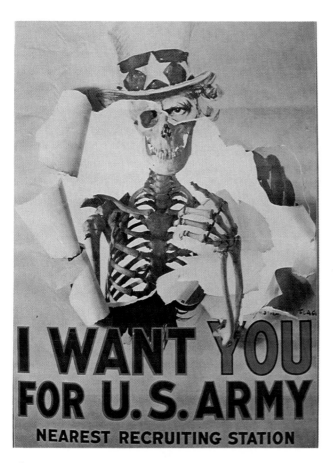

☝ **Plate 298. "E R A"**
Artist: Mario Uribe. Circa 1980. 26" x 20". Condition: Excellent. **$75.00 – 125.00.**

☝ **Plate 297. "I Want You for U. S. Army "**
"Nearest Recruiting Station." Vietnam War protest poster. 40" x 30". Circa 1968. **$125.00 – 150.00.**

☞ **Plate 299. "Mad"**
"Who Needs You." Full color. Published and distributed by O.S.P. Publishing, Monterey Park, California, E. C. Publications, Inc. 35" x 23". Circa 1989. Condition: Excellent. **$10.00 – 15.00.**

Pipes and Tobacco Tin-Tags

Two great examples of what you can expect to find in the area of Uncle Sam tobacco pipes are the "two-mold" clay pipe and the hand-carved and painted wooden pipe. It is interesting to note the incredible differences of the images on each pipe yet how you readily relate to the both of them being Uncle Sam. Both are very rare and should be considered a true find.

Beginning in the middle-to-late nineteenth century P. Lorallaird Tobacco Company began to use tin-tags affixed to their bulk tobacco sacks being shipped to market. These tin-tags soon took on the identity and image of Uncle Sam, as they were, in actuality, a form of an inspection tag. This of course is a similar scenario to that of Sam Wilson being a government meat inspector and supplier of goods to the U. S. Army, becoming known as Uncle Sam because of his Stamping "US" on all of his crates as a form of an inspection mark. These tin-tags existed in large quantities. Yet some of them are extremely rare.

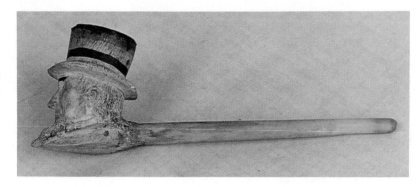

☞ **Plate 300. Smoking Pipe**
Two-mold clay. 2" x 6". 1876 Philadelphia Centennial Exposition era. Condition: Very good. **$350.00 – 375.00.**

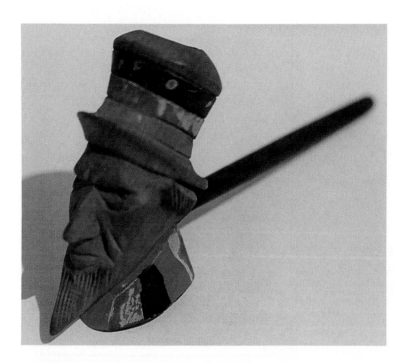

Plate 301. Smoking Pipe
Hand carved and painted hard-wood with ebony stem. Artist: unknown. Circa 1890. Condition: Very good. Carved head: 2⅛" x 6¼". **$250.00 – 275.00.**

☝ **Plate 302. Tobacco Tin-Tag**
Baked paint on tin. Maker: P. Lorallaird. Circa 1890. ¾". Condition: Very good. **$15.00 – 20.00.**

☝ **Plate 303. Tobacco Tin-Tag**
"Uncle Sam satisfying." Baked paint on tin. Circa 1900. 1" in diameter. Condition: Very good. **$35.00 – 50.00.**

✍ **Plate 304. Tobacco Tin-Tag**
"Uncle Sam." Baked paint on tin. Circa 1900. 1¼". tall. Condition: Very good. *Note: Very rare. **$75.00 – 100.00.**

☝ **Plate 305. Tobacco Tin-Tag**
Baked paint on tin. Circa 1900. ⅞". Condition: Very good. **$40.00 – 50.00.**

✍ **Plate 306. Tobacco Tin-Tag**
"Uncle Sam." Baked paint on tin. Circa 1900. 1½" long. Condition: Very good. **$10.00 – 15.00.**

Military and Political Badges, Pinbacks, Watch Fobs, and Jewelry

This is a category of Uncle Sam collectibles that has an extremely broad interest. Practically every antique or collectible shop has one or more showcase displaying "Smalls" which will inevitably include military and political badges and pin-backs. You will find that the most expensive ones will be those that have an image of Uncle Sam along with a political candidate or major military leader. You want to acquire the best condition possible in order to insure your investment.

A great variety of jewelry items depicting Uncle Sam in one form or another have been produced since the World War I era. Most all of it was made of lesser expensive materials and would fall more so in the classification of costume jewelry. However, the earlier pieces of better quality design and construction will fetch good prices.

☞ **Plate 307. Pin**
Round, metal. Full color. 1¼". Circa 1898. Condition: Excellent. **$125.00 – 140.00.**

☞ **Plate 308. Lapel Pin**
"Bound for Cuba." Bronze. 1½". Circa 1898. Condition: Excellent. **$60.00 – 75.00.**

☞ **Plate 309. Lapel Pin**
Uncle Sam. "Bound for Cuba." Metal. Circa 1898. 2⅛" x 1½". Condition: Excellent. **$85.00 – 95.00.**

☞ **Plate 310. Patriotic Pinback**
Circa 1900. 1½". Condition: Very good. **$125.00 – 150.00.**

☞ **Plate 311.
Patriotic Pinback**
Circa. 1900. 1¼". Condition: Very good. **$100.00 – 125.00.**

Plate 312. Political Pinback
"The Spirit of the Republic — Success —
President of all the people." Full color.
Date: Circa 1904. 2⅜". Condition: Very
good. **$1,200.00 – 1,500.00.**

Plate 313. Campaign Button
"No Third Term." F. D. Roosevelt's third
term against Wendel Wilke. ¾". Condition:
Excellent. **$35.00 – 45.00.**

Plate 314. Political Pinback
"Let's pull together." Lever on left side acti-
vates Hitler's hanging. Circa 1942. 1½". Condition: Very good. **$100.00 – 125.00.**

Plate 315. Jewelry Set – Costume
Earrings, pin, and ring, synthetic ruby, sap-
phire, and rhinestones set in a gold base
metal. Top hat pin – 1¼" x 1½". Circa 1950.
Ring – 1 x ⅝". Adjustable band. Earrings –
¾". Clip-on. Condition: Excellent. **$125.00
– 150.00.**

Plate 316. Jewelry – Costume
Pierced earrings – Uncle Sammy earring set. Enameled, cast brass bas-relief image. Copyright 1991. by "Lunch at the Ritz Earware," Inc., Chicago, IL, USA. Condition: Excellent. **$15.00 – 20.00.**

Plate 317. Celluloid Pin
Hand painted. Spanish/American War. Circa 1898. 2⅝" x 1". Condition: Very good. **$125.00 – 150.00.**

Plate 318. Jewelry – Costume
Enameled cast brass pin. Made by 1928, Inc., USA. Circa 1976. 2½" x 1". Condition: Excellent. **$25.00 – 30.00.**

Plate 319. Watch Fob
"1915 Panama Pacific." Exposition. Silver on copper on a leather strap. 1¾" x 1⅜". Condition: Excellent. **$600.00 – 700.00.**

114

Original Works of Art

Most important and most expensive in this category are original works of art by James Montgomery Flagg utilizing his image of Uncle Sam. Bear in mind that the exceedingly high prices for James Montgomery Flagg's art is based on the fact that there is very little of it out there. Though other works by Flagg not including Uncle Sam, will sell for much lesser prices, his Uncle Sam images are his best and most noted works. This of course is because of his most famous "I Want You" poster of 1917. Other artists' original works in this category will vary in price according to their notoriety, the quality of the individual piece, the period of time in which it was produced, its historic significance, or simply what the market has already established as its approximate value. Acquiring proper authenticity should be a must to the serious buyer.

☞ **Plate 320. Watercolor (In half-tone)**
"Come on America. We've Got a Big Job to Do!" Artist: James Montgomery Flagg. 24" x 20". Circa 1918. Condition: Excellent. **$18,000.00 – 20,000.00.**

✄**Plate 321. Pen and Ink**
"Home from the War." Artist: James Montgomery Flagg. 18½" x 13½". Circa 1918. Condition: Excellent. **$12,000.00 – 15,000.00.**

Plate 322. Watercolor
"I Need You Now!" Artist: James Montgomery Flagg. 26" x 28". Circa 1952. Condition: Excellent. **$21,000.00 – 24,000.00**

Plate 323. Watercolor
"Intergrity – Honesty – Service." "Every arrow feels the pull of the earth – To hit the mark, aim high." Artist: James Montgomery Flagg. 18½" x 23½". Circa 1917. Condition: Excellent. **$20,000.00 – 22,000.00.**

Plate 324. Watercolor
"Alert." Artist: James Montgomery Flagg. 11" x 8½". October 1941. Condition: Excellent. **$8,000.00 – 10,000.00.**

☞ **Plate 325. Watercolor**

"You Want <u>Me</u>." Known to be the very last image of Uncle Sam executed by J. M. Flagg shortly before his death. Artist: James Montgomery Flagg. 14" x 10". May 1960. Condition: Excellent. **$7,000.00 – 9,000.00.**

✎ **Plates 326 & 327. Pen and Ink**

Actor Robert Taylor being finger printed by Uncle Sam. In line are Lionel Barrymore in trench coat, a young John Wayne in his western attire, and behind him Ethel Barrymore along with other personalities all who were close friends of this socialite artist. Two-piece illustration. Artist: James Montgomery Flagg. Each 25" x 29", totalling 25" x 58". Circa. 1952. Condition: Excellent. **$18,000.00 – 20,000.00.**

☞ Plate 328. Pen and Ink
"1867 – 1947." Artist: James Montgomery Flagg. 24" x 28".
Circa 1947. Condition: Excellent. **$10,000.00 – 12,000.00.**

☞ Plate 329. Political Cartoon
Uncle Sam quoting President Roosevelt. Wolff
pencil on coquille board, 13¼" x 10¾". Circa
1940. Artist: Rollin Kirby. Condition: Very Good.
$700.00 – 900.00.

☞ Plates 330 & 331. James Cagney
Limited edition print of a portrait profile of James Cagney, incorporated with vignettes of Cagney as Uncle Sam in
character from the motion pictures, *Yankee Doodle Dandy* and *Public Enemy Number One*. An original pencil
"remark" drawing of Cagney as Uncle Sam in the lower right corner. This print is number 197 of an edition of 302
which the artist, Everett Raymond Kinstler, produced gratuitously, and likewise Mr. Cagney modeled for Mr. Kinstler, for the benefit of the Player's Club at Gramercy Park in New York, New York in 1980. **$500.00 – 700.00.**

☞ **Plate 332. Oil Painting**
"Uncle Sam — I. R. S." Artist: Robert Gunn. Date: 1986.
24" x 20", oil on canvas. Condition: Excellent.
$7,000.00 – 9,000.00.

 **Plate 333. Oil Painting**
Original cover art for *Working Woman* magazine,
1995. Artist: Robert Gunn. Signed: Monogram signature "R" over "G." 1994. 18" x 14", oil on canvas.
Condition: Excellent. **$4,000.00 – 5,000.00.**

☞ **Plate 334. Plaster Sculpture**
"Little Yankee Doodle, 1876." Fully colored sculpture of a little boy dressed in the top hat, vest, and coat of Uncle Sam,
carrying a thirteen star American flag. The artist/sculptor,
Gerald Czulewicz Sr., has captured the spirit of a little boy
doing his bit in celebrating what would then be the centennial of his country. Hand painted. Signed on the base, CZ,
1988. 10" x 4½". Condition: Excellent. **$800.00 –
1,200.00.**

☜ **Plate 335. Pen and Ink and Watercolor**
"Get behind Uncle Sam." Original art for World War I poster. Artist: William Henry Walker. 30" x 21". Condition: Very good. **$7,000.00 – 9,000.00.**

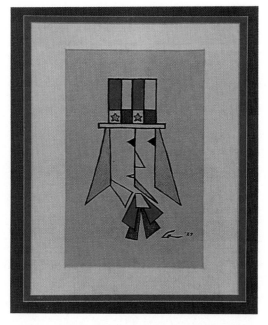

☝ **Plate 336. Pen and Ink and Watercolor**
Non-partisan Uncle Sam. Signed CZ '89. Artist: Gerald E. Czulewicz Sr. 12¾" x 15⅛". Condition: Excellent. **$600.00 – 700.00.**

☜ **Plate 337. Pen & Ink – Watercolor**
Uncle Sam as an integral part of the national emblem, original illustration for the title page of this book. Artist: Gerald E. Czulewicz Sr. Date: 1988. Signed: "C. Z. '88." Size: 16" x 14". Condition: Excellent. **$600.00 – 900.00.**

☞ **Plate 338. Pen and Ink**
"Political Chestnuts" cover illustration for magazine publication. Uncle Sam looking up into a chestnut tree holding the figures of Andersen, O'Brien, and Grant. Donohue and Quintard "chestnuts" are on the ground. Artist: C. deGrimm. 20" x 15". Condition: Very good. Circa 1887. **$1,500.00 – 2,000.00.**

☞ **Plate 339. Pen and Ink**
"The Pie of Plenty, 1887 – 88" cover illustration for magazine publication "Political Chestnuts." Uncle Sam with Columbia, dressed as an Indian. "Labor Gruel. Poor Crops, No Food, No Work, No Money." Artist: C. deGrimm. 20" x 15". Condition: Very good. **$1,500.00 – 2,000.00.**

☞ **Plate 340. Pen and Ink**
"Cuba – Go 'Way. I Don't Like You." Artist: Alexander VanLeshout. Circa 1901. 20" x 18". Condition: Excellent. **$2,100.00 – 2,400.00.**

☜ **Plate 341. Pen and Ink**
Original art for reproduction as a cartoon in a major periodical "Total Exports July $109,031,158, Total Exports Seven months $830,883,816, Excess Exports $324,526, 625." August 17, 1901. Artist: C. J. Newman. 22⅝" x 17⅝". Condition: Excellent. **$2,000.00 – 2,400.00.**

☞ **Plate 342. Pen and Ink**
Original editorial illustration for the *Washington Post*. Artist: Ole May. 20¾" x 15¾". Circa 1898. Condition: Excellent. **$2,300.00 – 2,500.00.**

☜ **Plate 343. Pen and Ink**
Original art for Brown & Bigglow calender. Artist: Stan Ekman. 13½" x 11". Circa 1954. Condition: Excellent. **$600.00 – 900.00.**

☞ **Plate 344. Charcoal and Pen and Ink**
"100th anniversary of the birth of President Rutherford B. Hayes — A Father of Industry in America." Artist: Howard Sanden. 26" x 20". Circa 1922. Condition: Very good. **$900.00 – 1,200.00.**

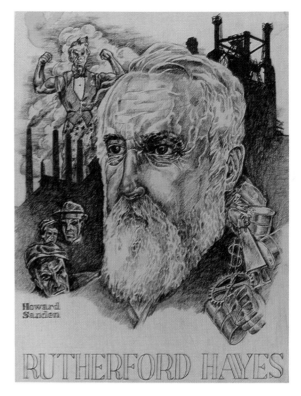

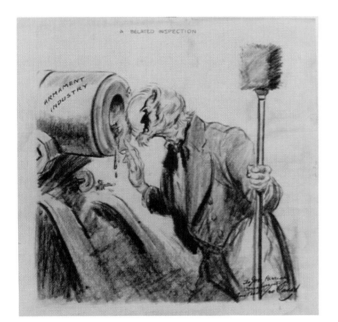

✍ **Plate 345. Artist's Crayon and Charcoal**
"A Belated Inspection." Artist: Jonathan Cassell. 14¼" x 14¼". Circa 1899. Condition: Very good. **$3,000.00 – 4,500.00.**

☞ **Plate 346. "The Spirit Of 1943"**
Comprehensive oil sketch for painting commissioned by the Pennsylvania Railroad. Reproduced in *Saturday Evening Post* in 1943 as advertisement. Oil painting on "stat" paper mounted on board. 16½" x 23". Artist: Dean Cornwell. 1943. Condition: Excellent. **$3,000.00 – 3,500.00.**

☞ **Plate 347. Artist's Crayon and Tempra**
Heightened with white. "Tanker Sinkings."
Artist: Lute Pease. Size: 16" x 20". Circa
1940. Condition: Excellent. **$500.00 –
700.00.**

☞ **Plate 348. Artist's Crayon and Tempra**
Heightened with white. Uncle Sam pulling a
"sweet tooth" from a young boy, U.S. Public.
Uncle Sam depicts sugar rationing. "Hurt? No,
Not Much." Artist: Lute Pease. 15" x 18". Circa
1941. Condition: Excellent. **$900.00 –
1,100.00.**

☞ **Plate 349. Charcoal Heightened with Tempra**
Drawing for the *New York Post*, Monday, February
19, 1948, by M. Lubovsky. "President Truman's twice
repeated statement about the immediate admittance
of 100,000 Jews to Palestine. October 4, 1946."
McMillan, seated in a jeep, is handing a rifle to Saud.
In the background, standing next to a barrel of Arabi-
an oil is Uthandt. Uncle Sam's hat is inverted on the
top of the barrel. 19" x 25¾". Condition: Excellent.
$3,000.00 – 4,000.00.

☞ Plate 350.
Pen & Ink and Watercolors
Drawing for the *Minneapolis Star and Tribune*. Victory Parade with Uncle Sam in the lead, along with Miss Liberty and Franklin Roosevelt. A mother and child looking on, are saying, "Mommy! Where's all the funny clowns?" "This is no circus son, this is the 1942 'all out for victory' parade!" Artist: Silas Olson. 9½" x 13". Condition: Excellent. **$400.00 – 450.00.**

☞ Plate 351. Plaster Model
Plaster production piece identical to the bronze sculpture (whereabouts unknown) commissioned by F. W. Eichorn in 1917 to be used as a flag-holder in storefront window displays during World War I. Model executed by sculptor, Guido Rebechini, signed on base. Copyright 1917 by F. W. Eichorn on back of base. "Rollin' 'em Up!" Hole in left rear of base to hold the flag. 12⅝" tall, base measures 3½" x 3⅝". Condition: Very good. **$400.00 – 450.00.**

☜ Plate 352. Bronze
Diameter, 7"; height 2¼". Mounted on wood with incised, carved chevron, hand enameled red, white, blue, and gold. Overall size, 17¼" x 20½". Circa 1900. Condition: Excellent. **$4,000.00 – 5,000.00.**

Plate 353. Oil Painting
"I Want You for U. S. Army." "Nearest Recruiting Station." Three section oil painting used during WWII for the Brooklyn, New York Recruiting Center. After James Montgomery Flagg, Circa 1944. 17' x 10', oil on canvas. Condition: Very good. **$3,000.00 – 4,000.00**

Plate 354. Watercolor
Black Uncle Sam selling cigars, very rare illustration. Artist: unknown. Circa 1885. 16" x 12". Condition: Very good. **$1,200.00 – 1,500.00.**

Folk Art and Primitives

One of the most enjoyable yet most controversial areas of collectibles, with or without the applied image of Uncle Sam, is that of folk art or primitives. The prices being realized at auctions, antique shows, and in antique shops for eighteenth, nineteenth, and early twentieth century American folk art and primitives have led to the extremely profitable activity of the production of fakes and frauds. However, folk art or primitives in actuality can and are being produced at this present time just as they were during any period of time in the past. It's truly a matter of representation, whether you are being offered a piece of folk art stated as being old or new. Buying folk art or primitives of Uncle Sam items, one should be knowledgeable enough to begin with or should seek professional opinions. There are equally as great folk art pieces being produced by contemporary artists as have been produced over the past two hundred years. Prices will vary in a most unpredictable manner. Let your heart guide your pocketbook.

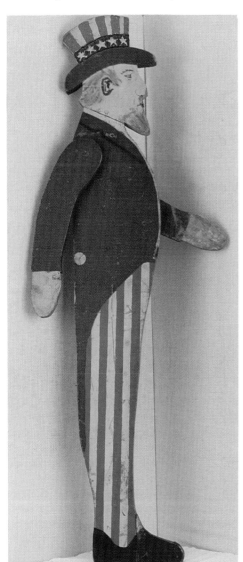

Plate 355. Flag Pole Holder
All wood profile of Uncle Sam with moveable arms that swing out to hold flag pole. All original paint. Overall height: 60". Condition: Very good. Circa 1918. 1920. **$650.00 – 750.00.**

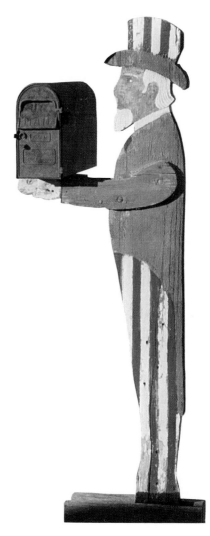

Plate 356. Mailbox Holder
All wood profile of Uncle Sam, original paint with minor restoration, original cast-iron mail box mounted on wooden swivel arms of Uncle Sam. Overall height: 60". Circa 1918. Condition: Very good. **$750.00 – 850.00.**

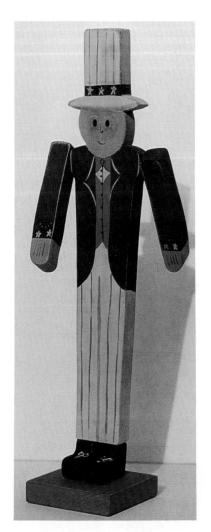

Plate 357. Whirligig
Hand painted, wood on a wood base. Uncle Sam's arms swing. 15" x 4¾" on a 3⅜" x 3⅜" base. Circa 1940. Condition: Excellent. **$50.00 – 70.00.**

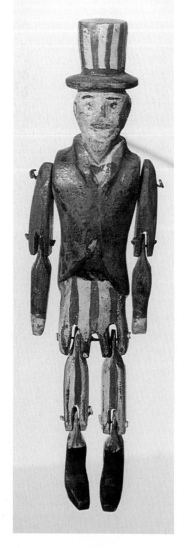

Plate 358. Dancing Uncle Sam
Hand carved and painted wood Uncle Sam dancing figure. Arms jointed at shoulders and elbows, legs jointed at knees and ankles. All original paint. Figure is extended by ¼" dowel rod, 40" long from back side. Overall height: 12½". Circa 1880. Condition: Very good. **$900.00 – 1,200.00.**

**Plate 359.
Dancing Uncle Sam**
Wood and metal. Uncle Sam figure extending from a stars and stripes post, dances on moveable legs and arms when board is snapped. 15½" x 28" x 8½". Condition: Excellent. Circa 1885. **$3,000.00 – 3,500.00.**

☞ **Plate 360. Uncle Sam on Big Wheel Bicycle**
Hand carved and hand painted. Bicycle made of cast iron with oak rim spoked wheels. Uncle Sam's jacket tails made of hand painted tin. Twentieth century (contemporary). Overall height: 52". Condition: Very good. **$450.00 – 500.00.**

☞ **Plate 361. Papier Maché Head**
Over-sized head of Uncle Sam made of wire mesh and papier maché. All original paint. Overall height: 25". Circa 1890. *Note: This head was used in Mardi Gras carnivals and parades. **$450.00 – 550.00.**

☞ **Plate 362. Uncle Sam – Hitler Whimsical Woodcarving**
Folk art woodcarving of Uncle Sam holding sledgehammer to hit head of Hitler on bell ringing device. Original natural wood finish. Artist: August Jackson, Hurley, Wisconsin. Signed and dated on base. Dated 1942. Overall height: 15". Condition: Very good. **$600.00 – 700.00.**

☜ **Plate 363. Wood Carving**
"A Match for All." Original paint. 12⅞" x 6⅞". Condition: Very good. Circa 1945. **$100.00 – 125.00.**

☝ **Plate 364. Whirligig**
Hand carved, full wood figure of Uncle Sam. Mounted on a wood block. 17¾" x 5" with an arm spread of 13". Circa 1935. Condition: Very good. **$175.00 – 225.00.**

☜ **Plate 365. Folk Art Shadow Dancer**
Twentieth century, hand painted, tin shadow dancer. Full figure of Uncle Sam seated. Signed in gold on the back of the left leg, "Young." 14" x 6". Condition: Excellent. **$100.00 – 120.00.**

☞ **Plate 366. Card Tray Holder**
Hand carved, hand painted wooden figure of Uncle Sam holding a red card tray, painted on the inside with the American flag – eight stars. Overall height, 13", 4" front to back. Card holder measures 4½" x 5¼". Circa 1976. Condition: Excellent. **$60.00 – 80.00.**

☞ **Plate 367. Wooden Nutcracker**
Fake fur hair, mustache, and beard. Coat tails open his mouth to crack the nut. Made in Taiwan. Overall height 14¾". Figure of Uncle Sam, 13⅜" high x 4½" wide. Circa 1975. Condition: Excellent. **$65.00 – 75.00.**

☞ **Plate 368. Wood Carving**
Hand painted. 4⅛" x 1¾". Circa 1976. Condition: Excellent. **$15.00 – 18.00.**

☞ **Plate 369. Wood Doll**
Painted face and dressed in felt suit. 3¼"
tall. Condition: Very good. Circa 1960.
$8.00 – 12.00.

Sheet Music

The image of Uncle Sam on the cover as well as the music itself was intended to inspire and instill in all Americans the necessary patriotic spirit to become victorious in all of our conflicts. Collecting sheet music in general has become a significant part of the antique and collectible market. The quality of the illustrations on the covers, the artists, and the subjects depicted, are their main attraction. It won't be long before sheet music covers with Uncle Sam illustrated images will be selling for close to the price range of posters having similar patriotic art work. The song titles, the artists, the illustrations, and in some cases, the historic significance, all or in part, will influence the prices. Condition is extremely important in this category. Near mint is most desirable.

🖘 **Plate 370. "Are You a True American?"**
Words and music by Margaret Jeffries Timmons, Mishawaka, Indiana. 12" x 9¼". Condition: Excellent. **$20.00 – 25.00.**

☞ **Plate 371. "Yankee Doodle Dandy"**
Warner Bros. presents James Cagney. Jimmy Cagney
pictured on front cover with his Uncle Sam hat. Based
on the story of George M. Cohan. Lyrics and music by
George M. Cohan. Inscribed: To Jerry, A true "Yankee
Doodle Dandy" (Jerry Czulewicz). Given to the author
for his book by Mr. Cagney. Signed, James Cagney. 13¼"
x 10½". Condition: Excellent. **$200.00 – 250.00.**
Regular original issue, not signed, **$35.00 – 45.00.**

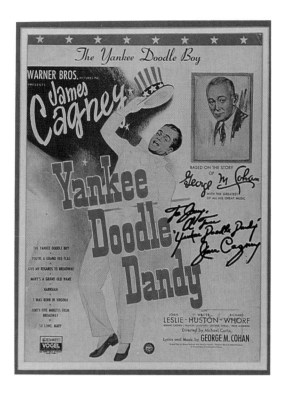

☜ **Plate 372. "We're Going to Kick the
Hell out of Will-Hell-Em"**
Words and music by Louis Matthew Long.
McGarry-Long Music Pub. Co. 14 x 11". Con-
dition: Excellent. **$35.00 – 40.00.**

☞ **Plate 373. "The Sammies Are Coming"**
The song hit of the allied countries. Words by Walter
S. Hunt. Music By E. A. Powell. Published by Hunt
& Powell, 102 University St., Peoria, Ill. 14" x 11".
Condition: Excellent. **$30.00 – 35.00.**

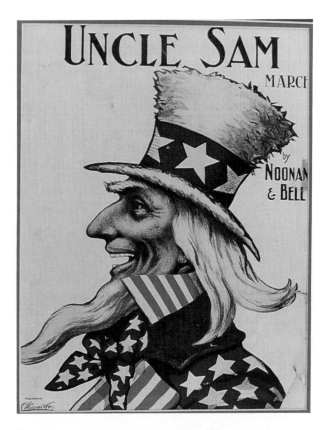

☙ **Plate 374. "You'll Be There"**
Lyrics by J. Keim Brennan. Music by Ernest R. Ball. M. Witmark & Sons, New York, Chicago, London. 14" x 11". Condition: Excellent. **$60.00 – 70.00.**

☞ **Plate 375. "Uncle Sam March"**
By Noonan & Bell. 14" x 11". Condition: Excellent. **$75.00 – 85.00.**

☙ **Plate 376. "I Think We've Got Another Washington and Wilson Is His Name"**
"A Popular Patriotic Song." Words and music by Geo. Fairman. Kendis-Brockman Music Co., Inc., New York. Einsen, N. Y. 13¼" x 10¼". Condition: Excellent. **$60.00 – 70.00.**

☞ **Plate 377. "Give a Bonus to Our Men"**
In honor of U. S. Veterans, Buck Privates Society. By Rus. Collier & Ben Seigel. Artist: E. D. Sullivan. Published by Collier & Seigel 2421 No. Clark St., Chicago. 12" x 9½". Condition: Excellent. $20.00 – 25.00.

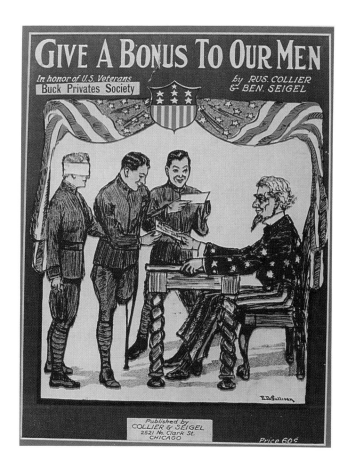

✐ **Plate 378. "We'll Carry the Star Spangled Banner thru the Trenches"**
Words and music by Daisy M. Erd, Chief Yeoman U.S.N.R.F. Published by District Welfare Aide, Bldg. 5, Boston Navy Yard. 14" x 11". Condition: Excellent. $25.00 – 35.00.

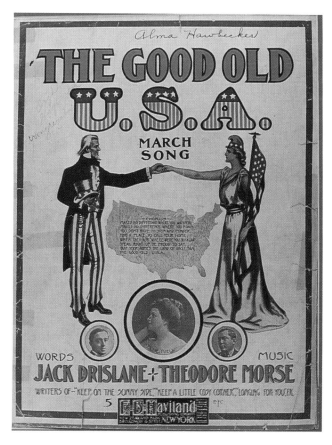

☞ **Plate 379. "The Good Old U.S.A. March Song"**
Words by Jack Drisland. Music by Theodore Morse. F. D. Haviland, New York. 14" x 11". Condition: Good. $50.00 – 60.00.

☞ **Plate 380.**
"I'm Just an Old Jay from the U.S.A."
Words by Ed Moran & Vincent Bryan. Music by Harry Von Tilzer. Harry Von Tilzer Music Publishing Co. Artist: E. H. Pfeiffer. 14" x 11". Condition: Excellent. **$60.00 – 70.00.**

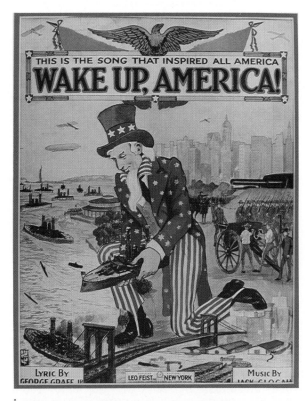

☞ **Plate 381. "Wake Up, America!"**
"This is the song that inspired all America." Lyrics by George Graff, Jr. Music by Jack Glogall. Popular Edition. Leo. Feist, New York. 14" x 11". Condition: Excellent. **$60.00 – 70.00.**

☞ **Plate 382. "I Am An American!"**
"Dedicated to every real American." Words and music by Benjamin Edwards Neal. Neal Publishing Company. The Boston Music Co., sole selling agents. 12¼" x 9¼". Condition: Excellent. **$25.00 – 30.00.**

☞ **Plate 383. "We'll Build a Little Home in the U.S.A. "**
"The hit of F. Ziegfeld Jr.'s Ziegfeld Follies." As introduced
and sung by Bernard Granville. Words by Howard Wesley.
Music by Chas. Elbert. Published by Leo. Feist, New York.
14" x 11". Condition: Excellent. **$20.00 – 25.00.**

❧ **Plate 384. "Dear Old America"**
"You played the winning hand. Waltz Song." Words
and music by J. J. Frederick. Published by J. J.
Frederick, Prophetstown, Ill. Browntone. 14" x 11".
Condition: Excellent. **$40.00 – 50.00.**

☞ **Plate 385. "What Kind of an American Are You?"**
"What are you doing over here?" Words by Lew. Brown
and Chas. McCarron. Music by Albert Von Tilzer.
Broadway Music Corporation. 14" x 11". Condition:
Excellent. **$27.00 – 32.00.**

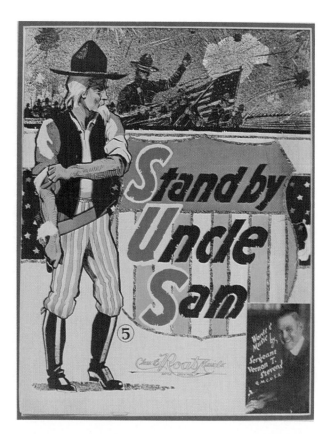

🎵 **Plate 386. "Stand By Uncle Sam"**
Charles Roat Music Co., Battle Creek, Mich. Words and Music by Sergeant Vernon T. Stevens, Q.M.C.U.S.A. 14" x 11". Condition: Very good. **$40.00 – 45.00.**

☞ **Plate 387.**
"Are you Lending a Hand to Yankee Land?"
Words by J. Will Callahan. Music by Blanche M. Tice. Blanche M. Tice Music Pub. Co., Sioux City, Iowa. 14" x 11". Condition: Excellent. **$20.00 – 25.00.**

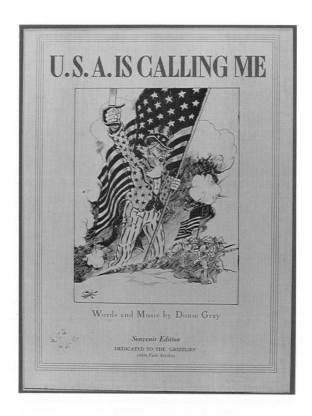

🎵 **Plate 388. "U.S.A. Is Calling Me"**
Words and music by Donie Gray. Souvenir edition. Dedicated to the "Grizzlies," 14th Field Artiliary. Hand dated, 12/28/17. 11" x 14". Artist: Tigner. Condition: Excellent. **$80.00 – 100.00.**

☞ **Plate 389. "To Our Army and Navy U.S.A."**
March song by Kate Baldwin, arranged by Harry J. Lincoln. Published by Harry J. Lincoln Music Co., Williamsport, Penn. 14" x 11". Condition: Excellent. **$35.00 – 40.00.**

🖋 **Plate 390. "Uncle Sam Won't Go To War"**
Words by Casper Nathan. Music by F. Henri Klickman. Frank K. Root & Co., Chicago, New York. 14" x 11". Condition: Excellent. **$30.00 – 35.00.**

☞ **Plate 391. "For Your Country and My Country"**
"The Official Recruiting Song." by Irving Berlin. Artist: Barbelle. 14" x 11". Condition: Excellent. **$45.00 – 50.00.**

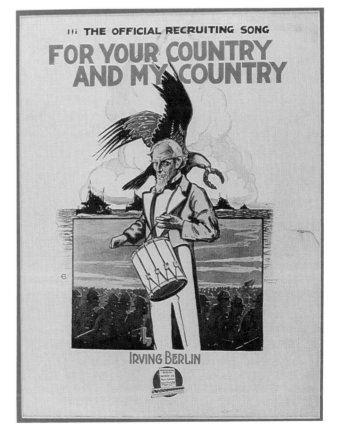

139

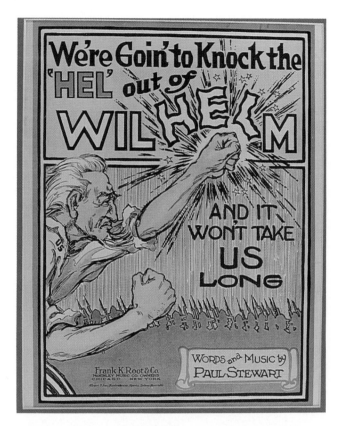

☞ **Plate 392. "Any Bonds Today?"**
Theme song of the National Defense Savings Program. Souvenir Copy. Words and music by Irving Berlin. Copyright by Henry Morgenthau, Jr., Secretary of the Treasury, Washington D.C. 12" x 9". Condition: Excellent. **$20.00 – 25.00.**

☝ **Plate 393. "We're Goin' to Knock the 'Hel' out of Wilhelm and it Won't Take Us Long"**
Words and music by Paul Stewart. Frank K. Root & Co. McKinley Music Co., Owners, Chicago, New York. 14" x 11". Condition: Excellent. **$50.00 – 60.00.**

☞**Plate 394.**
"You Can't Beat Us, if it Takes Ten Million More"
Lyrics by J. Keirn Brennan. Music by Ernest R. Ball. M. Witmark & Sons, New York, Chicago, London. Artist: Dunk, New York. 13⅝" x 10½". Condition: Very good. **$60.00 – 70.00.**

☞ **Plate 395.**
"What Are You Going to Do to Help the Boys"
Lyrics by Gus Kahn. Music by Egbert Van Alstyne.
Jerome H. Remick and Co., Detroit and New York.
14"x 11". Condition: Very good. **$30.00 – 35.00.**

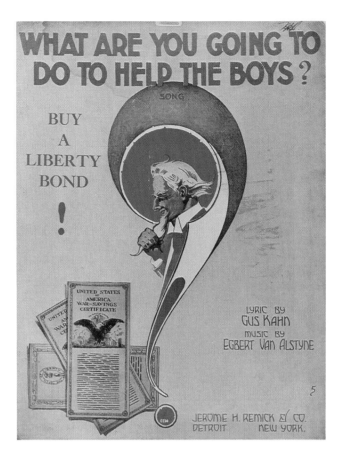

☞ **Plate 396. "America, He's for You!"**
By Andrew B. Sterling. Joe Morris Music Co., 145 W.
45th St., N.Y. Artist: E.H. Pfeiffer. Copyright 1918 by
the Joe Morris Music Co. 14" x 11". Condition: Excellent. **$20.00 – 25.00.**

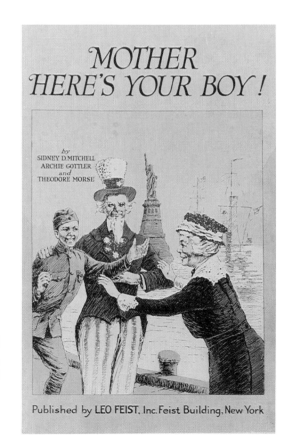

☞ **Plate 397. "Mother, Here's Your Boy!"**
By Sidney D. Mitchell, Archie Gottler, and
Theodore Morse. Published by Leo Feist, Inc.,
New York. Copyright 1918. 10½" x 7". Condition:
Excellent. **$50.00 – 55.00.**

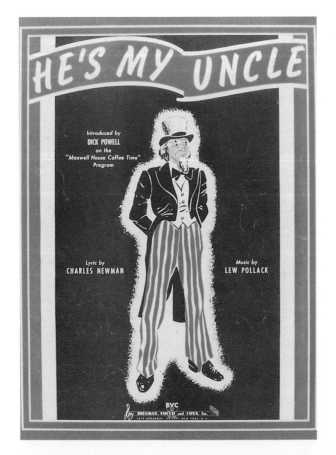

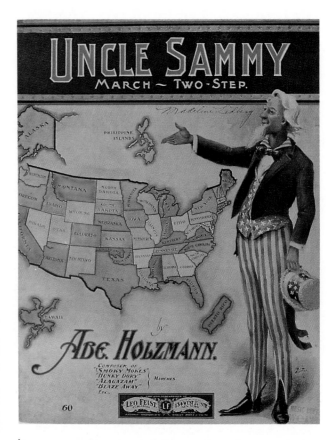

🙠 **Plate 398. "He's My Uncle"**
Introduced by Dick Powell on the "Maxwell House Coffee Time" program. Lyrics by Charles Newman. Music by Lew Pollack. BVC – Brigman, Vocco and Conn, Inc. 14" x 11". Condition: Excellent. **$18.00 – 25.00.**

👆 **Plate 399. "Uncle Sammy"**
By Abe Holzmann. Published by Leo Feist, New York. Artist: Helene Carter. 14" x 11". Condition: Excellent. **$50.00 – 60.00.**

🙠 **Plate 400. "The New Star"**
"March Two Step" By J.C. Halls. "To our President, Theo. Roosevelt. Artist: H. R. Smith. Copyright 1908, six pages. 14" x 11". **$45.00 – 50.00.**

☞ **Plate 401. "That International Rag"**
Words and music by Irving Berlin. Artist: E. H.
Pfeiffer, New York. Copyright 1913 by Waterson,
Berlin, and Snyder Co., New York. Six pages. 14" x
11". Condition: Very good. **$40.00 – 45.00.**

🎵 **Plate 402. "The Tuneful Yankee"**
A Monthly Magazine devoted to the interests of Popu-
lar Music. Vocal, Instrumental, Mechanical. Vol. 1, No.
10, November, 1917. Forty pages. Artist: Andre C.
DeTakach. Published by Walter Jacobs, Boston, Mass.
Atlantic Printing Co., Boston. 13" x 10". Condition:
Excellent. **$45.00 – 50.00.**

☞ **Plate 403. "America United"**
March. By Sam A. Perry. Published by Belwind
Inc., New York. Copyright 1921. Artist: Irwin D.
Hoffman. 14" x 11". Condition: Excellent. **$30.00
– 35.00.**

⊶⊲ **Plate 404. "The Badge of Honor"**
By M.L. Breon. Artist: H. R. Smith. 14" x 11". Condition: Very good. **$45.00 – 50.00.**

☛ **Plate 405. "March of Victory"**
Song by Betty Nelson. Published by P. B. Story, New York City. Copyright 1918 by Betty Nelson. 14" x 11". Condition: Excellent. **$70.00 – 80.00.**

⊶⊲ **Plate 406. "My Uncle Sammy Gals"**
Lyrics by Jack Frost. Music by F. Henri Klickman. 14" x 11". Condition: Excellent. $**18.00 – 23.00.**

☞ **Plate 407. "We'll Fight for Uncle Sammy"**
Words by Howard Reese. Music By Keith Reese.
Published by Howard Reese, Lafayette, Minnesota.
12" x 9". Condition: Very good. **$15.00 – 20.00.**

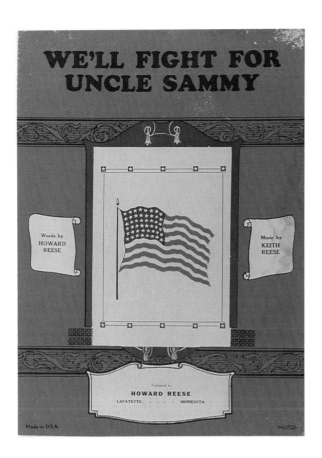

🎵 **Plate 408. "You Flew Over"**
Uncle Sam Takes His Hat Off to You. Published by
The Ted Browne Music Company, Chicago, Illinois.
Copyright 1928. 14" x 11". Condition: Very good.
$70.00 – 80.00.

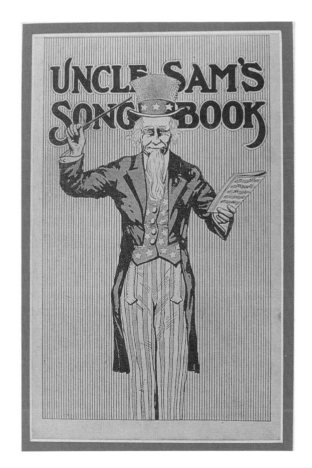

☞ **Plate 409. "Uncle Sam's Song Book"**
11" x 8". Condition: Excellent. **$35.00 – 40.00.**

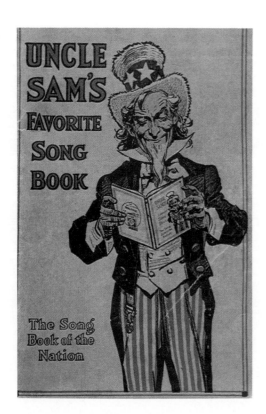

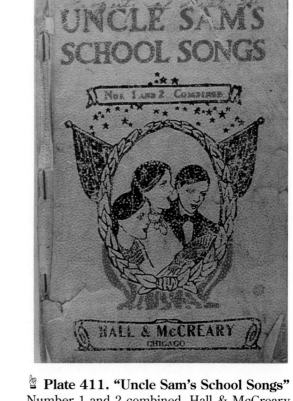

👉 **Plate 410. "Uncle Sam's Favorite Songbook"**
The Songbook of the Nation. Over 170 songs. Copyright 1919, Hall and McCreary Co., Chicago, IL, USA. 10" x 7". Condition: Very good. **$40.00 – 45.00.**

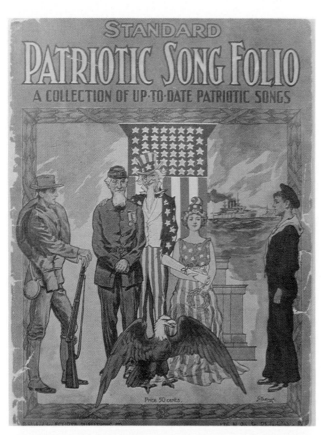

☞ **Plate 411. "Uncle Sam's School Songs"**
Number 1 and 2 combined. Hall & McCreary, Chicago. 8" x 6". Condition: Good. **$20.00 – 25.00.**

👉 **Plate 412.**
"Standard Patriotic Song" Folio
"A Collection of Up-to Date Patriotic Songs."
Artist: Starmer. 14" x 11". Condition: Very good.
$35.00 – 40.00.

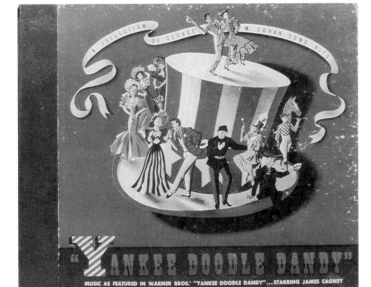

☞ **Plate 413. Record Set**
"Yankee Doodle Dandy" music as featured in Warner Bros. *Yankee Doodle Dandy* starring James Cagney. Victory Records. 10½" x 12". Three 78 RPM records. Condition: Very good. **$30.00 – 50.00.**

Puck Magazine Covers

Puck magazine covers are, without question, the finest illustrated covers by some of the best artists of the nineteenth century. Their value continues to rise rapidly as collectors and dealers alike, have become increasingly aware of the quality and desirability of this periodical. Condition is very important. The Uncle Sam *Puck* covers are the most desirable of all. All covers measure 14" x 10½". Condition is excellent unless otherwise indicated.

Plate 414. February 2, 1881, Vol. VIII, No. 204
"The Best Remedy" Uncle Sam—"I guess a change of operators is wanted here." Artist: J. A. Wales. **$100.00 – 125.00.**

A BIRD WHOSE WINGS NEED CLIPPING.

☞ **Plate 415. March 16, 1881, Vol. IX, No. 210.**
"Bird Whose Wings Need Clipping." Artist: "S."
$100.00 – 125.00.

NOW WE **HAVE** WHIPPED ALL CREATION!

☝ **Plate 416. June 8, 1881, Vol. IX, No. 222**
"Now we have whipped all creation." Artist: F. Opper.
$75.00 – 100.00.

FROM THE OLDEST TO THE YOUNGEST NATION.

☞ **Plate 417. July 6, 1881, Vol. IX, No. 226**
"From the oldest to the youngest nation. Freedom."
Artist: F. Opper. $90.00 – 125.00.

☞ **Plate 418. February 1, 1882, Vol. X, No. 256**
"Left in Charge. Chairman of Naval Affairs Committee." Artist: Bernard Gillam. **$90.00 – 115.00.**

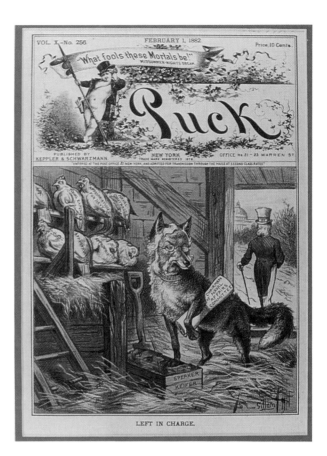

LEFT IN CHARGE.

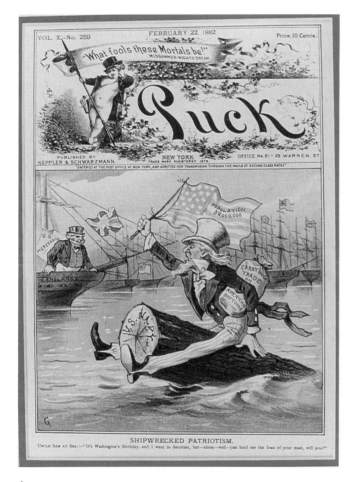

SHIPWRECKED PATRIOTISM.

Uncle Sam at Sea:—"It's Washington's Birthday, and I want to decorate, but—ahem—well—just lend me the loan of your mast, will you?"

☜ **Plate 419. February 22, 1882, Vol. X, No. 259**
"Shipwrecked Patriotism." Artist: Bernard Gillam.
$125.00 – 150.00.

☞ **Plate 420. March 15, 1882, Vol. XI, No. 262**
"Arthur's Awkward 'White Elephant.'" Artist: Bernard
Gillam. **$90.00 – 115.00.**

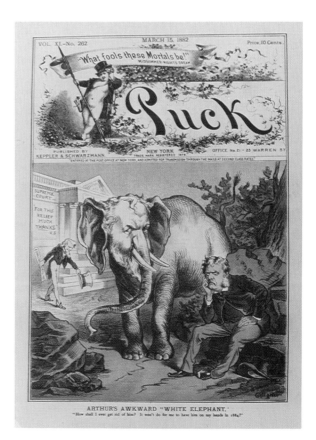

ARTHUR'S AWKWARD "WHITE ELEPHANT."

"How shall I ever get rid of him? It won't do for me to have him on my hands in 1884?"

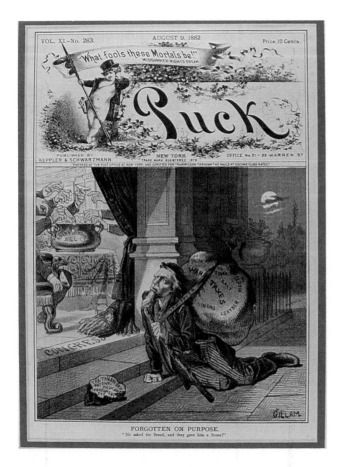

🖬 **Plate 421. August 9, 1882, Vol. XI, No. 283**
"Forgotten on Purpose. He asked for bread and they gave him a Stone." Artist: Bernard Gillam. **$75.00 – 100.00.**

☞ **Plate 422. September 13, 1882, Vol. XII, No. 288**
"Bullets and Bull's Eyes." Artist: F. Graetz. **$90.00 – 110.00.**

🖬 **Plate 423. March 21, 1883, Vol. XIII, No. 315**
"What's in it. Tariff Bill. That's one of those things which no fellow can find out." Artist: Bernard Gillam. **$100.00 – 125.00.**

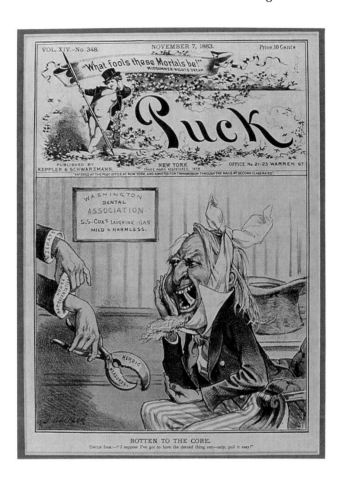

ROTTEN TO THE CORE.
Uncle Sam:— " I suppose I've got to have the derned thing out—only, pull it easy!"

☞ **Plate 424.**
November 7, 1883, Vol. XIV, No 348
"Rotten to the Core. I suppose I've got to have the darn thing out — only pull it easy." Artist: J. Keppler. **$125.00 – 150.00.**

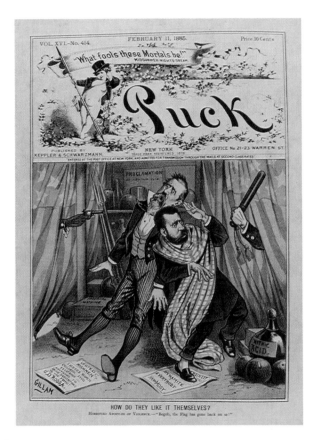

HOW DO THEY LIKE IT THEMSELVES?
Horrified Apostles of Violence.—"Begob, the Flag has gone back on us!"

✍ **Plate 425. February 11, 1885, Vol. XVI, No. 414**
"How do they like it themselves?" Horrified Apostles of Violence — "Begob, the flag has gone back on us!"
Artist: Bernard Gillam. **$75.00 – 100.00.**

☞ **Plate 426. June 17, 1885, Vo. XVII, No. 432**
"Canada as Mother Mandelbaum." Artist: J. Keppler. **$125.00 – 150.00.**

CANADA AS "MOTHER MANDELBAUM."

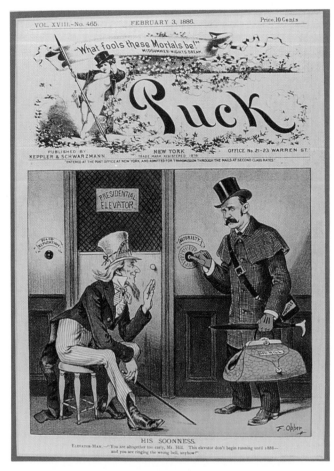

Plate 427. February 3, 1886, Vol. XVIII, No. 465 "His Soonness." Artist: F. Opper. **$125.00 – 150.00.**

Plate 428. April 14, 1886, Vol, XIX. No. 475 "Still they come. How many blood sucking vampires can Uncle Sam support?" Artist: C. J. Taylor. **$110.00 – 135.00.**

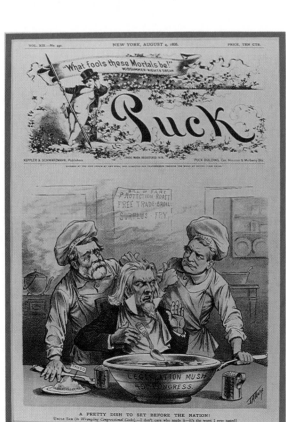

Plate 429. August 4, 1886, Vol. XIX, No. 491 "A pretty dish to set before the nation. 49th Congress." Artist: J. A. Wales. **$125.00 – 140.00.**

☞ **Plate 430.**
January 11, 1893, Vol. XXXII, No. 827
"Smash 'Em." Artist: W. A. Rogers. **$100.00 –
125.00.**

☝ **Plate 431.**
February 1, 1893, Vol. XXXII, No. 830
"The Task of Diogenes Not in it. Uncle Sam looking for
a statesmen in the United States Senate." Artist: F.
Opper. **$125.00 – 150.00.**

☞ **Plate 432. March 8, 1893, Vol. XXXIII, No. 835**
"It came High, but we had to Have It!" Artist: L. Dalrymple.
$100.00 – 125.00.

Plate 433.
April 12, 1893, Vol. XXXIII, No. 840
"The Russian Bear Asks too Much." Artist: W. A. Rogers. **$120.00 – 140.00.**

Plate 434. June 14, 1893, Vol. XXXIII, No. 849
"At it Again." Artist: Bernard Gillam. **$100.00 – 125.00.**

Plate 435.
September 13, 1893, Vol. XXXIV, No. 862
"Out of the Silver Flood!" Artist: L. Dalrymple. **$100.00 – 125.00.**

☞ **Plate 436. September 20, 1893, Vol. XXXIV, No. 863**
"It doesn't look much like it. Has the mouth of avarice, the canker of greed, so eaten into the hearts of this generation that they are unmindful of these men? God forbid!" From Harrison's Speech to the G. A. R. Encampment. Artist: C. J. Taylor. **$125.00 – 140.00.**

☞ **Plate 437. October 4, 1893, Vol. XXXIV, No. 865**
"A Senatorial Desperado. Take my silver or I'll take your life!" Artist: L. Dalrymple. **$110.00 – 125.00.**

☞ **Plate 438. October 25, 1893, Vol. XXXIV, 868**
"Not up to the Mark Yet." Artist: J. Keppler. **$100.00 – 120.00.**

☙ **Plate 439. February 21, 1894, Vol. XXXV, No. 885**
"Up to Date! Truthful Bill – I can not tell a lie, Uncle –
Grover did it." Artist: C. J. Taylor. **$100.00 – 115.00.**

☚ **Plate 440. June 20, 1894, Vol. XXXV, No. 902**
"An unpromising pair of racers." Artist: F. Opper.
$110.00 – 125.00.

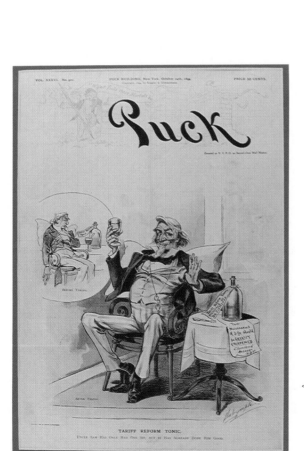

☙ **Plate 441.**
October 24, 1894, Vol. XXXVI, No. 920
"Tariff Reform Tonic." Artist: L. Dalrymple.
$125.00 – 140.00.

☞ **Plate 442.**
August 21, 1895, Vol. XXXVIII, No. 963
"Uncle Sam's Summer Girl for '95 The New Tariff." Artist:
L. Dalrymple. **$125.00 – 150.00.**

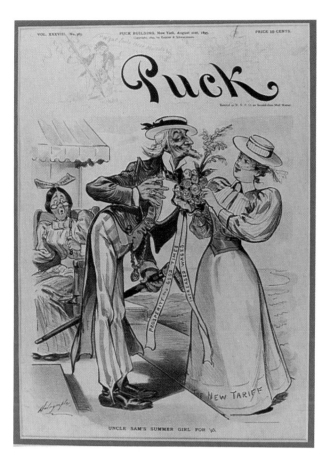

☝ **Plate 443.**
September 4, 1895, Vol. XXXVIII, No. 965
"That Coveted Cup." Artist: Sid Ehrhart. Condition:
Good. **$120.00 – 140.00**

☞ **Plate 444.**
February 19, 1896, Vol. XXXIX, No. 989
"Greedy Johnnie." He has got a lot of good things –
But how long can he keep them to himself?" Artist:
J. S. Pughe. **$125.00 – 150.00.**

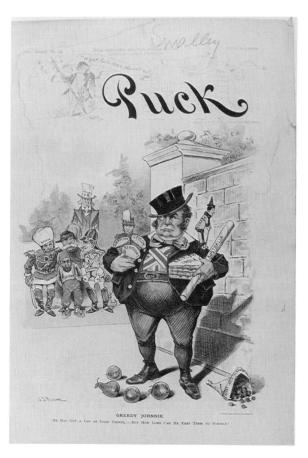

☞ **Plate 445.**
February 26, 1896, Vol. XXXIX, No. 990
"After the Carnival." Artist: F. Opper. $150.00 –
175.00.

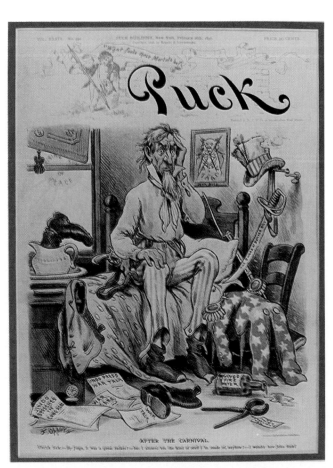

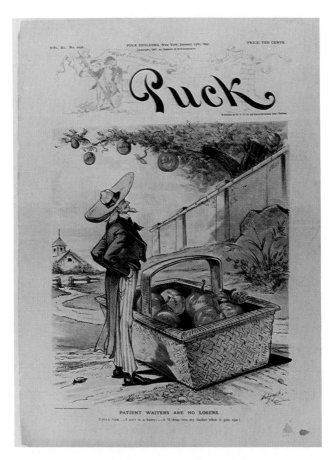

☝ **Plate 446. January 13, 1897, Vol. XL, No. 1036**
"Patient waiters are no losers." Artist: L. Dalrymple.
$100.00 – 120.00.

☞ **Plate 447. October 13, 1897, Vol. XLII, No. 1075**
"Time Nearly Up." Artist: J. Keppler. $150.00 – 175.00.

☞ **Plate 448.**
December 11, 1901, Vol. L, No. 1293
"The Canal Situation." Artist: K. (Keppler).
$140.00 – 160.00.

Puck Centerfolds

All Puck centerfolds are 14″ x 21″ and in excellent condition unless otherwise indicated.

Puck centerfolds, extracted from *Puck* magazines, are of the finest quality stone lithography of the nineteenth century. The political, economic, and social history of the United States during the last half of the nineteenth century is magnificently captured by the best illustrators, cartoonists, and writers of this period, within these centerfolds.

Their prices have been rapidly rising because of their quality, and the somewhat limited number of surviving issues. The Uncle Sam images in this periodical are the best. You can definitely expect these prices to increase substantially within the next few years. Condition, once again, is very important. Try to acquire lithographs in the best possible condition to insure future appreciation of their value.

🐚 **Plate 449. February 10, 1880**
"The one man power in our jury system." Artist: J. Keppler.
$125.00 – 150.00.

Plate 450. February 23, 1881
"The Two Philanthropists." Artist: J. Keppler.
$125.00 – 150.00.

Plate 451. March 23, 1881
"Solid on the hog question." Artist: S.
$150.00 – 200.00.

☞ **Plate 452. June 22, 1881**
"The kind of dog catching we would like to see." Artist: J. Keppler. **$125.00 – 150.00.**

☜ **Plate 453. November 9, 1881**
"Our Indian Policy – A House of Cards."
Artist: J. Keppler. **$300.00 – 350.00.**

☞ **Plate 454.**
November 16, 1881
"European notions of American manners and customs."
Artist: F. Opper. **$100.00 – 125.00.**

☞ **Plate 455. November 23, 1881**
"Uncle Sam's great moral and historical show." Artist: Keppler.
$125.00 – 150.00.

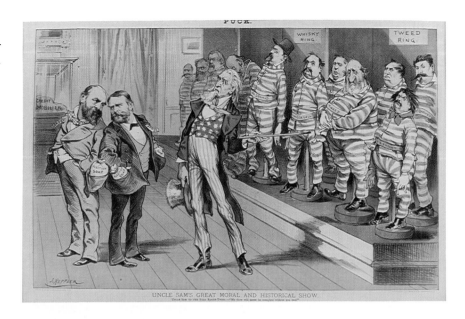

☜ **Plate 456. November 30, 1881**
"The Modern Moses." Artist: "O. K."
(refer to "K. O.") also Joseph Keppler.
$125.00 – 150.00.

☞ **Plate 457. December 7, 1881**
"The Pension Swindle." Artist: J. Keppler.
$100.00 – 125.00.

☞ **Plate 458. February 22 1882**
"The Modern Prometheus." Artist: Bernard
Gillam. **$150.00 – 175.00.**

☞ **Plate 459. February 22, 1882**
"A Fair Exchange." Artist: J. Keppler. **$125.00 – 150.00.**

☞ **Plate 460. March 20, 1882**
"U. S. Wringer." Artist: J. Keppler.
$100.00 – 125.00.

☞ **Plate 461. March 22, 1882**
"Under False Colors." Artist: J. Keppler. $150.00 – 175.00.

✎ **Plate 462. May 24, 1882**
"Speaker Keifer's Kaleidoscopic Speech, at the N. Y. Chamber of Commerce. Banquet, held at Delmonicos, May 9th, 1882." Artist: J. Keppler. $100.00 – 125.00.

☞ **Plate 463. June 19, 1882**
"Coney Island and the Crowned Heads." Artist: F. Graetz. $125.00 – 150.00.

☞ **Plate 464. August 16, 1882**
"Congressional Cracksmen. Police-
man Puck to Uncle Sam: This is the
work of professionals!" Artist: J. Keppler. **$100.00 – 125.00.**

✒ **Plate 465. August 23, 1882**
Uncle Sam's neglected farm." Artist: J.
Keppler. **$150.00 – 175.00.**

☞ **Plate 466. August 30, 1882**
"A Losing Business." Artist: F. Opper.
$250.00 – 300.00.

☜ **Plate 467.**
November 29, 1882
In sight of the promised land." Artist:
"G." (Gillam). **$150.00 – 175.00.**

☞ **Plate 468. Copyright 1883**
"Put 'em on ice." Artist: Bernard
Gillam. **$125.00 – 150.00.**

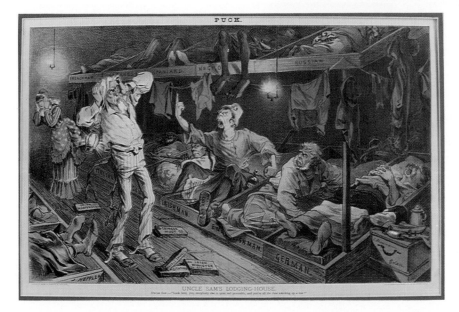

☜ **Plate 469. Copyright 1891**
"Uncle Sam's lodging house."
Artist: J. Keppler. **$125.00 –
150.00.**

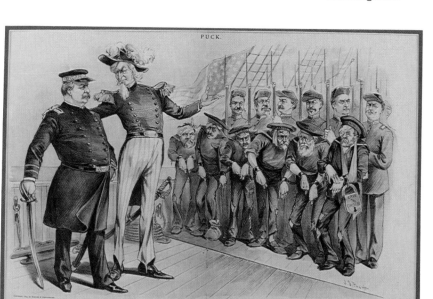

☞ **Plate 470. Copyright 1894**
"Master of the situation." Artist:
J. S. Pughe. $150.00 – 200.00.

🖙 **Plate 471. December 1, 1884**
The World's International Cotton Centennial and Exposition. New Orleans, LA from Dec. 1 to May 31, 1885. Artist: J. Keppler. **$150.00 – 200.00.**

☞ **Plate 472. June 27, 1883**
"Nursing our infant industries."
Artist: F. Graetz. **$100.00 –**
125.00.

Plate 473. August 8, 1883
"The Old Ticket." Artist: F. Opper.
$150.00 – 175.00.

Plate 474.
August 15, 1883
"Tit for Tat." Artist: F. Graetz.
$125.00 – 150.00.

Plate 475. October 3, 1883
"A Family Party." Artist: F. Graetz.
$150.00 – 175.00.

☞ **Plate 476. October 24, 1883**
"'Puck' is not going to be left — he has a horse-show of his own." Artist: Bernard Gillam. **$100.00 – 125.00.**

Plate 477. November 28, 1883
"Thanksgiving." Artist: J. Keppler. **$150.00 – 175.00.**

☞ **Plate 478.**
December 31, 1884
"Puck's review of the past year." Artist: J. Keppler. **$100.00 – 125.00.**

⇛ **Plate 479. February 25, 1885**
"Noxious Growths in Liberty's Grounds." Artist: J. Keppler. **$150.00 – 175.00.**

☞ **Plate 480. July 15, 1885**
"The new leader and the old chorus." Artist: Bernard Gillam. **$125.00 – 150.00.**

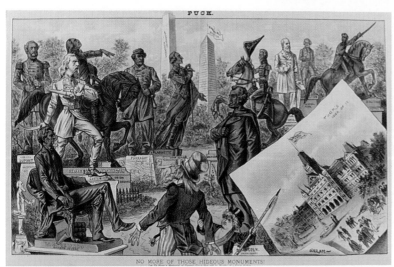

⇛ **Plate 481. August 19, 1885**
"No more of those Hideous Monuments." Artist: Bernard Gillam. **$125.00 – 150.00.**

☞ **Plate 482. October 28, 1885**
"A great past and a pitiful present." Artist:
Bernard Gillam. **$150.00 – 175.00.**

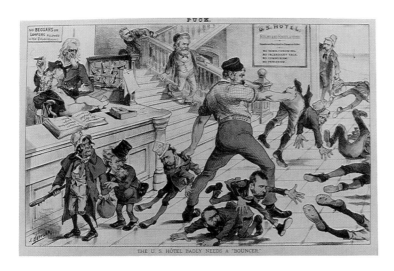

THE U. S. HOTEL BADLY NEEDS A "BOUNCER."

✑ **Plate 483. Copyright 1885**
"The U. S. hotel badly needs a 'bouncer.'" Artist: J. Keppler.
$100.00 – 125.00.

SNOWED IN.

✑ **Plate 484. January 20, 1886**
"Snowed in." Artist: J. Keppler. **$125.00 –
150.00.**

**☜ Plate 485.
June 23, 1886**
"Serving Two Masters."
Artist: J. Keppler. **$150.00 –
175.00.**

☞ Plate 486. July 14, 1886
"An Apparition of To-day." Artist: J.
Keppler. **$175.00 – 200.00.**

☜ Plate 487. Copyright 1888
"In Danger." Artist: J. Keppler.
$150.00 – 175.00.

☞ **Plate 488. December 28, 1892**
"What is needed — A thorough sifting." Artist: W. A. Rogers. **$150.00 – 200.00.**

✒ **Plate 489. February 1, 1893**
"Tammany is with Cleveland." Artist: W. A. Rogers. **$125.00 – 150.00.**

🐚 **Plate 490. July 5, 1893**
A funny lot of life-savers." Artist: L. Dalrymple. **$125.00 – 150.00.**

☞ **Plate 491. September 6, 1893**
"Coroner Harrison is a little too previous." Artist: L. Dalrymple. **$125.00 – 150.00.**

🐚 **Plate 492. February 14, 1894**
"Puck's Valentines for 1894." Artist: F. Opper. **$100.00 – 125.00.**

☞ **Plate 493. March 28, 1894**
"A Senate for Revenue Only." Artist: F. Opper. **$150.00 – 175.00.**

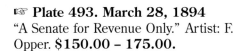

Plate 494. April 11, 1894
"Another hide to be taken." Artist: L. Dalrymple. **$175.00 – 200.00.**

☞ **Plate 495.**
November 28, 1894
"A Glad Thanksgiving of some Personages from Puck's Pages." Author: F. Opper. **$125.00 – 150.00.**

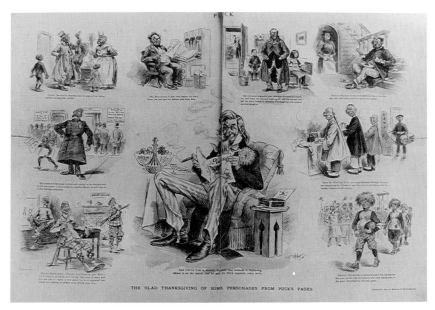

☞ **Plate 496. April 10, 1895**
"The Universal Epidemic of Jingoism."
Artist: F. Opper. **$125.00 – 150.00.**

☞ **Plate 497. May 29, 1895**
"Progress and Poverty — A Decoration Day Study." Artist: L. Dalrymple.
$175.00 – 200.00.

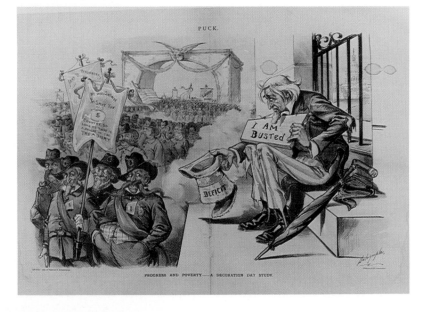

☞ **Plate 498. July 24, 1895**
"A Rival who has Come to Stay."
Artist: L. Dalrymple. **$150.00
– 175.00.**

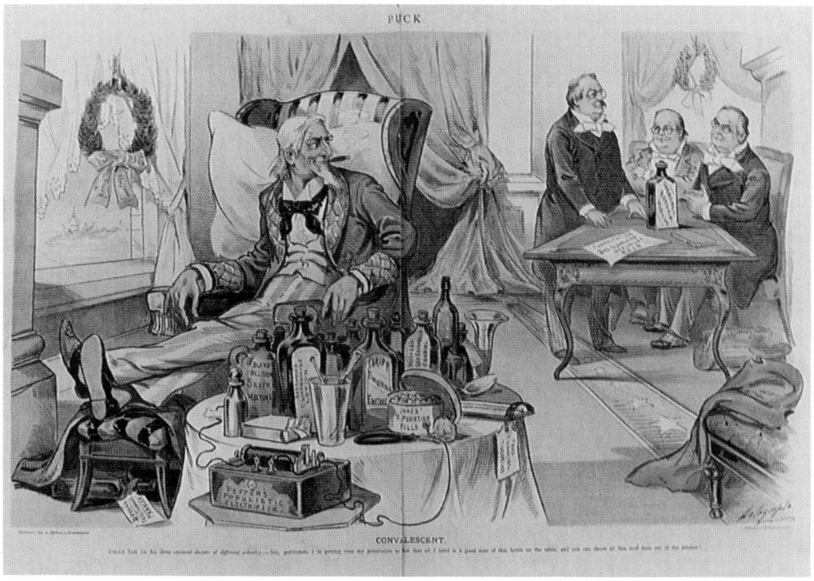

☞ **Plate 499.**
December 23, 1896
"Convalescent." Artist: L. Dalrymple. Condition: Very good. $**150.00 – 175.00.**

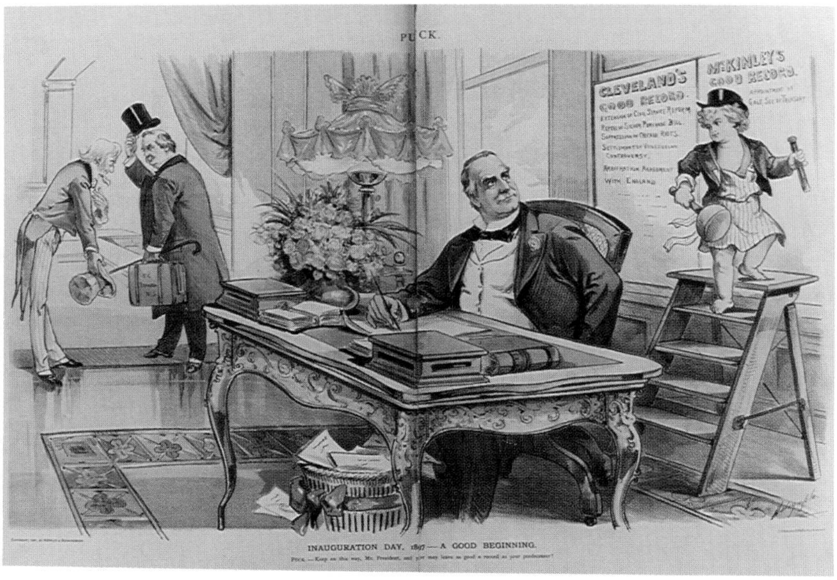

☞ **Plate 500. March 3, 1897**
"Inauguration Day 1897 — A Good Beginning." Artist: L. Dalrymple. Condition: Very good. **$125.00 – 150.00.**

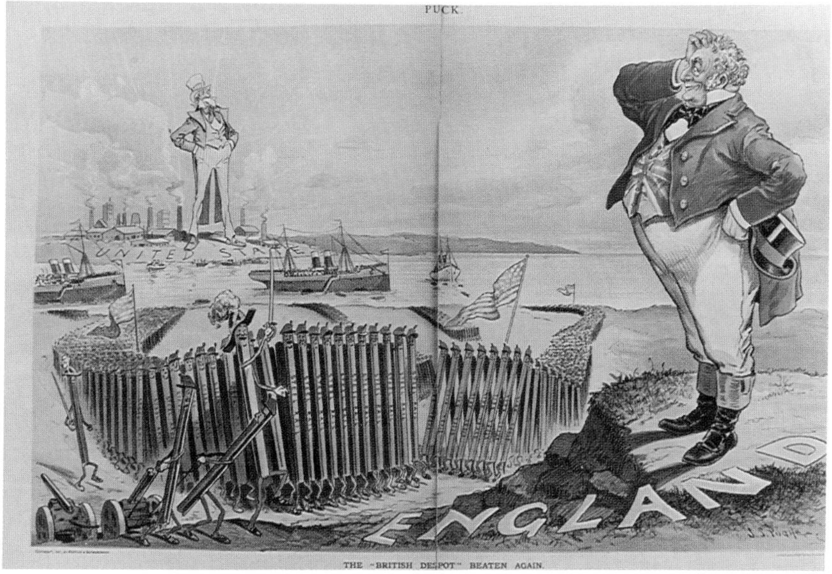

☞ **Plate 501. March 24, 1897**
"The British Despot Beaten Again." Artist: J. S. Pughe. **$150.00 – 175.00.**

🐚 **Plate 502. March 31, 1897**
"Two obstacles that must be removed before Uncle Sam can drive on." Artist: L. Dalrymple. **$125.00 – 150.00.**

☞ **Plate 503. June 2, 1897**
"The Tantalus of To-day." Artist: J. S. Pughe. **$175.00 – 200.00.**

🐚 **Plate 504. September 15, 1897**
"A Self-Evident Fact." Artist: J. S. Pughe. **$150.00 – 175.00.**

☞ **Plate 505. Copyright 1910**
"Good Government vs. Revolution! —
An Easy Choice." Artist: Keppler.
$125.00 – 150.00.

✒ **Plate 506. Copyright 1909**
"His Foresight." Artist: J. S. Pughe.
$150.00 – 175.00.

☞ **Plate 507. Copyright 1910**
"The Best Balance for Uncle
Sam." Artist: J. Keppler. $175.00
– 200.00.

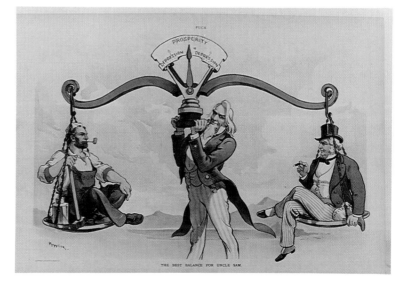

179

Puck Back Covers

Puck magazine back covers can in many instances have a greater collectible demand mainly because they are usually a full and complete image without the magazine title and other printed information not pertinent to the illustration. The quality of the full-color lithographic process as well as the best artists of the time was utilized in the same manner of the *Puck* covers and centerfolds. Condition, once again is most important along with the artist and subject matter in determining values. Back covers measure 14" x 10½". Condition is excellent unless otherwise indicated.

☞ **Plate 508. October 5, 1881**
"Press Rumors about Arthur." Artist: F. Opper.
$60.00 – 90.00.

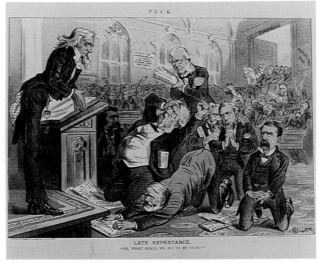

☞ **Plate 509. December 12, 1882**
"Late Repentance. Oh, what shall we do to be saved?" Artist: Bernard Gillam.
$100.00 – 120.00.

☞ **Plate 510. November 3, 1896**
"Obstructing the Public Highway."
Artist: F. Opper. **$120.00 – 135.00.**

☞ **Plate 511. August 22, 1883**
"A New Version of an Old Story." Telegraph Monopoly. Artist: Bernard Gillam. **$100.00 – 125.00.**

☞ **Plate 512. January 6, 1886**
"An Awkward Vehicle." Artist: J. A. Wales. **$150.00 – 175.00.**

☞ **Plate 513. January 8, 1886**
"A New Year's Present to Uncle Sam." Modified Tariff. Artist: "B" (Frank Beard).
$150.00 – 175.00.

Leslie's Weekly Magazine Covers

One of the finer illustrated periodicals of the late nineteenth century *Leslie's Weekly* utilized the artwork of some of the best and most noted illustrators of the period. The full-color cover art was most appealing. Some of the best Uncle Sam images can be found on the covers of this magazine. Try only to acquire the best condition possible.

All covers are in excellent condition and 14" x 11" unless otherwise stated.

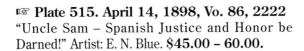

Plate 514. March 17, 1898
"Uncle Sam is Ready." Artist: E. N. Blue.
$45.00 – 60.00.

☞ **Plate 515. April 14, 1898, Vo. 86, 2222**
"Uncle Sam – Spanish Justice and Honor be Darned!" Artist: E. N. Blue. $45.00 – 60.00.

☞ **Plate 516. April 21, 1898, Vol. 86, No. 2223**
"Better Rags with Honor than Patches with Dishonor." Artist: E. N. Blue. **$45.00 – 60.00.**

☛ **Plate 517.**
April 28, 1898, Vol. 86, No. 2224
"Remember the Maine." Artist: E.N. Blue.
$75.00 – 90.00.

☞ **Plate 518. May 26, 1898**
"Rally Round the Flag, Boys!" Artist: E. N. Blue.
$45.00 – 60.00.

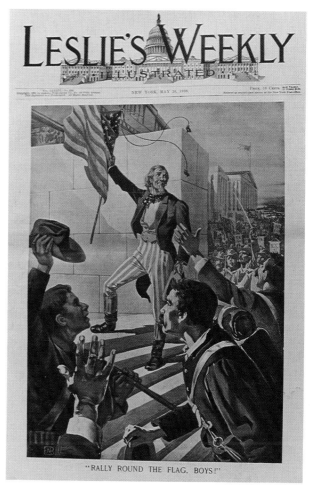

☞ **Plate 519.**
May 5, 1898, Vol. 86, No. 2225
"On to Cuba! Remember the Maine." Artist: E.N.
Blue. **$75.00 – 90.00.**

A BICYCLE BUILT FOR TWO.

☞ **Plate 520. June 2, 1898**
"A Bicycle Built for Two." Artist: E.N. Blue.
$45.00 – 60.00.

☞ **Plate 521. June 9, 1898, Vol. 86, No. 2230**
"Uncle Sam – Guess I'll Keep 'em!" Artist: E.N. Blue.
$45.00 – 60.00.

☞ **Plate 522. July 4, 1912**
"The Youngest Republic Receives Its New Flag."
Artist: Will Jones. **$35.00 – 45.00.**

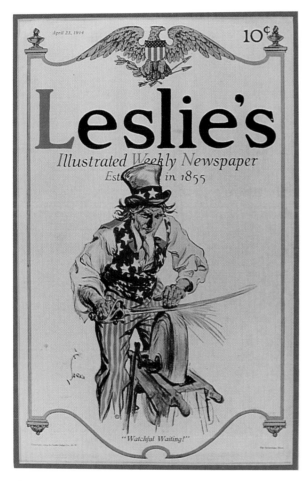

☝ **Plate 523. April 23, 1914**
"Watchful Waiting." Artist: Sarka. **$45.00 –
60.00.**

☞ **Plate 524. November 25, 1915**
"I ought to be thankful." Artist: Grant E. Hamilton. **$45.00 – 60.00.**

☙ **Plate 525. December 23, 1915**
"Best Wishes." Artist: Grant E. Hamilton.
$45.00 – 60.00.

☝ **Plate 526. July 6, 1916**
"What are you doing for preparedness." Artist: James
Montgomery Flagg. *Note: First appearance of J.M.
Flagg's "I Want You" pose which later became used on
his most famous poster. **$250.00 – 300.00.**

☙ **Plate 527. February 15, 1917**
"I Want You." Artist: James Montgomery
Flagg. *Note: First appearance of J.M.
Flagg's "I Want You," image and caption.
Later to be used on most famous recruiting
poster of all times. **$300.00 – 350.00.**

☞ **Plate 528. March 29, 1917**
Artist: Sarka. $40.00 – 50.00.

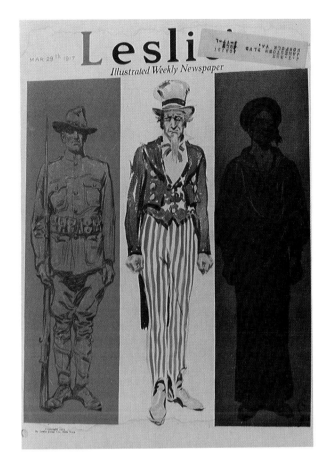

☝ **Plate 529. December 29, 1917**
"Get off that throne!" Artist: James Montgomery
Flagg. *Note: First variation by J. M. Flagg of "I want
You" pose. **$150.00 – 200.00.**

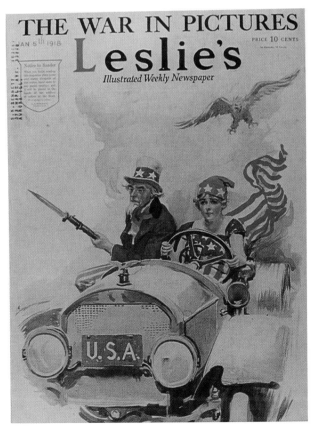

☞ **Plate 530. January 5, 1918**
"U.S.A." Artist: James Montgomery Flagg.
$60.00 – 75.00.

Plate 531. January 26, 1918
"Help the horse to save the soldier." Artist: James Montgomery Flagg. **$75.00 – 100.00.**

Plate 532. February 2, 1918
"Uncle Sam's Burden." Artist: Orson Lowell. **$35.00 – 45.00.**

Plate 533. March 2, 1918
"This Spring." Artist: Clyde Forsythe. **$65.00 – 75.00.**

☞ **Plate 534. April 27, 1918**
"The Great American Game." Artist:
Clyde Forsythe. **$65.00 – 75.00.**

☝ **Plate 535. May 18, 1918**
"Come Across." Artist: Orson Lowell. **$65.00 –
75.00.**

☞ **Plate 536. May 29, 1918**
"Business Germany To-Day." Artist: Sarka.
$65.00 – 75.00.

☞ **Plate 537. July 6, 1918**
"Which? Red Cross or Iron Cross." Artist: Orson
Lowell. **$65.00 – 75.00.**

☞ **Plate 538. January 4, 1919**
"New World, Old World." Artist: Orson Lowell.
$50.00 – 60.00.

☞ **Plate 539. June 28, 1919**
"Stars & Stripes or the Red Flag." Artist:
James Montgomery Flagg. **$60.00 –
70.00.**

☞ **Plate 540. November 22, 1919**
"The best table in today's world." Artist: Sarka.
$50.00 – 60.00.

Plate 541. April 24, 1920
"The Red Success in Russia." Artist: James Montgomery
Flagg. $65.00 – 75.00.

Life Magazine Covers

This particular publication of *Life* magazine was the early predecessor of the photo illustrated publication of *Life*. *Life* magazine of the late nineteenth and early twentieth century had numerous covers with Uncle Sam images in black and white as well as full color, created by some of the most popular artists of this period. Condition is a most important factor in relationship to price. All covers are 11" x 9" and in excellent condition.

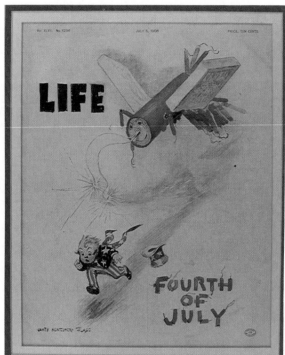

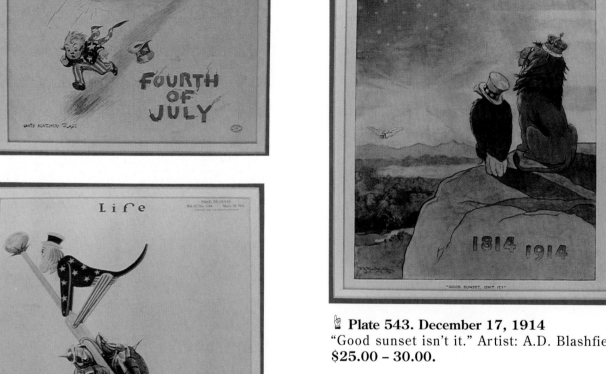

Plate 542. July 5, 1906
"Fourth of July." Artist: James Montgomery Flagg.
$30.00 – 40.00.

Plate 543. December 17, 1914
"Good sunset isn't it." Artist: A.D. Blashfield.
$25.00 – 30.00.

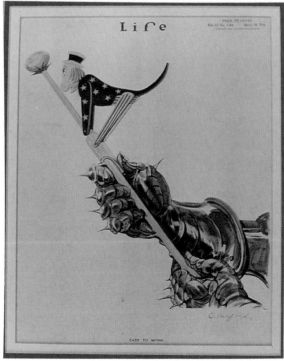

Plate 544. March 30, 1916
"Easy to Work." Artist: O. Herford. **$30.00 – 40.00.**

☞ **Plate 545. May 11, 1916**
"Not so deaf as he used to be." Artist: Charles Dana
Gibson. **$75.00 – 85.00.**

☝ **Plate 546. February 1, 1917**
"Where wealth accumulates." Artist: Ellison
Hoover. **$25.00 – 30.00.**

☞ **Plate 547. May 24, 1917**
"With Thy help, Amen." Artist: Angus
MacDonnall. **$40.00 – 50.00.**

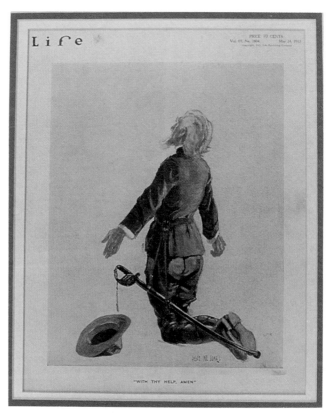

Plate 548. November 16, 1922
"The return of the school master." Artist: Charles
Dana Gibson. $75.00 – 85.00.

Plate 549. June 22, 1905
"Meditative." Artist: J. Conacher. 10½" x 8½".
$40.00 – 50.00.

Plate 550. January 20, 1905
"Life Inauguration Number." Artist: William
Walker. $75.00 – 85.00.

Harper's Weekly

Magazine Covers
Centerfolds and Full Pages
Miscellaneous Engravings

For almost six decades *Harper's Weekly* was probably the most popular illustrated periodical of its day. From the 1850s to the turn of the century, this periodical utilized the artwork and wood block illustrations of some of the greatest American illustrators of the nineteenth century, Winslow Homer and Thomas Nast being among the most noted. The best and most popular images of Uncle Sam found in this periodical were produced by Thomas Nast. All of the illustrations were produced in wood block or steel engraving, all without color. However you may, at times stumble on to *Harper's Weekly* illustrations that were hand colored in water color at a later date. Some of you may find these more appealing but, in actuality, the serious collector may find them less desirable. The centerfolds found in this periodical, containing Uncle Sam images, are some of the most historically significant of all. Other illustrations of Uncle Sam found on full pages or smaller within this periodical are also desirable to many collectors and historians.

Prices will vary in accordance to the size, artist, subject matter, and the quality of the illustration. All *Harper's Weekly* covers and full pages measure 16½" x 11½". All centerfolds measure 16½" x 23". All other engravings vary in size as individually indicated. All illustrations in this section are in excellent condition. *Note you can expect a rapid increase in prices for Thomas Nast engravings in the same manner as the prices of Winslow Homer engravings from this periodical have gone up!

☞ **Plate 551. June 29, 1872 — Cover** "The Sage of Chappaqua." Artist: Thomas Nast. **$75.00 – 85.00.**

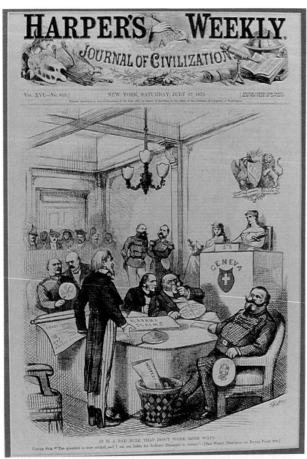

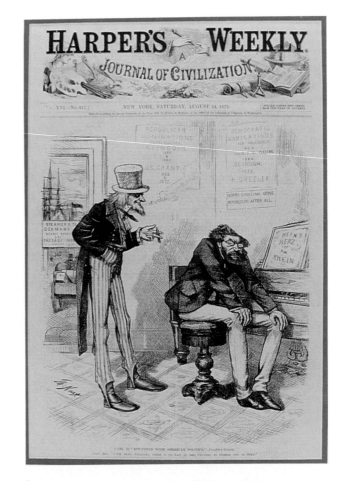

☞ **Plate 552. July 27, 1872 — Cover**
"It's a Bad Rule that Don't Work Both Ways." Artist: Thomas Nast. **$40.00 – 45.00.**

☞ **Plate 553. August 24, 1782 — Cover**
"Carl is Disgusted with American Politics." Artist: Thomas Nast. **$60.00 – 70.00.**

☞ **Plate 554. September 21, 1872 — Cover**
"General Orders." Artist: Thomas Nast. **$50.00 – 60.00.**

☞ **Plate 555. October 11, 1873 — Cover**
"Keeping the Money Where it Will Do Most Good." Artist: Thomas Nast. **$45.00 – 50.00.**

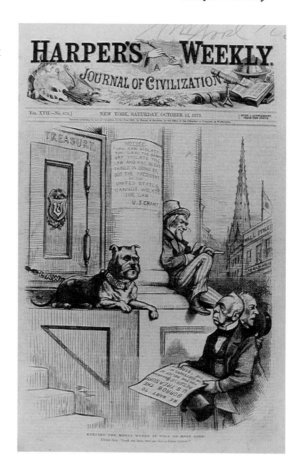

☜ **Plate 556. May 23, 1874 — Cover**
"The Next Thing in Order." Artist: Thomas Nast.
$50.00 – 60.00.

☞ **Plate 557.**
April 1, 1876 — Cover
"The Minuteman — Fixed by the Spirit of '76." Artist: Thomas Nast.
$90.00 – 100.00.

☞ **Plate 558. October 21, 1876 — Cover**
"The Solid South — Gaunt & Hungry."Artist:
Thomas Nast. **$50.00 – 60.00.**

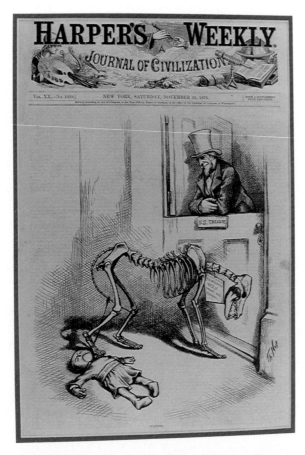

☞ **Plate 559. November 25, 1876 — Cover**
"Waiting." Artist: Thomas Nast. **$45.00 – 50.00.**

☞ **Plate 560. February 16, 1878 — Cover**
"The First Step Toward National Bankruptcy."
Artist: Thomas Nast. **$60.00 – 70.00.**

☞ **Plate 561. April 12, 1879 — Cover**
"History repeats Itself — A Little Too Soon." Artist: Thomas Nast. **$50.00 – 60.00.**

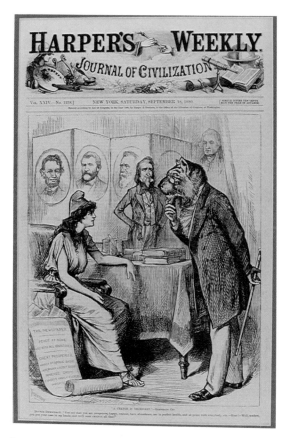

☝ **Plate 562. September 18, 1880 — Cover**
"A Change is Necessary." Artist: Thure Thulstrup. **$60.00 – 70.00.**

☞ **Plate 563. February 12, 1881 — Cover**
"Death to Monopoly!" "Uncle Sam Hercules, 'That's right, my boy. That's the way to crush him; and, if you fail, I'll see what I can do.'" Artist: Bernard Gillam. **$60.00 – 70.00.**

☜ **Plate 564. January 14, 1882 — Cover**
"The Queen of Industry, or, the New South." Artist:
Thomas Nast. **$60.00 – 70.00.**

☝ **Plate 565. June 3, 1871 — Centerfold**
"The Wolf in Sheep's Clothing." Artist: Thomas Nast. **$75.00 –
85.00.**

☜ **Plate 566. December 2, 1871 — Full Page**
"To Whom it May Concern." Artist: Thomas Nast.
$50.00 – 60.00.

☞ **Plate 567. July 13, 1872 — Partial Page**
"Romish Ingratitude." Artist: Thomas Nast. 7½" x
6¾". **$35.00 – 45.00.**

☝ **Plate 568. October 12, 1872 — Centerfold**
"Tied to His Mother's Apron Strings." Artist: Thomas Nast.
$90.00 – 100.00.

☞ **Plate 569. November 16, 1872 — Full Page**
"It Never Rains but it Pours." Artist: Thomas Nast.
$90.00 – 100.00.

Plate 570. July 15, 1876
"The Glorious Day We Celebrate."
Supplement. Artist: Thomas
Worth. 16½" x 23". **$150.00 –
175.00.**

☞ **Plate 571. December 16, 1876 — Full Page**
"The Lionzed Asinus Vulgaris." Artist: Thomas Nast.
$65.00 – 75.00.

Plate 572. August 19, 1876 — Full Page
"A Financial Lesson." Artist: Thomas Nast.
$75.00 – 85.00.

☞ **Plate 573. December 9, 1876 — Full Page**
"The Indifference of Uncle Sam." Artist: Thomas
Nast. **$35.00 – 45.00.**

☝ **Plate 574. March 30, 1878 — Full Page**
"Our Uncle's Honor Touched." Artist: Thomas
Nast. **$100.00 – 110.00.**

☞ **Plate 575. December 20, 1879 — Partial Page**
"There's Healthy 'Resumption.' " 8″ x 6″. Artist: Thomas
Nast. **$35.00 – 40.00.**

☜ **Plate 576. May 15, 1880 — Full Page**
"The Republic is always going to the dogs according to those who cannot run it." Artist: Thomas Nast. **$40.00 – 50.00.**

☝ **Plate 577. October 30, 1880 — Partial Page**
"The New Pilgrim's Progress." Artist: Bernard Gillam. 6½" x 9½". **$30.00 – 35.00.**

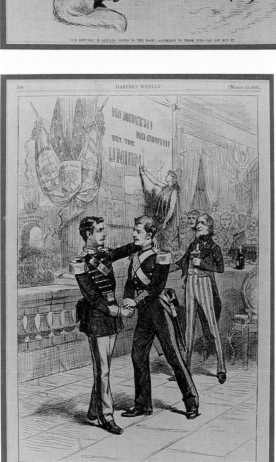

☜ **Plate 578. March 19, 1881 — Full Page**
"New York and New Orleans. No North, No South, but the Union." Artist: Thomas Nast. **$90.00 – 110.00.**

☞ **Plate 579. July 2, 1881 — Partial Page**
"Enough to make a horse laugh." Artist:
Thomas Nast. 10" x 9". **$40.00 – 50.00.**

✍ **Plate 580. April 30, 1881 — Partial Page**
"A Distinction Without a Difference." Artist:
Bernard Gillam. 6½" x 9". **$35.00 – 45.00.**

☞ **Plate 581. June 2, 1882 — Full Page**
"The Lion's Generosity." Artist: Thomas Nast.
$45.00 – 50.00.

☞ **Plate 582. August 16, 1884 — Full Page**
"The So-Called 'Intensely American Candidate.'" Artist: Thomas Nast. **$50.00 – 60.00.**

☝ **Plate 583. January 16, 1864 — Partial Page**
"New Year's Gift to Little J. B." Artist: Frank H. T. Bellew. 6½" x 7". **$25.00 – 35.00.**

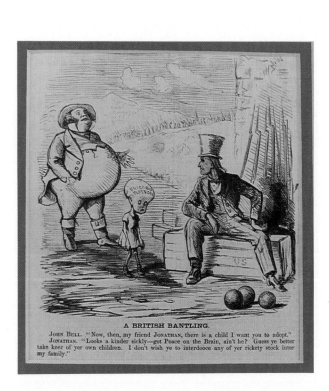

☞ **Plate 584.**
October 15, 1864 — Partial Page
"A British Bantling." 6½" x 5½". Artist: unknown. **$15.00 – 20.00.**

☞ **Plate 585.**
November 12, 1864 — Partial Page
"Don't Swap Horses." Artist: Frank H. T.
Bellew. 5½" x 7½". **$25.00 – 35.00.**

DON'T SWAP HORSES.

JOHN BULL. "Why don't you ride the other Horse a bit? He's the best Animal."
BROTHER JONATHAN. "Well, that may be; but the fact is, OLD ABE is just where I can put my finger on him; and as for the other—
though they say he's some when out in the scrub yonder—I never know where to find him."

UNCLE SAM. "I'd like to have you fix this Coat for me, MR. JOHNSON. I've worn it ne
about sixty-nine years, and it's getting rather too small. But it's a good one yet. Couldⁿ
you fix a sort of Amendment to it?"
A. JOHNSON. "No, I'd rather not; I'm not in the Jobbing line now."

✏ **Plate 586. November 3, 1866 — Partial Page**
"Old Coats Turned on the Shortest Notice." 6½" x
5½". Artist: unknown. **$15.00 – 20.00.**

☞ **Plate 587. December 1, 1866 — Partial Page**
"Andy Makes a Call on Uncle Sam." Artist: F. G.
$15.00 – 20.00.

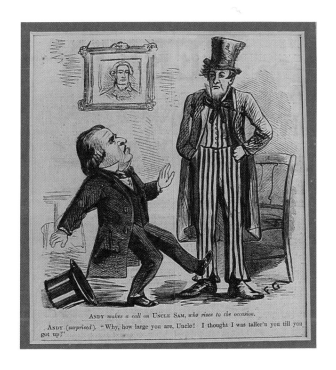

ANDY *makes a call on* UNCLE SAM, *who rises to the occasion.*

ANDY (*surprised*). "Why, how large you are, Uncle! I thought I was taller'n you till you
got up!"

☜ Plate 588. September 28, 1872 — Partial Page
"News from Vermont & Maine." 6½" x 5½". Artist:
Thomas Nast. **$25.00 – 30.00.**

**☞ Plate 589.
October 25, 1872 — Partial Page**
"Alabama Claims." 6½" x 6½". Artist:
Thomas Nast. **$25.00 – 30.00.**

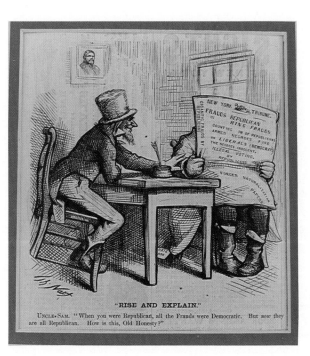

☜ Plate 590. October 26, 1872 — Partial Page
"Rise & Explain." 6½" x 6½". Artist: Thomas Nast.
$25.00 – 30.00.

☞ **Plate 591.**
November 2, 1872 — Partial Page
"The Same Old Smell." 6½" x 5½". Artist:
Thomas Nast. **$20.00 – 25.00.**

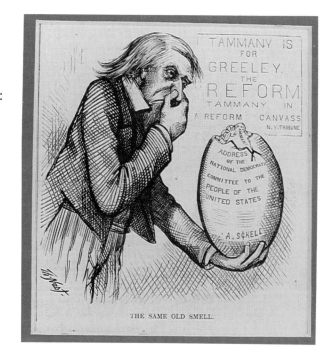

THE SAME OLD SMELL.

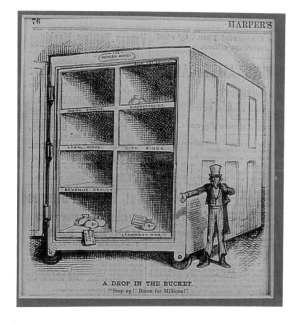

A DROP IN THE BUCKET.
"Step up! Room for Millions!"

☞ **Plate 592. January 22, 1876 — Partial Page**
"A Drop in the Bucket." 6" x 5½". Artist: Thomas
Nast. **$15.00 – 20.00.**

☞ **Plate 593.**
September 9, 1876 — Partial Page
"Box and Cox." 6½" x 6½". Artist:
Thomas Nast. **$25.00 – 30.00**

"BOX AND COX."
U. S. "Why we laugh—again."

THE MISTAKE OF HIS LIFETIME.

UNCLE SAM. "You may as well give it up, General; the American people will never vote to let you into the White House in such a coat as that."

☜ **Plate 594. October 9, 1880 — Partial Page**
"The Mistake of His Lifetime. "6½" x 5½". Artist: Bernard Gillam. **$20.00 – 25.00.**

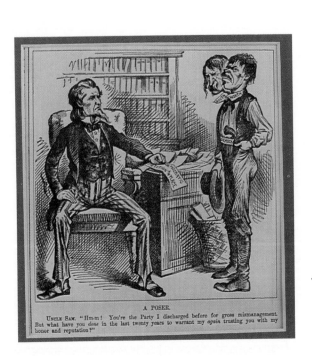

A POSER.

UNCLE SAM. "Hm-m! You're the Party I discharged before for gross mismanagement. But what have you *done* in the last twenty years to warrant my *again* trusting you with my honor and reputation?"

TO THIS COMPLEXION HAS IT COME AT LAST?

HON. BEN. HILL. "My dear sir, just honor him, let him have his own way, and let him boss over the other boys, and I'll promise you he won't rebel again."

[In his speech at Tammany Hall, Senator HILL said: "*If* HANCOCK *is elected, I guarantee that the South will never secede again.*"]

☞ **Plate 595.**
October 23, 1880 — Partial Page
"To This Complexion Has It Come at Last?" 6½" x 5½". Artist: Bernard Gillam. **$15.00 – 20.00.**

☜ **Plate 596.**
November 6, 1880 — Partial Page
"A Poser." 6½" x 5½". Artist: Thomas Nast. **$15.00 – 20.00.**

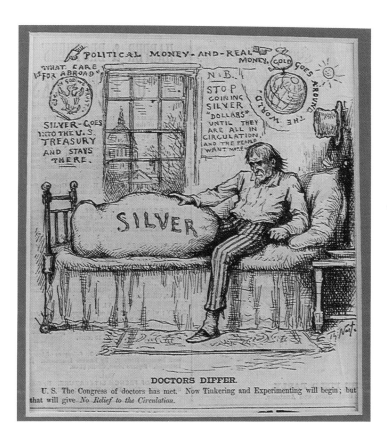

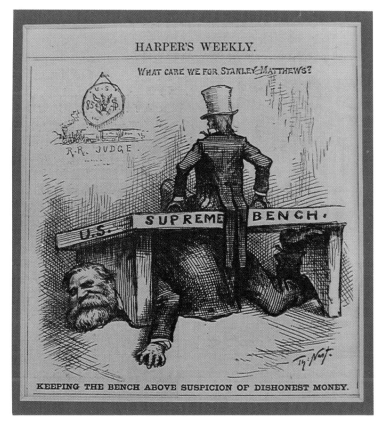

Plate 597.
December 25, 1880 — Partial Page
"Doctors Differ." 6½" x 6½". Artist:
Thomas Nast. **$20.00 – 25.00.**

Plate 598.
March 10, 1881 — Partial Page
"Keeping the Bench Above Suspicion of
Dishonest Money." 6½" x 6½". Artist:
Thomas Nast. **$15.00 – 20.00.**

Magazine Covers – Miscellaneous Publishers

Other than *Puck, Leslie's Weekly, Life,* and *Harper's Weekly,* a great number of popular magazines from the late nineteenth century to this present day have utilized Uncle Sam images by some of the most noted as well as some relatively obscure artists and illustrators.

This category contains some of the more popular publications produced during this period. You will also find some short-lived and somewhat rare periodicals of significant historic interest included in this section. Prices will vary in accordance to the cover artist, the illustration, and in some instances the periodical itself. Acquire the finest condition possible.

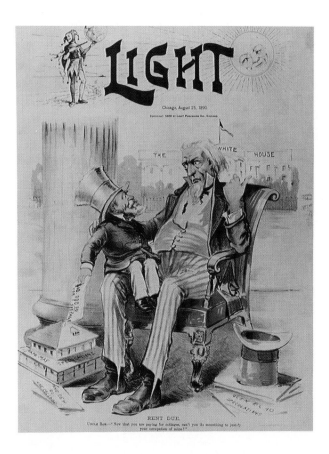

Plate 599. Light
August 23, 1890, Vol. 3, No. 53. "Rent Due."
Unsigned. 14" x 11". Condition: Excellent.
$100.00 – 120.00.

☞ **Plate 600. New England Homestead**
January 2, 1897. "Happy New Year Prosperity."
Artist: Maxfield Parrish. From an original pen and ink. Captioned: "Uncle Sam's New Suit and what He Hopes to Secure From It." Reduced for publication from original size of 15" x 15". 10" x 10" (image size). Condition: Excellent. **$200.00 – 250.00.**

☞ **Plate 601. Judge**
June 8, 1918. "The Nation's Perpetual Smileage Book." 14" x 11". Artist: James Montgomery Flagg. **$75.00 – 90.00.**

✍ **Plate 602. Milestones**
July, 1917. "The Conscript." Artist: Clyde Forsythe. 12" x 9". Condition: Excellent. **$90.00 – 100.00.**

☞ **Plate 603. Saturday Evening Post**
July 4, 1936. "Flight." Uncle Sam and the American Eagle. Artist: J. C. Leyendecker. 14" x 11". Condition: Excellent. **$75.00 – 85.00.**

☞ **Plate 604. Opportunity**
July 1935. "The New Declaration of Independence – Salesmanship." Artist: R. James Stuart. 14" x 11". Condition: Excellent. **$20.00 – 30.00.**

☞ **Plate 605. Fortune**
May, 1935, Vol. 11, No. 5. Uncle Sam on stilts in the circus. Artist: Norman Reeves. Magazine, 14" x 11¼". Condition: Excellent. **$35.00 – 45.00.**

☞ **Plate 606. Truth, The American Weekly**
July 20, 1898, Vol. 17, No. 587. "The Foremost Star." Artist: "W.G.S." 12" x 9". Condition: Good. **$40.00 – 60.00.**

☞ **Plate 607. The Country Gentleman**
June 16, 1917. "Upon the farmers of this country, therefore in large measure, rest the fate of the war and the fate of the nations." – President Wilson. Artist: Herbert Johnson. 14" x 11". Condition: Excellent. **$75.00 – 85.00.**

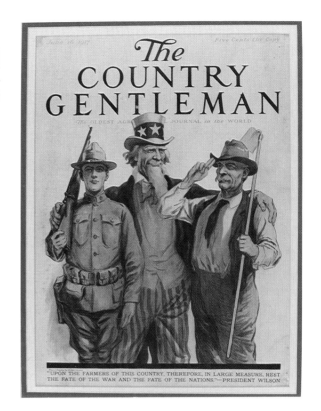

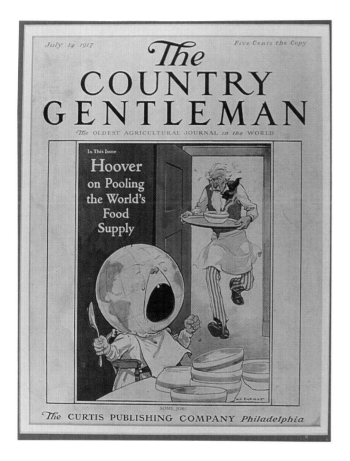

☞ **Plate 608. The Country Gentleman**
July 14, 1917. "Hoover on pooling the world's food supply. Some Job." 14" x 11". Condition: Excellent. Artist: Walter J. Enright. **$60.00 – 75.00.**

☞ **Plate 609. The Country Gentleman**
October, 1936. Artist: Frank Lea. 14" x 11". Condition: Very good. **$50.00 – 60.00.**

◆━ **Plate 610. The Etude Music Magazine**
July, 1944. 14" x 11". Unsigned. Condition: Very good. **$25.00 – 30.00.**

✎ **Plate 612. The Etude**
July 1917. "Pressers Musical Magazine". Artist: E.H. Kreps. 14" x 11". Condition: Excellent. **$40.00 – 45.00.**

☞ **Plate 611. Liberty**
February 13, 1932. "Our appalling crisis — What would Lincoln do?" Magazine. Artist: James Montgomery Flagg. Mr. Flagg places Lincoln in the "I want you" pose. 12" x 9". Condition: Excellent. **$60.00 – 75.00.**

☞ **Plate 613. Liberty**
January 19, 1935. "The World Menace of the SAAR." Artist: F.G. 12" x 9". Condition: Excellent. **$75.00 – 90.00.**

☝ **Plate 614. Liberty**
November 7, 1936. "Election 1936." Artist: Scott Evans. 12" x 9". Condition: Very good. **$50.00 – 70.00.**

☞ **Plate 615. KEN**
January 12, 1939. Full color. Artist: Corsair. 13½" x 10⅝". Published by KEN, Inc., 919 N. Michigan Avenue, Chicago, IL, USA. Condition: Very good. **$60.00 – 80.00.**
*Note *KEN* Magazine was a Socialist publication with a limited circulation and is very scarce.

☞ **Plate 616. KEN**
January 26, 1939. Full color. Artist: Stephan Broder.
13½" x 10⅝". Condition: Very good. **$75.00 –
90.00.**

☞ **Plate 617. KEN**
March 9, 1939. Full color. Artist: Russell T. Limbach.
Condition: Very good. **$75.00 – 90.00.**

☞ **Plate 618. MAD**
No. 182, April, 1976. "I Want, Too." Mimicking a James Montgomery Flagg
poster, signed with a symbol of a fish. "Another Mad Mini-Poster." 10⅝" x 8".
Condition: Excellent. **$15.00 – 20.00.**

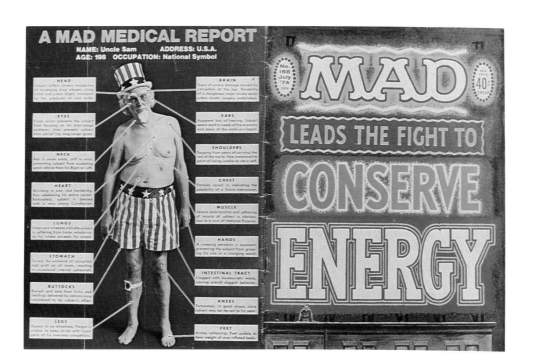

☞ **Plate 619. MAD**

No. 168, July, 1974. "A Mad Medical Report." Unsigned. 10⅝" x 8". Condition: Excellent.
$10.00 – 15.00.

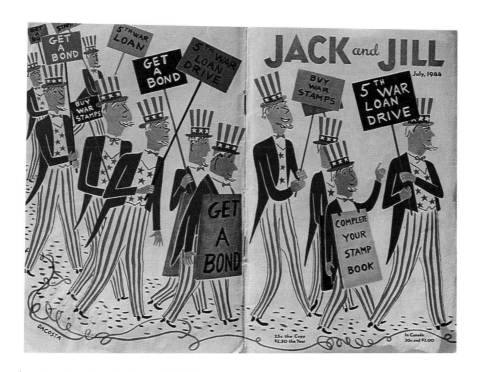

☞ **Plate 620. JACK and JILL**

July, 1944. Artist: Dacosta, Stella May. 10" x 13½". Condition: Excellent.
$25.00 – 30.00.

☞ **Plate 621. The Postal Record**
November, 1979. "NALC Needs You to Win the War."
11" x 9". James Montgomery Flagg type. Condition:
Excellent. **$8.00 – 10.00.**

☞ **Plate 622. The American Legion Magazine**
January, 1941. "All for one, one for all." Artist: J.W.
Schlaikjer. 12" x 9". Condition: Excellent. **$35.00 –
40.00.**

☞ **Plate 623. TIME**
May 2,1977. "Uncle Jimmy Wants You, but will
America enlist?" Referring to President Carter's
policy on the draft. 10⅞" x 8⅛". Condition: Excellent. **$10.00 – 12.00.**

☞ **Plate 624. Venture**
November, 1980. "Uncle Sam wants to put you in business. The biggest venture capitalist of all." Story on page 30. 10⅞" x 8". James Montgomery Flagg style. Condition: Excellent. **$8.00 – 10.00.**

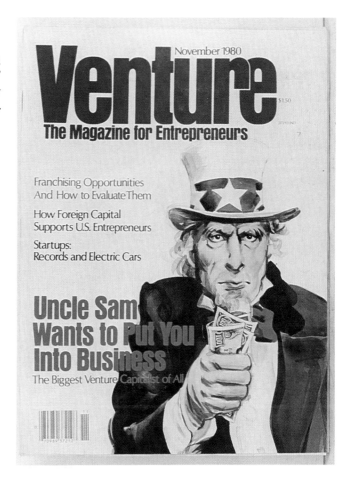

✎ **Plate 625. Personal Computing**
October 1986. Special Issue. 12" x 9". Condition: Very good. **$5.00 – 10.00.**

☞ **Plate 626. Nation's Business**
November, 1976. "Zero-Base Budgeting. One Way to Erase Needless Government Programs." Unsigned. 12" x 9". Condition: Excellent. **$5.00 – 8.00.**

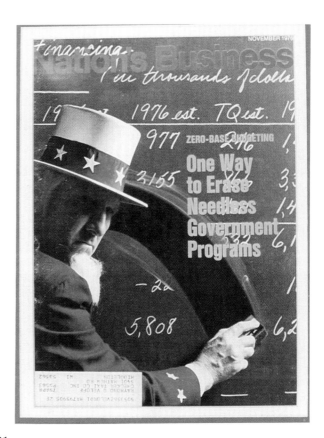

Plate 627. The New Yorker
July 3, 1989. 10¾" x 8¼". Artist: Lee Lorenz.
Condition: Excellent. **$10.00 – 12.00.**

Plate 628. U. S. Army Recruiting Journal
September, 1974. "I Want Quality!" Artist: James
Montgomery Flagg. 11" x 8½". Condition: Excellent. **$15.00 – 20.00.**

Newspapers

Newspapers have a multitude of collecting applications, from full-color comic sections to major personalities to tragedies in the headlines. In relationship to Uncle Sam, the best finds would be mid-nineteenth century special event issues or early twentieth century full-color front page images. There are not a great deal of them around, but they do show up in most every major city's newspaper. There are bargains in this category, but they are difficult to find in good condition because of the perishability of the paper and how little of it was kept.

☞ **Plate 629. Bunker Hill Centennial**
This edition of 100,000 copies printed and published by Rand, Avery & Co., 117 Franklin Street, Boston, June 17, 1875. Copyright 1875. 1775 – 1875. Artist: Frank Henry Temple Bellew. Front cover measures 22¾" x 31". Condition: Good. **$250.00 – 300.00.**

Plate 630. The Saturday Blade
"Thanksgiving in the USA — Peace and Prosperity." Chicago. Full front page. November 20, 1915. Artist: A. Bowles. 22" x 28". Condition: Excellent. **$75.00 – 100.00.**

Plate 631. The Saturday Blade
"Is the pen mightier than the word and the submarine." Chicago. April 19, 1916. Artist: A. Bowles. Front page 22" x 28". Condition: Excellent. **$50.00 – 70.00.**

Plate 632. The Philadelphia Inquirer
War Atlas. Front page of special section. Artist: Weinberg. Size: 14" x11". Date: Feb. 13, 1942. Condition: Very good. **$75.00 – 100.00.**

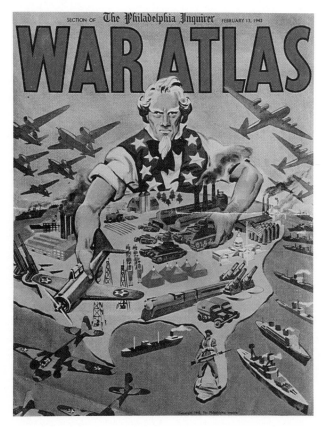

☞ **Plate 633. The Daily News**
"The Roosevelt Bears Abroad." New York.
June 1, 1907. Full page. Artist: R. K. Culver. Article by Seymour Eaton. Full page
22½" x 30". Condition: Good. **$75.00 –
100.00.**

✇ **Plate 634.**
Chicago Daily Tribune
"Good Work, General!"
May 8, 1945. Uncle Sam
with General Eisenhower.
Artist: Parrish. Drawing
6¼" x 5⅞". Condition:
Excellent. **$40.00 –
50.00.**

Prints and Engravings – Individually Published

A great variety of prints and engravings by a multitude of different artists of the nineteenth and twentieth centuries depicting Uncle Sam in one form or another have been published to coincide with the current events of the times. Usually for political or military applications, some of the best images of Uncle Sam can be found on these one-time and somewhat limited publications of prints. This section includes a representational cross section of examples that you may discover in your collecting pursuits. Prices will vary extensively depending upon the period of time produced and the significance of the artist and the subject matter. The finest condition is a must.

Plate 635. Uncle Sam with La Grippe — Broadside
Hand-colored impression of the lithograph published by Henry R. Robinson, circa 1838. Size: 17½" x 25½". Condition: Very Good. **$4,500.00 – 5,000.00.** *Note: Refer back to the introduction for additional information on this.

☞ **Plate 636. "Springfield to Washington. Lincoln vs. Douglas Democrats"**
Greve Litho. Co., Milwaukee, WI, Poster No. 421. 24" x 19" with 1" margins. Artist: Archibald M. Willard, 1892. Condition: Very good. **$1,000.00 – 1,200.00.**

☝ **Plate 637. "All Nations are Welcome to the World's Columbian Exposition Chicago 1893"**
Colorplate print. Copyright J. M. Campbell, 1892 – 93. 7¾" x 12". Condition: Excellent. **$125.00 – 150.00.**

☞ **Plate 638. Yankee Doodle 1876**
Black and white stone lithograph. Artist: Edward Harrison May. 13½" x 10". Published by Haskell & Allen, 61 Hanover St. Boston, Mass. April 5, 1876. **$1,000.00 – 1,200.00.**

Plate 639. "I Need You"
Supplement to *The North American*. Philadelphia. Sunday, December 2, 1917. 14" x 11". Artist: James Montgomery Flagg. Condition: Excellent. **$300.00 – 350.00.**

👆 **Plate 641. "Navy!"**
"Uncle Sam is calling you! Enlist in the Navy! Do it Now! I Want You." Copyright 1917, Leslie – Judge Co., N.Y. July 6, 1916. Artist: James Montgomery Flagg. 14" x 11". Condition: Excellent. **$300.00 – 350.00.**

👆 **Plate 640. "The Call to Arms!"**
"The Most Striking of the Allied Nations Calling for Men, Money and Munitions in the Death-grapple for Democracy. I Want You." Copyright Leslie – Judge Co. Artist: James Montgomery Flagg. 8" x 6¼". 1941. Condition: Excellent. **$60.00 – 75.00.**

☞ **Plate 642. "I Want You for the U. S. Army. United States Army Recruiting Service"**
Artist: James Montgomery Flagg. 13" x 10". Copyright 1941. Condition: Excellent. **$70.00 – 90.00.**

☝ **Plate 643. "The Love of Freedom"**
Artist: Ezio Anichini, Florence, Italy. Copyright 1917 by M. A. Stern, Chicago. Size: 19½" x 15½". Full-color lithograph. Condition: Very good. **$150.00 – 200.00.**

☞ **Plate 644. "Pershing in France Berlin or Bust"**
Artist: E. G. Renesch. Copyright 1917 by E. G. Renesch, Chicago. Full–color rota-gravier. 20½" x 15". Condition: Very good. **$200.00 – 250.00.**

☞ **Plate 645. Uncle Sam**
Artist: A. W. Nunemaker. 10" x 8". Condition:
Very good. **$30.00 – 35.00.**

👆 **Plate 646. Flying Uncle Sam**
Original proof sheet for the 1928 *Saturday Evening
Post* cover. Artist: Norman Rockwell. 13½" x 10½".
Condition: Excellent. **$150.00 – 200.00.**

☞ **Plate 647.**
"Yankee Kid March and Two Step"
Artist: Charlotte Blake. Copyright applied for.
14" x 11". Copyright 1917. Condition: Excellent.
$40.00 – 50.00.

☞ **Plate 648. "Lindbergh"**
Charles Lindbergh dressed as Uncle Sam along with a poem, "Our Brave Lindy" by Elsie J. Miller. Image of Lindbergh as Uncle Sam. Artist: James Stuart. 12" x 9". Condition: Excellent. Circa 1928. **$40.00 – 50.00.**

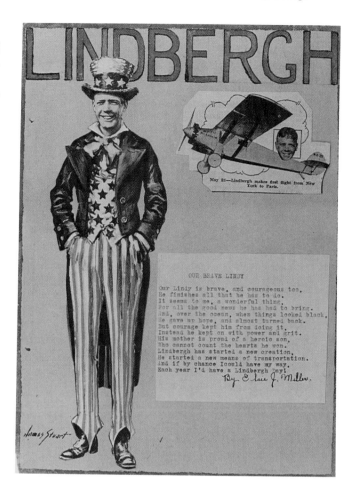

👉 **Plate 649. I Think We've Got Another Washington and Wilson is His Name"**
20" x 16". Circa 1917. Condition: Excellent. **$175.00 – 200.00.**

☞ **Plate 650. "Making the World Safe for Democracy"**
"Carrying the World to Victory." Copyright 1918 by D. H. Johnson, Oak Park, Illinois. 19½" x 15½". 1917. Condition: Excellent. **$275.00 – 300.00.**

☞ **Plate 651. "His speech was short, but generous. We want you back, you belong to us"**
Copyright 1908 by Edward Stern & Co., Inc. 12" x 9".
Condition: Excellent. **$60.00 – 75.00.**

☞ **Plate 652. "Gentlemen, Our Country!"**
Copyright 1916. Morris & Bendien, New York. 10" x 8".
Condition: Excellent. **$50.00 – 60.00.**

☞ **Plate 653. "We've Made a Monkey Out of You!"**
Artist: J. H. King. Copyright 1943. 20" x 15". Condition:
Excellent. **$200.00 – 250.00.**

☞ **Plate 654. "Uncle Sam is on the Job"**
"Hon. Uncle Sam, Me Velly, Velly, Solly." Uncle Sam states, "I'll Give You Something to Remember." Copyright 1942 by Adrian Groot, Manchester, CT. 3-D figure. 12" x 9½". Condition: Very good. **$225.00 – 250.00.**

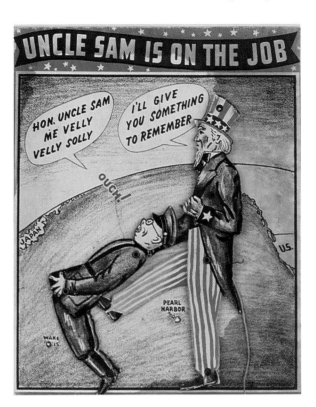

👆 **Plate 655. "Help China! China is Helping Us!"**
"Give to United China Relief, 1790. Broadway New York." 14" x 11". 1938. Artist: James Montgomery Flagg. Condition: Good. **$100.00 – 125.00.**

☞ **Plate 656. Pennant**
"Welcome Home." Silkscreen on paper: red, white and blue stars and stripes. "Well done my boys – We thank thee for the victory. God bless you all my boys and girls." Made by BB Bonter, 30 W. Harrison St., Chicago, 5, IL, USA. Copyright 1945. 34½" x 15". **$55.00 – 75.00.**

☞ **Plate 657. "Help him to help U.S.!"**
"Help the Horse to Save the Soldier. The American RED STAR Animal Relief. National Headquarters. Albany, N. Y." 14" x 11". Artist: James Montgomery Flagg. Circa 1917. Condition: Excellent. **$100.00 – 125.00.**

☞ **Plate 658. "I Want Out"**
Anti-Viet Nam War. Full color. After James Montgomery Flagg. 13" x 10". Circa 1973. Condition: Excellent. **$65.00 – 85.00.**

☞ **Plate 659. Photograph**
Uncle Sam costumed man leading a parade float advertising Paul Davis Dry Goods Company. First prize – Oct. 2, 1917. Size: 8" x 10". Photographer Flint. **$40.00 – 45.00.**

☞ **Plate 660. "Vote"**
In stars and stripes. 11" x 8½". James
Montgomery Flagg type. Circa 1960. Con-
dition: Excellent. **$10.00 – 15.00.**

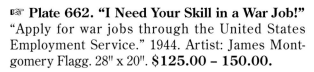

☞ **Plate 661. "Have You Had Your Pill Today"**
30" x 24". James Montgomery Flagg. Circa 1964.
$50.00 – 70.00.

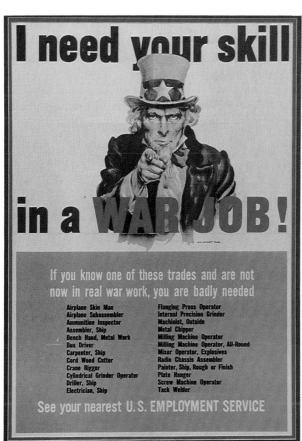

☞ **Plate 662. "I Need Your Skill in a War Job!"**
"Apply for war jobs through the United States
Employment Service." 1944. Artist: James Mont-
gomery Flagg. 28" x 20". **$125.00 – 150.00.**

⚞ **Plate 663. "Uncle Sam Wants You"**
Red, white, and blue silkscreen on black, "I Want You"
pose, with a pistol. 36" x 24". James Montgomery
Flagg type. Circa 1971. Condition: Very good.
$150.00 – 175.00.

Prints – Magazine or Book Extracts

More for the historian or specialty collector, but also for the general collector of Uncle Sam images and items,
this section tries to show respect for the artist-illustrator whose images of Uncle Sam may have only appeared with
in the context of a story line, in a book, or part of a short story or advertisement within a magazine. Some extremely rare images of Uncle Sam can, in fact, be found in this category. In general, prices will be on the lower end of the
scale, yet the eventuality of increased prices could be a possibility in the very near future.

☞ **Plate 664. Centerfold**
"Uncle Sam bids welcome to Mr.
Taft." Artist: Grant E. Hamilton.
Copyright 1909. 13⅞" x 20½". Condi-
tion: Very good. **$100.00 –
125.00.**

UNCLE SAM BIDS WELCOME TO MR. TAFT

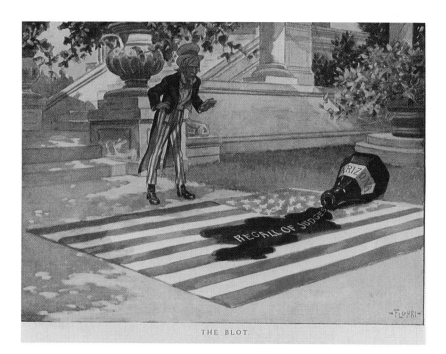

☞ **Plate 665. May 20, 1911**
"The Blot." Artist: Flohri. Color. 12" x 9". $40.00 – 45.00.

☝ **Plate 666. June 10, 1911**
"Insomnia." Artist: Flohri. 12" x 9". $40.00 – 45.00.

☝ **Plate 667. May 11, 1918**
"The Sword is Mightier than the Pen Just Now."
Artist: E. W. Kemble. Color cover. 14" x 10½".
$20.00 – 25.00.

Plate 668. "A Word to the Wives: Save"
Artist: Charles Dana Gibson. 11" x 8". Condition: Excellent. **$50.00 – 60.00.**

Plate 669. New York Evening Post
Artist: Oscar Edward Cesare. 1918. 11" x 8". Condition: Excellent. **$40.00 – 45.00.**

Plate 670. "Murder on the High Seas"
"Well, have you nearly done?" **$15.00 – 20.00.**

☞ **Plate 671. "Next to be kicked out – Dumba's Master." $15.00 – 20.00.**

THE NEXT TO BE KICKED OUT—DUMBA'S MASTER

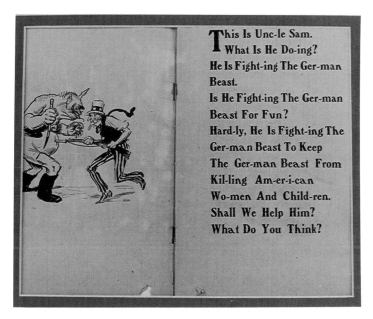

✌ **Plate 672. Liberty Loan Primer**
"This is Uncle Sam. What is he doing? He is fighting a German Beast." Unsigned. 8" x 10". Circa 1918. Condition: Excellent. **$25.00 – 30.00.**

☞ **Plate 673. "He is your Uncle Sam"**
The story of what Uncle Sam stands for by Frederic J. Haskin. 9" x 6". Circa 1918. Condition: Good. **$10.00 – 15.00.**

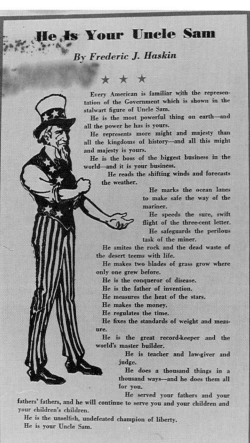

Plate 674. "I Need You Again"
"Your Army and Your Air Force Serve the Nation and Mankind in War and Peace." 1952. Artist: James Montgomery Flagg. 13" x 9¾". Condition: Good. **$18.00 – 22.00.**

Plate 675. Better Homes and Gardens
Family Money Management. February 1976. "New tax laws that can save you money." Color drawing of Uncle Sam. Artist: G. K. 5¼" x 4". Condition: Excellent. **$3.00 – 5.00.**

Plate 676. 1989 American Legion Calendar
"You've Got What it Takes Soldier. Now Take Care of What You've Got." U. S. Army Conservation Program – SAVE. Artist: Ernest Hamlin Baker. 10⅝" x 8¼". Condition: Excellent. **$3.00 – 5.00.**

☞ **Plate 677. 1988 American Legion Calendar**
"We're on our Way!" November, 1987. Artist:
Newell Convers Wyeth. Original art done approximately 1941. 10¾" x 8¼". Condition: Excellent.
$3.00 – 5.00.

☝ **Plate 678. "An Amusing Book."**
"How Spain will do us up." Artist: Homer C. Davenport. Copyright 1897. 15½" x 11½". Condition:
Excellent. **$70.00 – 90.00.**

☞ **Plate 679. "About Time To Get To Work."**
"War with Spain." Artist: Homer C. Davenport.
Copyright 1897. 15½" x 11½". Condition: Excellent. **$70.00 – 90.00.**

☜ **Plate 680. "Getting the Old Gun Ready"**
"Spanish-American War." Artist: Homer C. Daven-
port. Copyright 1897. 15½" x 11½". Condition:
Excellent. **$70.00 – 90.00.**

☞ **Plate 681.**
"And the Blow Almost Killed Uncle"
"Spanish-American War." Artist: Homer C. Daven-
port. Copyright 1897. 15½" x 11/½". Condition:
Excellent. **$70.00 – 90.00.**

☜ **Plate 682. "America, 1977"**
"The Bill for Vietnam." Artist: Edward
Sorel. Copyright 1977. 11" x 8". Condition:
Excellent. **$25.00 – 35.00.**

☞ **Plate 683. "Vietnam, 1973"**
President Nixon with a wounded Uncle Sam.
Artist: Edward Sorel. Copyright 1973. 11" x 8".
Condition Excellent. **$35.00 – 50.00.**

☜ **Plate 684. "Water-
gate Before...and After"**
Artist: Edward Sorel.
Copyright 1974. 11" x 8".
Condition Excellent.
$25.00 – 30.00.

✒ **Plate 685. March 15, 1976**
Seven-frame cartoon. Artist: Edward Sorel. 1" x 8".
Condition: Excellent. **$15.00 – 20.00.**

☞ **Plate 686.**
"Liberate New York City"
Artist: Edward Sorel. Copyright
1975. 6" x 8". Condition: Excellent. **$15.00 – 20.00.**

☞ **Plate 687. "The Bill"**
"Always goes to Uncle Sam." Artist:
Edward Sorel. Copyright 1977. 6" x 8".
Condition: Excellent. **$15.00 – 20.00.**

☝ **Plate 688. "The Moral Flabbiness"**
Artist: Edward Sorel. Copyright 1976. 8"
x 4". Condition: Excellent. **$15.00 –
20.00.**

☞ **Plate 689.**
Uncle Sam with Lyndon B. Johnson
Signed: M.R. 11⅝" x 9¼". Condition: Excel-
lent. **$12.00 – 15.00.**

Miscellaneous

The following group of categories include items of which I have discovered only one or two examples. Some of these items are most unique in their own right and some are extremely rare. Yet rarity does not always command a high price.

There are only a few chocolate molds in the image of Uncle Sam, most of which are made of pewter, lead, or tin. You may also discover Uncle Sam molds intended to be used for puddings, breads, or jello. Most of these molds were produced in the late nineteenth and early twentieth century.

The two-piece cast-iron corkscrew of Uncle Sam is the only example I have personally discovered. I feel certain there must be a variety of others out there somewhere waiting to be sought out.

Pencils, pencil sharpeners, and pencil boxes with an applied image of Uncle Sam have been manufactured in a variety of forms going back to the late nineteenth century. The rarest item in this category I believe to be the black Uncle Sam pencil sharpener made in Occupied Japan. I am sure there are many treasures to be discovered in this area that I myself have not had the opportunity to find.

It is only fitting that there should be Uncle Sam Christmas tree ornaments to hang on the tree along side of Santa Claus ornaments, since the artist, Thomas Nast, who was one of the most prolific cartoonist illustrators of early Uncle Sam images, was also the creator of our most accepted image of Santa Claus. Nast was illustrating both Uncle Sam and Santa Claus for *Harpers Weekly* as early as the 1860s.

There are only a few blown glass Uncle Sam ornaments known to have been produced between 1900 and 1930. All of these have also been reproduced within the past five to ten years. There are also a variety of other Uncle Sam ornaments made of wood, composition, celluloid, plastic, and paper. Many of the present day collectors find the best quality limited production ornaments being produced today just as desirable as the earlier original ornaments.

Another group of categories, for which there seems to be only one good example for each, are clocks, lamps, and postage stamp machines. The rarest and most desirable of these examples would be the Uncle Sam – Franklin D. Roosevelt electric clock. However, these examples have their own individual application to different collectors for different reasons. Historic significance and working condition are important in relationship to price.

Prices will vary greatly from the old to the new and condition should be as near perfect as possible.

Plate 690. Vote Watch
Pictorial dial of Uncle Sam pulling his shirt open to expose "Vote" written on his chest. Watch movement is mechanical with calendar dial. Full-color dial and original leather wrist band of red, white & blue. 1¼" diameter. Manufacturer: unknown. 1972. **$75.00 – 125.00.**

🖐 **Plate 691. Chocolate Mold**
Heavy metal mold with a full Uncle Sam. No. 514
on his back, S & Co. on the front of his hat. 5¼" x
3". Circa 1890. Condition: Excellent. **$140.00 –
160.00.**

🖐 **Plates 692 & 693. Chocolate Mold**
Solid Nickel – Silver. Two-piece No. 19. Made by
Thos. Mills & Bro., Inc., Philadelphia, PA. Circa 1918.
7½" x 3¼". Condition: Excellent. **$150.00 – 175.00.**

🖐 **Plate 694 & 695. Corkscrew**
Two-piece cast iron bust of Uncle Sam. Hat is removable corkscrew. Marks: Patent applied for 1932. 2⅞" x
1⅞" x 1¼". All original paint. Condition: Very good. **$250.00 – 300.00.**

☜ Plate 696. Bumper Ornament
Die-cut molded composition with gold, red, white, and dark blue paint. "Drive Ahead with Roosevelt." Manufactured by ARPO. Copyright 1936 by Nationwide Distributors, New York. 8" x 11¼". Condition: Very good. **$150.00 – 175.00.**

☞ Plate 697. Spoon
Souvenir spoon dated March 9, 1898. "500,000,000 for Defense" on a banner on the handle. "Feb. 15, 1898, Maine" with an eagle on the bowl. Marked, "Souvenir Co., New York" on the back. Sterling silver. 4" long. Condition: Excellent. **$100.00 – 125.00.**

☝ Plate 698. Ballot Box
Plastic tophat with "Deposit Tickets Here" slot. "Hats off to the past" on both sides. Ticket removal door on hatband. 15" x 15". Condition: Very good. Circa 1950. **$125.00 – 150.00.**

☞ **Plate 699. Mirror/Coat Rack**
Copper, Spanish American War. "Our Nations Pride." 18" square. Mirror, centered, is 8" square. Condition: Very good. Circa 1898. **$125.00 – 150.00.**

✍ **Plate 700. Doorstop**
Cast-iron doorstop with original paint. Circa 1900. 14" x 6½" x 4". Condition: Very good. **$350.00 – 450.00.**

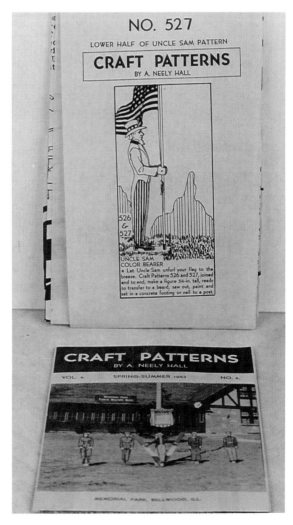

☞ **Plate 701. Pattern**
Craft Patterns, Elmhurst, IL. Uncle Sam wooden cut-out for a flagpole or mailbox holder. Includes folded flyer which contains nine photographs of the finished product. Vol. 4, No. 8, Spring - Summer, 1943. Pattern No. 527 by A. Neely Hall. Finished cut-out 54¼". Condition: Excellent. **$30.00 – 35.00.**

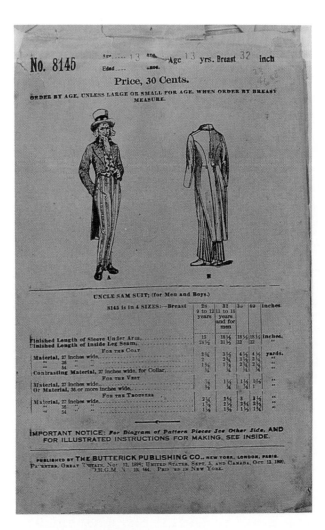

☞ Plate 703. Mechanical Pencil
"Souvenir Memphis Down in Dixie."
5⅝" x ⅝" in diameter. Condition:
Excellent. Circa 1945. **$20.00 –
25.00.**

☞ Plate 702. Pattern
Uncle Sam suit, pattern number 8145. The Butterick
Publishing Co., New York, London, Paris. Patented in
the United States September 5, 1898. Printed in New
York. 8½" x 5¼" (folded). Condition: Very good. Circa
1920. **$50.00 – 60.00.**

☞ Plate 704. Pencil
Plastic two-piece sleeve containing
wooden pencil and eraser. Outer image
of Uncle Sam knocking out "Hitler"
and "Tojo" while saying "now-you'll
remember Pearl Harbor." Opposite
side has advertisement for Farmers
Union Elevator Co. Valier, Montana.
3½" x ½". Manufacturer Sample #L-
303-V. 1943. Condition: Excellent.
$40.00 – 60.00.

☞ Plate 705. Pencil Sharpener
Uncle Sam – Darkie – Pencil sharpener. Cast iron. Marked inside
back of tophat, "Made in Occupied Japan." Circa 1948. All original
paint. 1⅞" x 1⅛". Condition: Excellent. **$450.00 – 550.00.**

Plate 706. Pencil Box
Paper on wood with tin top. Made by The Ozark Pencil Company, St. Louis, Missouri. Circa 1918. 12" x 1¼". Condition: Very good. **$75.00 – 85.00.**

☞ **Plate 707. Printer's Block**
Steel on wood ¾" x 1½". Condition: Excellent. Circa 1900. **$35.00 – 45.00.**

Plate 708. Printer's Block
Copper on wood. 1½" in diameter. Block, 1⅝" square. Condition: Excellent. Circa 1900. **$50.00 – 65.00.**

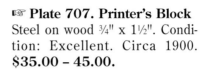

We haven't moved, we are still in the same old place.

Plate 709. Ink Blotter
"We haven't moved, we are still in the same old place." 3½" x 6⅜". Circa 1918. Condition: Excellent. **$30.00 – 35.00.**

Plate 710. Pencil Sharpener
Cast pot-metal standing figure of Uncle Sam walking. Copper plated finish. Also can be found in cold-painted red, white, and blue colors. 2" x 1" x ⅜". Manufacturer: Ever-Sharp MFG. Co., N.Y. 1918. **$120.00 – 150.00**

≋ **Plate 711. Ink Blotter**
"The More We Back 'em Up, the Sooner They'll Be Home." McCarthy Foundry Co., Chicago. 4" x 9". Copyright 1942. Condition: Excellent. **$10.00 – 15.00.**

☞ **Plate 712. Ink Blotter**
"The International WALK-OVER. The tie that binds." Advertisement for P. H. Severson, Lake Park, MN. Slogan: "When WALK-OVERS go on – Troubles go off." Circa 1915. 4" x 7½". Condition: Very good. **$35.00 – 45.00.**

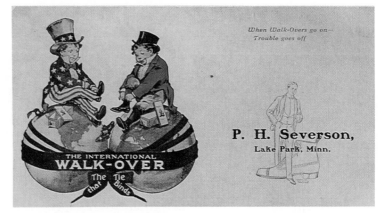

≋ **Plate 713. Ink Blotter**
Uncle Sam/Abraham Lincoln. 5" x 3⅜". Copyright 1932. Condition: Excellent. **$25.00 – 30.00.**

☞ **Plate 714. Ink Blotter**
"I Want Your Waste Paper." Edwin C. Price & Co. "Save Every Scrap of Waste! Shick Fire-proof Balers." 3½" x 5¾". Circa 1942. Condition: Excellent. **$12.00 – 15.00.**

🎄 **Plate 715. Cut-out Christmas Tree Ornaments**
4" x 1" with original box. Copyright 1918. Condition: Excellent. **$50.00 – 60.00.**

🖋 **Plate 716. Christmas Tree Ornament**
Molded and cold-painted pewter teddy bear as Uncle Sam. Label on bottom reads, "Storybook Collections TM Carolyn Carpin TM 1989. 1⅞" x 1¼" x 1⅜". Condition: Excellent. **$12.00 – 15.00.**

Plate 717. Christmas Ornament
Hallmark Uncle Sam Keepsake Ornament, pressed tin. Dated 1984. Copyright 1984 Hallmark Cards, Inc. Kansas City, Missouri 64141. Made in Hong Kong QX449-1. Issue price $6.00. Original box pictures ornament on both sides Marked. "©1984 Hallmark Cards, Inc." on the back of his right trouser leg. 5" x 2½". Condition: Excellent. **$25.00 – 30.00.**

Plate 718. Christmas Tree Ornament
Standing Uncle Sam, an individually mouth-blown and hand painted glass ornament. This ornament was produced in the family workshop of Inge-glas of Lauscha, Bavaria, exclusively for "Old World Christmas" in a limited edition. Circa 1994. 4½" x 1½". **$25.00 – 35.00.**

Plate 719. Christmas Tree Ornament
An individually mouth-blown and hand painted glass ornament. Produced by Christopher Radko in a limited edition. Ca. 1994. 7" x 1¾". **$25.00 – 35.00.**

☞ **Plate 720. Pot Metal Clock**
United Clock Company. Circa 1944. The face of the clock on the right marked, "United" with an eagle and star above it. Eagle and star light up. Base marked, "Our Uncle Sam." This clock commemorates Roosevelt's involvement in the North Atlantic Treaty Organization. 11½" x 13" x 3¾". Condition: Very good. **$400.00 – 500.00.**

☜ **Plate 721. Lamp**
Uncle Sam's "Pledge of Allegiance" Portable Lamp. Plastic. 7⅞" x 4⅜" x 4". Condition: Excellent. Circa 1950. $50.00 – 60.00.

☞ **Plate 722. Stamp Machine**
Ca. 1945. Uncle Sam measures 2½" x 4½". Automatic Dispenser Co., Los Angeles, Serial No. 4819 Nickle and dime slots. 20½" x 7⅞" x 4¼". Condition: Excellent. **$100.00 – 150.00.**

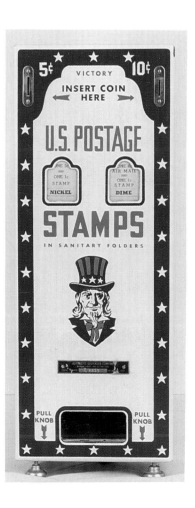

BIOGRAPHIES OF UNCLE SAM ARTISTS

This section includes biographical sketches of over 200 artists who have created or utilized images of Uncle Sam, in one form or another, from 1838 to the present time. Over 100 of these artists' works are represented within the text of this book. The remaining artists not here-in represented have all produced a great variety of images of Uncle Sam. Should you discover any of them in your collecting pursuits, this additional reference information should be of some value to you in doing further research on your acquisitions. Please be aware that you may find little-to-no-information on many artists who have created Uncle Sam images, as they may not have received any public or published recognition for their work.

A., H.
Illustrator, cartoonist who contributed to *Life* magazine from 1910 through 1925. Research has concluded nothing as to the identity of this artist.

ALEXANDER, Will (1883 – 1938)
Born: Haddonfield, NJ. Studied: Drexel Institute; Pennsylvania Academy of Fine Arts. Member: Philadelphia Society of Allied Artists.

ANTHONY, Francis N.
Active from 1890 through 1915 as a cartoonist for major book publishers, as well as magazine and newspaper publishers in New York, Pennsylvania, Ohio, and Illinois. Did the frontispiece of Uncle Sam in T. R. in Cartoon by Raymond Gros in 1910 for the Saalfield Publishing Company.

BAKER, Ernest Hamlin (1889 – 1975)
Baker was a self-taught artist who developed his own intricate approach as typified by the nearly 400 cover portraits painted from photographs of subjects taken from all possible angles, then studied, even with a magnifying glass, to provide him with the knowledge of the entire face and head. Residing in Carmel, NY, Baker worked with the United States Post Office, Federal Art Project of the Works Progress (later Projects) Administration, the large government programs set up during the Great Depression to provide jobs for artists. See plate 676.

BALCHLOR, S. O.
Active as a cartoonist for various magazine publishers including *Life* from approximate 1902 through 1915.

BALFOUR-KER, William
Illustrator active in 1904 in New York City.

BARBELLE
Artist and illustrator active in New York between 1905 and 1925.

BARCLAY, McKee (1870 – 1947)
Born: Louisville, KY. Residence: Baltimore, MD. On the staff of several newspapers in Kentucky. Political writer/cartoonist for the *Baltimore Sun* from 1908 – 1920.

BARTHOLOMEW, Charles L.
Born: 1869 in Chariton, IA. Residence: Minneapolis, MN Studied: Burt Harwood; Douglas Volk Illustrator of children's books, author of Bart Chalk Talk System, Crayon Presentation. Editor: Textbooks on illustrating and cartooning. Position: Dean Federation School of Illustrators and Cartoonists; *Minneapolis Journal.*

BEARD, Frank (1842 – 1905)
When only 18 years old, Frank Beard drew a cartoon, "Why Don't You Take It," which was published by Currier and Ives lithographers and distributed by the Republicans as a campaign document. During the Civil War he was a special artist for *Harper's Weekly*, contributing ideas for the back page. In the 1870s Beard was one of the most prolific cartoonists for the various short-lived comic

papers such as Phunny *Phellow, Wild Oats,* and *Leslie* comic magazines. Beard returned to lithography when *Judge* was founded in 1881, creating handsome and sophisticated material until 1886. Frank Beard is credited with being the originator of the chalk-talk, a popular form of public entertainment for a generation. For years he was a professor of fine arts at Syracuse University, eventually giving up politics, but not cartoons. See plate 513.

BELLEW, Frank Henry Temple (1828 – 1888)
Born in Cawnpore, India, to an English family, Bellew came to America in 1850 and immediately embarked on a career in cartooning and humorous illustration. Settling in New York City, he contributed cartoons to the new illustrated monthlies, most notably, *Harper's,* the *Illustrated American News,* and children's books. He was founder of cartoon and humor magazines such as *Lantern, Vanity Fair,* and *Nick Nax.* In the 1870s he was a mainstay of the *New York Graphic,* the first illustrated daily in America. Bellew wrote and illustrated, *The Art of Amusing* in 1866, an interesting treatise on his craft. Bellew was as important to his field — the magazine panel cartoon, which he practically created — as Nast was to the editorial cartoon. He was among the earliest and most prolific of woodcut cartoonists, one who broke the bonds of anonymity and whose signature (a triangle) became as famous as the names of writers who shared a masterful caricaturist. To him belongs the mantle of "Father of American Cartooning." See plates 2, 3, 583, 585, 629.

BERRYMAN, Clifford Kennedy (1869 – 1949)
Pulitzer Prize-winning cartoonist born in Kentucky. Berryman's first job in art was with the U.S. Patent Office in Washington, D.C. delineating patent entries for $30 a month. When a cartoon was submitted to the *Washington Post,* he was paid $25 and his career was chosen. Berryman joined the *Post* staff as an editorial cartoonist in 1891. In 1907 he switched to the *Washington Star* where he remained until 1949. Berryman is remembered as a Washington institution. His cartoons were largely without malice, his caricatures belabored, betraying a lifelong amateurish tint to his work. He always drew with pen and ink and relied on the crosshatch. His most famous cartoon, in 1902, depicted one of Teddy Roosevelt's bear hunts. He began including the little bear as a mascot in his Roosevelt cartoons. The bear was mass-produced and became an essential element of childhood. As its originator, Berryman never realized a cent from its success. Among other honors, Berryman was the first cartoonist to hold the position of President of the Gridiron Club.

BIR, D
Active as a cartoonist/illustrator for *Life* magazine, as well as numerous other magazines and newspaper periodicals from approximately 1900 through 1920.

BISHOP, Daniel
Residence: Portland, OR. On the staff of The Oregon Journal, Bishop was an active cartoonist and illustrator from approximately 1920 to 1940.

BLASHFIELD, Albert Dodd (1860 – 1920)
Cartoonist, illustrator born in Brooklyn, NY. He was educated and received his art training from the Art Students League. In the early 1890s, he joined the staff of *Life* magazine, becoming a fixture there until his death. Blashfield illustrated several of J. A. Mitchell's books

(the founder and editor of *Life*). His major contribution was his delineation of *Life* magazine's cupid. See plates 255, 543.

BLUE, E. N.
Prolific artist, illustrator and cartoonist who produced hundreds of illustrations for *Puck, Leslie's Weekly, Harper's,* and the United States Government Printing Department, as well as numerous publishing companies. Although little is known of Blue's academic background, his work indicates a definite influence of academic study and accomplishment. See plates 187, 509, 510, 511, 514 – 518.

BONTE, H.
Commercial artist and illustrator active in New York 1890 – 1915. Bonte was reproduced lithographically by Prang, Raphael Tuck, and Buffalo Litho. Company. See plate 92.

BOR
Bor was on the staff of the *Boston Globe* during the late 1800s. One of his drawings was illustrated in the book, Exciting Experiences in *Our Wars with Spain and the Filipinos, The Life of Admiral Dewey.* No record or information pertaining to Bor's academic training and background are known to exist.

BOURMAN, R. C.
Prolific cartoonist, illustrator active in St. Paul and Minneapolis, MN, from 1880 through 1920. Most noted for his political and satirical cartoons in regional newspapers, including the *Minneapolis Tribune.*

BOWLES, A.
Artist, cartoonist and illustrator active in the Chicago, IL, area from 1910 through 1930 for the *Saturday Blade,* as well as other regional periodicals. See plates 630, 631.

BOWMAN, R. P.
Active in the Minneapolis, St. Paul, MN area from approximately 1890 through the early 1900s. Illustrated, through the *Minneapolis Tribune,* in *Exciting Experiences in our Wars with Spain and the Filipinos, The Life of Admiral Dewey.*

BRAAKENSEIK, Johan
Born: 1858 in Amsterdam. Considered in other European countries to be the outstanding Dutch political cartoonist. Studied: Amsterdam Academy, 1876 to 1881; *Het Politienieuws;* and *De Amsterdammer Weekblad voor Nederland,* as well as other magazines. For decades he did one large and one small drawing for each weekly issue. Braakenseik covered events in Dutch politics and every important occurrence in Europe and the world. He published an album consisting entirely of his cartoons on the Spanish-American War.

BRANDT, Gustav (1861 – 1919)
Born: Hamburg, Germany. Brandt's career was completely dedicated to Berlin's satirical magazine, *Kladderadatsch.* Studied: Academies of Dusseldorf and Berlin. At the turn of the century, he had become a specialist in celebrity caricatures. Declared by Eduard Fuchs, a historian of humorous art, to be the greatest living German caricaturist and the first one of world rank.

BRINKERHOFF, Robert Moore
Born: 1880 in Toledo, OH. Residence: New York NY. Studied: Art Students League; Academy Colarossi, Paris. Member: Society of Illustrators, 1912; Dutch Treat Club. Illustrator: *The Saturday Evening Post, Redbook.* Author: *Dear Mom* and *Little Mary Mixup in Fairyland.* Published: Duffield, 1926. Contributor: cartoons, *New York World-Telegram.* Position: staff, United Features Syndicate, New York.

BRONSTRUP
Cartoonist working in the San Francisco area in the early 1900s until approximately 1935, primarily for the *San Francisco Cronicle.*

BROUGHTON
Active from 1890 through the 1920s producing numerous illustrations for *Life* magazine, *Leslie's Weekly, Harper's Weekly,* and other periodicals of this time. Most noted for his depictions of historic and political subjects.

CADY, Harrison (Walter)
Born: 1877 in Garner, MA. Member: Society of Illustrators; Society of American Etchers; American Watercolor Society; Salmagundi Club. Exhibited: National Academy of Design, 1944, 1945 (prize), 1946; Macbeth Gallery (one-man); Kleeman Gallery (one-man); World's Fair, New York, 1939. Work: New York Public Library, Library of Congress, University of Nebraska. Author: Caleb Cottontail, as well as other children's stories. Contributor: *Life, Saturday Evening Post, Ladies' Home Journal.*

CAMERINI
Italian cartoonist who drew for the *Il Travaso* in Rome, Italy during the 1920s.

CARTER, Helene
Produced numerous advertising illustration art pieces for minor publishing houses and original art for sheet music. See plate 399.

CASSELL, Jonathan H. (1875 – 1940)
Born: Nebraska City, NE. Although he signed his work "Jno. Cassell" he was known as John Cassell. Educated at Doane College of Crete, NE (1892 – 94), Cassell studied art at the Art Institute of Chicago and began drawing cartoons for the *Ram's Horn.* In the 1890's Cassell began freelancing to *Puck, Judge,* and *Life* magazines and illustrating for popular monthlies and books. Around 1913, along with Rollin Kirby, he worked as editorial cartoonist. Although eclipsed by Kirby, he was a respectable and forceful cartoonist in his own right. When the *World* went to a single edition, Cassell joined the *Brooklyn Eagle.* Cassell had a handsome crayon line and shaded his drawings neatly. There was a great deal of animation in his figures and he had a way of endowing his targets with squint-eyed, dour expressions. See plate 345.

CESARE, Oscar Edward (1885 – 1948)
American cartoonist born in Linkoping, Sweden, Cesare studied art in Paris, then moved to America at the age of eighteen and continued his art studies in Buffalo. He took his first jobs in Chicago and worked for several newspapers, including the *Tribune.* Drawing editorial cartoons for the *World, The Sun, The Post, Harper's Weekly,* and *The New Times,* Cesare gained much fame with *The Times* as an interviewer-sketcher. His most famous interview was with Lenin in 1922. He also visited General Billy Mitchell, Orville Wright, and Benito Mussolini. *One Hundred Cartoons by Cesare,* a collection dealing mostly with war-related issues, was published in 1916 by Small, Maynard. Cesare died at the age of 63 in Stamford, CT. Lamentably, his brilliant work is largely forgotten today. See plate 669.

CHAPIN, H.
Active in the Los Angeles, CA, area from approximately 1890 through 1920 as a political, satirical cartoonist. Chapin created cartoon illustrations for numerous periodicals published in the Los Angeles area. Also a staff artist, illustrator for the *Los Angeles Times.*

CHILD, Charles Jesse
Born: 1902 in Montclair, NJ. Residence: Bucks County, PA. Member: Philadelphia Arts and Crafts Guild; Federal Art Project of the Works Progress Administration. Exhibited: American Painters Today, Exhibition; Worcester Museum of Art, 1938. Illustrator: *A Book of Americans, 1934.*

CHRISTY, Howard Chandler
Studied: National Academy of Design; Art Students League; Chase School of Art. Member: Society of Illustrators, 1915. Exhibited: Paris Expo, 1900 (medal); Pan-Am. Expo., Buffalo, 1901 (prize). 1873 – 1952

Christy made his early reputation by accompanying U.S. troups to Cuba during the Spanish-American War when articles illustrated by his works were published by *Scribner's* and *Leslie's Weekly*. When his Christy Girl became famous in *Scribner's*, the subject of his art became almost entirely that of beautiful girls. Christy's painting technique was sumptuous and he was in great demand as a portraitist. Among his best known portraits are of Mrs. William Randolph Hearst of New York and Secretary of State Charles Hughes, as well as Mrs. Calvin Coolidge and Amelia Earhart. In later years he produced several murals, the most famous of which is "The Signing of the Constitution" which hangs in the rotunda of the Capitol in Washington D.C. He was elected to the Society of Illustrators Hall of Fame in 1980.

CHUBB

Research produced little information on the life of this artist other than the fact that, through the *Rochester Herald*, his work was reproduced in *Leslie's* in the early 1900s.

CONACHER, John C. (1876 – 1947)

Although Conacher was classically trained, he developed a style which was full of comic detail, apparent in his numerous pen and ink drawings for magazines in the early 1900's. His drawings appeared in *Judge* and *Everybody's* magazines and his work for the Seaboard National Bank advertisements was selected for the ADC Annuals of Advertising Art. See plate 549.

CORNWELL, Dean (1892 – 1960)

Painter, illustrator, decorator, instructor, and lecturer. Born: March 5, Louisville, Ky. Studied with Harvey Dunn and Carlton Chapman at the Art Students League in New York. Combining his academic illustration technique with his painterly post-impressionistic style, Cornwell became one of the most succcessful artist/illustrators of his time. Member: NA; NSMP, (Pres. 1954); SI (Pres. 1922); Arch. Lg; NAC; Mural P.; Players Club, NY; Chelsea Arts Club, London, Eng.; London Sketch Club; SC; AAPL; Calif. AC. Exhibited: Wilmington SFA, 1929, 1921 (prize); AIC, 1922; SC, 1927 (Prize); Allied Ar. Am., 1939 (Prize) Arch. Lg., 1939. Work: Murals, Los Angeles Public Library; Lincoln Memorial, Redlands, Calif.; Detroit Athletic Club; USPO, Mural, Morgantown, NC; Davidson County Court House, Nashville; General Motors Bldg.; WFNY, 1939. Illustrator: Magazines, newspapers, books, posters, and calenders. He was also very actively involved with the WPA as both artist and instructor. WWWAA. See plates 129, 346.

CORY, J. Campbell (1867 – ca. 1925)

Born: Waukegan, IL. Educated in Waukegan and began cartooning in New York in 1896. Along with Fred Morgan of the *Philadelphia Inquirer*, probably the last great crosshatch political cartoonist. Drew for many of America's largest newspapers and magazines, including the *New York World* and *Harper's Weekly*. Published the *Great West Monthly* in 1907 – 08 and *The Bee*, an oversized chromolithographed humorous weekly, during the Spanish-American War. Paid cartoonist for a political party for two decades. Cory started a syndicate, distributing his own cartoons and those of others. Ran a correspondence school and published books teaching the elements of cartooning, including *Cory's Hands* and *The Cartoonist's Art*.

CROSBY, Percy Leo

Born: 1891 in Brooklyn, NY. Residence: McLean, VA. Member: Society of Illustrators, Salmagundi Club. Exhibited: 10th Olympic Exhibition, Los Angeles, 1932 (medal)., Originator of the Cartoon: "Skippy."

CULVER, R. K.

Active in New York from 1900 through the 1920s, Culver was a staff artist of the *Daily News* of New York, producing illustrations for a feature article entitled, "The Roosevelt Bears Abroad." See plate 633.

CUSHING, Otho (1871 – 1842)

Born: Fort McHenry, MD. Died: in New Rochelle, NY. Studied:

Boston Museum of Fine Art. Schooled in France. Positions: Massachusetts Institute of Technology; *Life* staff for 25 years.

CZULEWICZ, Gerald E. (1944 – present)

Born: Erie, PA. Studied illustration, painting, and advertising design at Art Center College of Design, Los Angeles, CA, from 1963 – 1965; San Francisco State College, 1965; interior stage and set design under Edwin Willis of MGM Studios Hollywood, CA, and James McNaughton of NBC Television Network. Freelance artist, illustrator, and designer, 1964 – 1967 doing work for Macy's of Southern California; Bullock's; MGM Studios; Paramount Studios; Master Charge Credit Card Corp.; United Bank of California; KWAK International; Judy Spencer Co.; Rolling Stones and Grass Roots album & promotional arts; Hart, Schaffner & Marx, San Francisco; presently pursuing career in modern art and design in Isanti, MN. See plates 334, 336, 337 (cover page).

DACOSTA, Stella May

Painter and illustrator, Philadelphia, PA. Exhibited: WC Exh. Pa. Acad. FA, 1936, 1938; Germantown A. Lg., 1937; Intl. WC Exh. AIC, 1937 – 1939 (40). See plate 620.

DALRYMPLE, Louis (1861 – 1905)

Cartoonist born in Cambridge, IL. Educated at the Pennsylvania Academy of Fine Arts and at the Art Students League in New York. In 1886, Dalarymple was a staff member for *Puck* for 15 years. He was prolific and his style was full of native humor. There was much animation in his figures. Dalrymple handled lithographic political subjects, as well as black-and-white humorous cartoons. Just after the turn of the century, when he also dabbled in Sunday comic strips, he left *Puck* to draw for its rival, *Judge*. See plates 432, 435, 437, 441, 442, 446, 490, 491, 494, 497, 498, 499, 500, 502.

DARLING, Jay Norwood (J. N. Ding) (1876 – 1962)

Born: Norwood MI. Residence: Des Moines, IA. Member: Society of Illustrators; Century Association. Cartoonist: *Sioux City (Iowa) Journal*, 1901, 1906; *Des Moines Register*, 1913 — Twice a Pulitzer Prize winner, Jay Darling first signed himself "Ding" in a yearbook lampooning faculty members as chorus girls; he was suspended for a year. In 1900 Ding was a reporter for the *Sioux City Journal*. While tracking down a story, he sketched a lawyer who refused to be photographed. In so doing, he became a sketch artist for the paper on the strength of the quality of this sketch. In 1913 he accepted a position with the *New York Tribune*, one of the most prestigious papers in the country, as a regular cartoonist. He was syndicated by the *Herald-Tribune Syndicate*. In his day the great Ding Darling was one of the most influential and most often reprinted cartoonists in America.

DART, Harry Grant (1870 – 1938)

Born: Williamsport, PA. Dart's first job as an artist was making portraits of deceased personalities for the National Crayon Company. In the mid 1890s, he worked briefly for the *Boston Herald* and, in 1898, the *New York World* sent him to Cuba to cover the Spanish-American War as a sketch artist. After the war, Dart joined the *New York World*, rising to the rank of art editor, covering news events and court trials with his staff. He later worked for the *New York Recorder* and *Denver Times*, but was best remembered for his freelance magazine work, chiefly for *Life* magazine, during the first decades of the century, and for *Judge* and *Life* in the late 1920s. Member: Players and the Society of Illustrators.

DAVENPORT, Homer Calvin (1876 – 1912)

Born: Silverton, OR. Reared on a farm, he was a jockey, railroad fireman, and a clown in a circus. Employed in 1892 by the *San Francisco Examiner*, Davenport was taken to New York by William R. Hearst in 1895 and became a member of the staff of the *New York Journal* (American). He went to Europe in 1897, where he met and cartooned many public men, including Gladstone, and sketched the Dreyfus trial. Author: *Davenport's Cartoons* (Cartoons), *The Dollar of the Man*? Davenport admired Theodore Roosevelt and, in 1904, the cartoonist accepted a position with the *Republican New York Mail*, where he drew his most famous cartoon, "He's Good Enough for Me," Uncle Sam's endorsement of the Rough Rider for re-election. The cartoon was widely reprinted as a campaign document. See plates 678, 679, 680, 681.

DEAN
Cartoonist living and working in the Dayton, OH, area during a period from approximately 1915 to 1935. Dean was on the staff of the *News*, a Dayton publication.

DeGRIMM, C.
Illustrator and cartoonist active in New York City from 1875 to 1915 doing work for numerous periodicals including *Harper's, Puck, Political Chestnuts, Leslie's Weekly,* and *Country Gentleman.* See plates 338, 339.

DEHLL
As a cartoonist in Moscow, Dehll drew for *Pravda* during the 1920s and 30s.

DE MANUELE, Jos. B.
Contemporary, itinerate illustrator, artist of the Madison, WI, area.

DE MAR, John L. (1865 – 1926)
Born: Philadelphia, PA. Position: cartoonist, *Philadelphia Record,* 1903.

DE TAKACH, Andre C.
Artist/illustrator, active in the Boston, MA, area between 1910 and 1920. See plate 402.

DONNELL
Active from 1910 through 1925, Donnell produced numerous illustrations for *Leslie's Weekly,* as well as other periodicals of this period.

DUNK
Illustrator producing images for sheet music for M. Wilmark and Sons in the New York area. See plate 394.

DUVAL, L. E.
Active from 1880 through 1910, Duval produced numerous original illustrations for use in conjunction with advertising catalogs, brochures, trade cards, and postcards.

EHRHART, Sid
Residence: Brooklyn, NY. Ehrhart drew for *Puck* magazine in the 1890s. Along with Dalrymple and Taylor, he did most of the cartoons which attacked Bryan in 1896, the butts of *Puck's* satire in these years. See plate 443.

EKMAN, Stan
Artist, illustrator from Chicago, IL, who produced numerous pen and ink and watercolor illustrations for Brown and Bigelow Publishing Company, Dow Publishing Company, and McMillan Publishing Company from 1940 through 1960. Studied: Chicago Art Institute; St. Paul School of Art; Art Students League, New York. Most commonly known for his calendar illustration art. See plate 343.

ENRIGHT, Walter J.
Born: 1879 in Chicago, IL. Studied: Art Institute of Chicago; Armour Institute, Chicago. Member: Society of Illustrators, 1910; Players Club. Position: cartoonist, *Miami Herald.* See plate 608.

EVANS, Raymond Oscar (1887 – 1954)
Born: Columbus, OH. Evans received his B.A. from Ohio State University in 1910 and became an advertising artist in Columbus. On the staff of the *Columbus Dispatch,* he received training from Billy Ireland and drew editorial cartoons for the *Dayton News* in 1912 and 1913. He also

drew for the *Baltimore News* and *American,* and freelanced for *Puck* until his death. Evans taught cartooning at the Maryland Institute.

EVANS, Scott
Illustrator, Westport, CT. See plate 614.

FEININGER
Cartoonist active in Berlin, Germany, from 1900 through 1920. Work: *Lustige Blatter,* Berlin. Produced numerous illustrations in German periodicals.

FELD, N.
Active in Syracuse, NY, from 1890 – 1910 with numerous periodicals, including the *Syracuse Herald,* for which he was a staff artist.

FLAGG, James Montgomery (1877 – 1960)
Born: Pelham Manor, NY. Studied: Art Students League, 1893; Herkomer in England; V. Marec in Paris. Member: Society of Illustrators, 1911; Lotos Club; Artists Guild. Illustrator: *City People, Kitty Cobb, Boulevards All the Way — Maybe.* Books of satire, *Liberty, Cosmopolitan,* other magazines. Collection of drawings published as, "The Well-Knowns." Flagg sold his first illustration to *St. Nicholas* magazine when he was only 12 years old. At 14, he began 20 years as a staff member of *Life.* Best known for his, "I Want You" poster of Uncle Sam, 1917 (One of 46 World War I posters), and for his creation, "The Flagg Girl." Although Flagg claimed to be firmly established on the staffs of *Life* and *Judge* at the age of 14, his work did not regularly begin appearing until the mid-1890s. He preserved his cartoon discipline for interior work in the magazines (paintings graced the covers); Nerby Nat was a colored comic strip with captions instead of balloons that ran in *Judge* for years and was wildly successful. In later years, Flagg was the toast of Broadway and Hollywood for his famous impromptu portrait sketches of celebrities. It was his poster art that gained Flagg his greatest recognition, particularly for "Uncle Sam Wants You!," a recruiting poster from World War I that first appeared as a cover for *Leslie's Weekly,* which was owned by *Judge.* He also did other posters during both World Wars and conservation posters in the 1930s. See plates 64, 265 – 283, 285, 320 – 329, 526, 527, 529, 530, 531, 539, 541, 542, 601, 611, 628, 639 – 642, 655, 657, 658, 660 – 663, 674.

FLOHRI, Emil (1869 – 1938)
Joined the staff of *Leslie's Weekly* as an artist at the age of 16 and soon switched to the affiliated *Judge* magazine, where he drew humorous panels in pen and ink before switching to stone. Flohri became an accomplished lithographer and his political cartoons in color are masterpieces of sublety. Around 1910, he took up the brush and executed many of *Judge's* last colored political cartoons. He painted portraits of silent film stars beginning in 1920. In the late 1920s, Flohri went to work for Walt Disney and remained there for nearly a decade. See plates 665, 666.

FORSYTHE, Clyde (1885 – 1962)
Born: Orange, CA. Studied: L. E. G. Macleod; Hl. Dunn; H. Giles; E. Bisttram; Art Students League with DuMond, 1904. Member: New York Society of Painters, Salmagundi Club, Allied Artists of America, California Art Club; Lagunda Beach Artists Association; Pasadena Society of Artists.,Exhibited: Painters of the West, 1927 (medal). Work: Municipal Artists Gallery, Phoenix. Creator: poster used in Fifth Victory Liberty Loan, "And They Thought We Couldn't Fight." Shared his California studio with Frank T. Johnson. See plates 533, 534, 602.

G., F.
Cartoonist, illustrator contributing artwork for *Harper's* magazine from 1860 through 1890, as well as other periodicals during this period. See plate 613.

GAHMAN, Werner
German cartoonist working in Berlin for the *Kladderadtsch* during the 1920s.

GALE
Cartoonist living and working in the Los Angeles, CA, area from approximately 1910 to 1935. Gale was on the staff of the *Los Angeles Times*.

GIBSON, Charles Dana (1867 – 1944)
Born: Roxbury, MA. Studied: Art Students League; Saint Gaudens; Academie Julian, Paris. Member: Cornish (NH) Colony; Society of Illustrators; National Association of Portrait Painters; Associate Member of the National Academy of Design, 1932. Exhibited: Pan-Am Expo., Buffalo, 1901 (medal). Author/Illustrator: "Sketches in London," "People of Dickens," "Education of Mr. Pipp." With Thomas Nast, Charles Dana Gibson had more impact on American life than any other artist or cartoonist. After two years of study, finally one cartoon — unsigned — was accepted by *Life* and ran in the March 25, 1886 issue. Thereafter, Gibson's cartoons appeared with greater frequency in *Life*, profusely in *Tid-bits* and *Time* and occasionally in *Puck* into 1887. In response to *Puck's*, "Taylor-made Girl" and Ehrhart's beauties in *Puck*, *Life* bestowed the monicker, "Gibson Girl," on its prize artist's creations. Soon Gibson was one of America's most famous celebrities. The Gibson Girl was merchandised widely, and amid much fanfare her creator signed a $100,000 contract to draw exclusively for *Collier's*, accepting work as he desired for *Life*; Gibson's loyalty to his discoverer was fierce. In 1920, after the death of *Life's* founders, Gibson became owner and editor of the magazine that had originally graced him with his first signs of encouragement. Gibson's contribution to American life was enormous. In the cartoonworld his influence can be assessed by the number of imitators in his wake, including James Montgomery Flagg and Orson Lowell. See plates 545, 548, 668.

GILLAM, Benard (1856 – 1896)
American cartoonist and publisher born in Branbury, England. Gillam sold his first cartoon in 1876, and was soon contributing to the *Leslie* publications and the *New York Graphic*. When James Wales left *Puck* to found *Judge* in 1881, Keppler hired Gillam from *Leslie's*, adding a new element to the predominantly German *Puck* staff. He soon became one of its stars through his powerful cartoons. In 1886, after Wales sold *Judge* to William Arkell, Arkell lured Gillam from *Puck* with a half-interest in the magazine. He was, for a short period of time, the most partisan cartoonist of his day. See plates 418-421, 423, 425, 434, 458, 467, 468, 476, 480 – 482, 509, 511, 563, 577, 580, 594, 595.

G.,F.
GODWIN, FRANK (Frances) (1899 – 1959)
Godwin divided his career between cartooning and illustration, moving from one field to the other with basically the same approach. Self-taught, Godwin became a master of pen and ink. Cartoon strips, "Connie" and "Rusty", as well as many others were by Godwin, sometimes under other by-lines. He worked in the studio of sculptor Gutzon Borglum, modeling busts in clay to make his characters realistic and consistent. Godwin started his art career as an apprentice of the *Washington Star* newspaper. Later, he studied at the Art Students League and the helping hand of James Montgomery Flagg got him his first work in New York, mostly for the humor magazines. Over the years, his work appeared in *Liberty, Cosmopolitan, Colliers* and many other periodicals. He also did advertising illustrations for clients such as Prince Albert Tobacco, Texaco, and Coca-Cola.

GOLIA
Active in the early 1900s, Golia was a staff artist of *Pasquino, Turin,* an Italian newspaper.

GOOLD, Paul (1875 – 1925)
Born: Casco Bay, ME. Goold began his cartooning career with the Portland, Maine *Sunday Press* and *Sunday Times* after graduating from high school. Later he studied at the Yale Art School. From 1899 to 1903, Goold was on the art staff of the *New York Times* before modestly entering the magazine field. He drew mostly for *Life*, but also for *Judge*. Goold was killed in a four-story fall from his Carnegie Hall studio in New York City.

GRAETZ, F
As an illustrator and cartoonist, Graetz came to *Puck* in 1882. When Keppler was in Europe in 1883, Graetz, along with Opper and Gillam, did all the cartoons for that periodical. He left *Puck* in 1886. See plates 422, 463, 472, 474, 475.

GROESBECK, Dan Sayre
Active in Philadelphia and New York up to the 1920s, Groesbeck produced illustrated art for numerous publications, as well as original poster art for the United States Department of Printing. See plates 287, 292.

GUNN, Robert (1945 – Present)
Artist and illustrator presently residing in Olathe, KS. The paintings of artist Robert Gunn speak of America of the early twentieth century, its values and ideals. Because of Gunn's ability to express priceless moments of good times, family and friends, he has been proclaimed by the publishers of the *Saturday Evening Post*, "the artist most likely to carry on the tradition of Americana established by Norman Rockwell." A master technician, Gunn is a firm believer in the importance of working from a detailed pencil drawing. The artist's concentration is most intense as he works on each character's face. The scope of artist Gunn's work includes several paintings that commemorate great past events from the Olympic games and hang in Olympic headquarters, New York City. In 1979, he was selected to paint President Carter's portrait for display in the presidential museum. Today, Gunn continues to seek America in his paintings, reflecting people who care about each other in the world they live in. It allows all of us a delightful look back at a valued way of American life. See plates 332, 333.

H., W.
Unidentified cartoonist on the staff of *Ulk*, Berlin, during the 1920s.

HALKE, F.
Cartoonist on the staff of *Ulk*, Berlin.

HAMILTON, Grant E. (1862 – ca. 1920)
Cartoonist and editor, born in Youngstown, OH. Hamilton graduated from Yale in 1880 and resided near Flushing, NY, where he and a group of other young cartoonists formed the Nereus Boat Club. He began contributing to *Judge* in 1881. *Judge* soon relied heavily on him for its political and social cartoons and, when the magazine changed hands in 1886, Hamilton was one of the very few staffers retained. He eventually became art editor of *Judge* and, after a merger, art editor of *Leslie's Weekly* as well. Hamilton contributed his own art for many years, except for the period during the election of 1904 when he drew anti-Republican cartoons for the rival, *Puck*. In the late 1880s and early 1890s, the back page of *Judge* was his. See plates 524, 525, 664.

HANNY, William F.
Cartoonist. Born: Burlington, IA in 1882. Work: Huntington Library, San Marion, CA. Hanny also resided in Philadelphia where he did some work for the *Philadelphia Inquirer*.

HART, J. F.
Hart was a newspaper illustrator who produced a pen and ink drawing in 1919 memorializing the death of Theodore Roosevelt. This illustration depicted Uncle Sam with his hat off, standing with Columbia in front of the White House paying homage. The image was published throughout the country.

HEDRICS
Illustrator active from approximately 1890 through 1905 in the St. Louis area for the *St. Louis Globe Democrat*.

HELGUERA,
Leon Illustrator who resided in New York City. See plate 293.

HERFORD, Oliver (1863 – 1935)
American cartoonist, poet, and epigrammist born in Sheffield, England. Educated at Lancaster College in England, and Antioch College in Ohio, Herford received art training at the Slade School in London and the Academie Julian in Paris. He sold his first cartoon to the *Century* magazine where only the most respectable cartoonists appeared, and soon became a regular contributor to *Life* and *Puck* (England). He became as famous as his pen and ink and wash creations. His most remembered books include: *Behind Time; Artful Antics; Pen and Inklings; An Alphabet of Celebrities; A Child's Primer of Natural History; Overheard on a Garden; The Cynic's Calendar.* Herford wrote a column, Pen and Inklings, for the *Saturday Evening Post,* under Norman Hapgood and a column for the March of Events section on the Hearst newspapers. He also wrote four successful plays. See plate 544.

HOFFMAN, Irwin D.
Born: 1901, Boston, MA. Residing in New York City. Studied: MBFA Sch. Member: SAE. Exhibited: GGE, 1939, SAE (prize); WMAA; New Sch. Soc. Res.; BM; PAFA; Los Angeles Mus. A.; Valentine Mus.; Honolulu Acad. A.; Dayton AI; Phila. SE; SAE; Assoc. AM.A., 1940 (oneman). Work: Kansas City AI; mural, Colo. Sch. Mines (in Golden), Gold Operators, Inc., New York; "Fine Prints of the Year." 1934. Position: Artist/Correspondent: Abbott Laboratories (47) See plate 403.

HESSE, Don (1918 – Present)
Born Belleville, IL. Hesse studied at the St. Louis School of Fine Arts at Washington University and joined the *Belleville Daily News-Democrat* as an artist-photographer in 1935. He remained until 1940. In 1946, he joined the *St. Louis Globe Democrat* art staff and has worked there ever since, becoming chief political cartoonist in 1951. He was syndicated for years by the McNaught Syndicate and is now distributed by the Los Angeles Times Syndicate. It is possible that he is the most published political cartoonist in America, as the Hesse Cartoon is picked up by hundreds of rural papers, as well as by big city dailies. He has won many Freedoms Foundation and National Headliners awards.

HOGAN, Inez
Residence: Washington, D. C.
Wrote and illustrated *Nicodemus Helps Uncle Sam*, copyright 1943. See plate 113.

HOOVER, Ellison (1890 – 1955)
Born: Cleveland, OH. Hoover studied art at the Art Students League in New York before landing a staff position with the *New York World.* Later, he worked for the *New York Evening News* and the *New York Herald-Tribune.* In the 1910s and 1920s, Hoover frequently drew for *Judge* and *Life.* One character, Otto, later starred in a short-lived strip for the *Herald-Tribune.* Syndicated cartoon: "Mr. and Mrs." See plate 546.

HUGGINS, Wilfrid
Huggins did numerous illustrations for *Puck*, as well as other periodicals during the early 1900s.

J., A.
These initials appeared on postcard illustrations in the early 1900s.

JONES, Will
New York City and Hackensack, NJ, resident. Born: 1888 in Philadelphia, PA. See plate 522.

K., G.
Contemporary illustrator who created a drawing of Uncle Sam which was published in *Better Homes and Gardens* in 1976. See plate 675.

K., O.
These initials appear to be O. K., however, in the author's opinion, the "O" is, in fact, a stylized "J," making the initials J. K., that of Joseph Keppler. The style of the art itself in this illustration is also that of Keppler.

KEMBLE, Edward Windsor (1861 – 1933)
Residence: New York City. Studied: Self-taught. Illustrator: *Uncle Tom's Cabin; Huckleberry Finn.* Author: *Kemble's Coons, Thompson St. Poker Club.* Illustrator: *Life*, ca. 1883. In 1880 four of Kemble's sketches were bought by Charles Parsons of the Harper's organization. He became the major (front-page) political cartoonist for the *New York Graphic* while receiving his only formal artistic training at the Art Students League, taking classes alongside Frederick Remington. In 1883, when *Life* magazine was founded, Kemble frequently contributed to the black and white weekly, drawing more cartoons for *Life* than for any other publication throughout his career. Through these lively cartoons, Mart Twain engaged Kemble to illustrate Huckleberry Finn. See plate 667.

KEPPLER, Joseph (1837 – 1894)
Born: Kieligenstadt, Austria. Studied: K. K. Akademie der Bildern Kunste. Drew for the paper, *Kikeriki.* In 1869, Keppler launched his first publishing venture, a weekly satirical sheet in German called *Die Vehme*, of which he was the principal cartoonist. This publication has the distinction of being the first American humorous journal with lithographic cartoons. Keppler introduced *Puck* magazine, which brought him to the attention of Frank Leslie, who invited him to join the staff of his magazines in New York. Keppler excelled at *Leslie's*, producing some outstanding cartoons and nurturing his dream of running his own cartoon magazine. Shortly after overseeing an impressive display — the erection of the Puck Pavilion at the Chicago World's Fair and the issuance of the World's Fair Puck — Keppler died. See plates 424, 426, 438, 447– 450, 452, 453, 455 – 457, 459 – 462, 464, 465, 469, 471, 477 – 479, 483 – 487, 505, 507.

KING, J. H.
Artist and illustrator active in New York and Philadelphia from the late 1930s through the mid 1950s who periodically did work for the United States Printing office. Numerous illustrations by King have been reproduced in the form of World War II posters. See plate 653.

KINSTLER, Everett Raymond
A native New Yorker, Kinstler began his career at the age of 16 drawing comic strips and went on to produce hundreds of magazine illustrations and book covers. He studied at the Art Students League with Frank Dumond and Sidney Dickinson. A protege of James Montgomery Flagg, Kinstler ultimately made the transition from illustrator to portraitist and soon established himself as one of the nation's foremost portrait artists. In 1983 he was awarded an honorary doctorate by Rollins College in Florida. Among Kinstler's more than 500 commissioned portraits are such well-known subjects as John Wayne, James Cagney, Paul Newman, Katharine Hepburn, and Liv Ullmann, Tom Wolfe, Tennessee Williams, Alan Shepard, Scott Carpenter, Secretary of State Cyrus R. Vance, and President Richard M. Nixon. Kinstler has painted from life, more than 30 United States cabinet members, more than any other artist in this country's history. He also painted the official portrait of President Gerald R. Ford. Kinstler is represented in many public and private collections, including the Metropolitan Museum of Art, The Brooklyn Museum, The White House, The Pentagon, and the National Portrait Gallery. He is Academician, National Academy of Design, and a member of the American Watercolor Society, the National Arts Club, Audubon Artists, Allied Artists of America, the Pastel Society of America, the Players Club, the Century Association, and the Lotos Club. The author of *Painting Faces, Figures, and Landscapes* (Watson-Guptill, 1981) He has been featured in numerous periodicals, including *American Artist* magazine, *Southwest Art, Success, People* magazine, and the *Saturday Evening Post.* See plates 330, 331.

KIRBY, Rollin
Cartoonist and three-time recipient of the Pulitzer Prize, Kirby was born in September 1875 in Galva, IL. Around the turn of the century, he worked as a freelance illustrator in Philadelphia and New York. During the next ten years, his work appeared frequently in *Collier's, McClure's, Harper's* and the *American* magazine and in *Life*, starting around 1909. It was with the *World* that Kirby became one of the most influential and republished of American editorial cartoonists. The cartoonist's glory days were on the *New York World* in the 1920s; he won three Pulitzer Prizes in the decade. In 1942 he semi-retired, doing occasional work for the *New York Times Magazine* and *Look* magazine. See plates 329.

KNOTT, John Francis (1878 – 1963)
Born in Austria. Knott studied at the Holmes School of Illustration in Chicago and at the Royal Academy of Art in Munich. In 1905 he joined the staff of the *Dallas News* as an editorial cartoonist. In 1936, Knott received an honorary mention from the Pulitzer Prize committee and, in 1939, the National Headliners Club Award.

KREPS, E. H.
Illustrator active in the early 1900s through 1925. See plate 612.

LAMBDIN, Victor
Illustrator working in the Denver, area from 1890 through 1905. Through his work with the Denver Republican, Lambdin was published in the book, *Exciting Experiences in Our Wars. The Life of Admiral Dewey.*

LEA, Frank
Lea was an illustrator born in Charlottesville, VA, in 1904, who resided in Philadelphia. See plate 609.

LEYENDECKER, Joseph Christian (1874 – 1951)
Leyendecker was born in Montabaur, Germany, coming to America at the age of eight. At the age of 16, he secured his first job in a Chicago engraving house on the strength of some large pictures he had painted on kitchen oilcloth. After work he studied under Vanderpoel at the Chicago Art Institute, saving for five years to attend the Academie Julian in Paris. Upon his return he had no difficulty obtaining top commissions for advertising illustrations and cover designs for the leading publications. His first *Post* cover was done in 1899, creating over 300 more during the next 40 years. Among the most famous of these was the annual New Year's baby series. His advertising illustrations made his clients famous, including the Arrow Collar man. In 1977, Leyendecker was elected to the Society of Illustrators Hall of Fame. The fascinating story of his personal life, along with that of his brother, Frank, is related in Norman Rockwell's, *My Adventures as an Illustrator.* See plate 603.

LIMBACH, Russell T.
Born in Middletown, CT, in 1904. Resided in Massillon, OH. Studied: Cleveland Sch. A. Exhibited: CMA, 1926-29 (prizes) 1931 (prize), 1934 (prize), 1935 (prize); Phila PM, 1928 (med); AIC, 1931. Work: CMA; AIC; BM; MMA; NYPL; WMAA; LOC; Yale; Wesleyan Univ.; SFMA; Herron Al; Glasgow Univ., Lyman Allyn Mus., Massillon Mus.; Hunter Col.; Univ. Wis.; Los Angeles Mus. Author/ Illustrator: "American Trees.", 1942, "But Once a Year," Am. A. Group, 1941. Position: T., Wesleyan, Middletown, CT (47). See plate 617.

LICHTENSTEIN, Roy
Born in New York, in 1923. Study and Training: Ohio State University, BFA, 1946, MFA, 1949. Work in Public Collections: Solomon R. Guggenheim Museum and Whitney Museum of American Art, New York; Pasadena Museum of Art; Tate Gallery, London, England; Stedelink Museum, Amsterdam, Holland; Albright-Knox Art Gallery, Buffalo, New York, plus others. Commissions: Outside wall for Circarama, New York State Pavilion; New York World's Fair, 1963; bill-

board for Expo. 1967, Montreal. Exhibitions: Retrospective, Pasadena Art Museum, 1967; Tate Gallery, London, 1968, Documenta IV, Kassell, Germany, 1968; Print Biennial, Brooklyn Museum, 1968; Solomon R. Guggenheim Museum, 1969.

LIFTON, George C.
American toy maker, manufacturer active during the late 1930s through the mid 1950s.

LITTLEMAN
Littleman was active during the late 1920s through approximately the mid 1940s producing numerous political images for a variety of publishers during the period. Illustrated: *Wet or Dry,* Copyright 1932.

LORENZ, Lee (1933 – present)
Born: Hackensack, NJ. Lorenz attended the Carnegie Institute of Technology 1950 – 51, receiving his B.F.A. in 1954 after transferring to the Pratt Institute in Brooklyn. He freelanced as a commercial artist, animator and cartoonist until 1958, when he became a staff cartoonist for the *New Yorker.* He was appointed art editor in 1973. An excellent stylist, Lorenz works mainly in what appears to be pen and wash. With several separately published collections of his work to his credit, Lorenz has served as president of the Cartoonists' Guild and as a member of the board of directors of the Museum of Cartoon Art. See plate 627.

LOUNSBURY, Fred C.
Artist active between 1885 and 1910 out of his studio in New York where he produced hundreds of book illustrations, as well as postcard and poster illustrations. See plates 74, 82.

LOWELL, Orson Byron (1871 – 1956)
Born: 1871 in Wyoming, IA. Resided in New Rochelle, NY; Stockbridge, MA. Studied: Art Institute of Chicago with Vanderpoel, O. D. Grover. Member: Society of Illustrators, 1901; Artists Guild: New Rochelle Art Association; Stockbridge Art Association Iowa Artists and Authors Club. Illustrator: Books, national magazines. From 1907 to 1915, Lowell was under exclusive contract to *Life* and was lured away by Judge with an exclusive contract from 1915 – 1923. He worked successively and successfully for the Ericson Advertising Agency (1921 – 1929), *American Girl* magazine (1935 – 1945), the George Matthews Adams Service (1937 – 1938), and the Churchman (1943 – 1946). See plates 532, 535, 537, 538.

LOYD, Sam
Illustrator and author of *Cyclopedia of Puzzles* published by Lamb Publishing Company, New York, 1914. Member of the New York Press Club and active 1900 to 1925 illustrating and writing for numerous newspapers and periodicals during this time.

LUBOVSKY, M. – Lubovsky, Mamin.
American Address, New York.
Lubovsky, Maxim H.
Painter, Bronx, New York. There are two people signing as M. Lubovsky, but not much is known about them. See plate 349.

M., W. (William Morris) (1874 – 1940)
Born: Salt Lake City, UT, William Morris attended public schools and received no art training. In 1904 he landed a job as sketch artist and cartoonist for the *Spokane Spokesman-Review,* where he remained until 1913. After moving to New York, Morris freelanced, working for *Puck, Harper's Weekly*, the *Independent,* the *Evening Mail.* The George Matthew Adams Service syndicated his cartoons widely. The Republican National Committee hired him in 1936 to draw propaganda cartoons for use by any papers wishing to print them. He seems to have been a gun for hire, as his political convictions changed as often and as simply as he changed employers. His books include: Spokesman-Review Cartoons (1908), The Spokane Book (1913), and One Hundred Men of Rockland County (1920).

MAC DONNALL Angus (1876 – 1927)
Born: St. Louis, MO. Residence: Westport, CT. Studied: St. Louis School of Fine Arts. Member: Society of Illustrators; Guild of Free Lance. Art: Chicago Watercolor Club; Author's League; Palette and Chisel Club. MacDonnall readily became a fixture in *Life* magazine where he hit his stride when he discovered the pencil as his medium for finished work. Soon he was regularly appearing in all the humor magazines. At the time of his death, his work was an advertised main attraction in *Judge* magazine. See plates 547.

MARCUS, Peter (1889 – 1934)
Born: New York City. Residence: New York City; Stonington, CT. Studied: Ecole des Beaux-Arts; Ecole des Beaux-Arts Decoratifs, Paris; C. H. Davis; H. W. Ranger. Member: Architects League; Connecticut Academy of American Etchers; American Artists Professional League. Exhibited: Connecticut Academy of Fine Arts, 1918 (prize). Author, Illustrator: *New York, the Nation's Metropolis.*

MAY, Ole (1873 – ca. 1920)
Born: Pleasanton, IA. Ole May began his cartooning career in the early 1890's for newspapers in Los Angeles and Houston; later he drew human interest and editorial cartoons for the *Washington Post.* He followed Charlie Payne into Pittsburgh to draw editorial cartoons for the *Gazette-Times,* before he joined the *Cleveland Leader.* Cleveland was blessed in the 1910's with a flock of talented cartoonists, May among them. His figures were sound, but comically drawn. An effective partisan (Republican), his ideas were clear and free of labels, making him one of the first political cartoonists to so liberate himself. May gave life to the symbol of Cleveland, Uncle Mose. See plate 342.

MC CUTCHEON, John T.
Born: 1870 in South Raub, IN. Residence: Chicago, IL. Studied: Purdue University with E. Knaufft. Member: Society of Illustrators, 1911; Art Institute of Chicago. Award: Cartoon Pulitzer Prize, 1931. Author: Stories of Filipino Warfare; Bird Center Cartoons; In Africa. Staff: *Chicago Tribune* and correspondent during the Spanish War and World War I. See plate 114.

MC KAY, R. D.
Artist, illustrator active in the New York area from the period of approximately 1885 through 1910. On the staff of the *Syracuse Herald,* McKay was illustrated in the book; *Exciting Experiences in Our Wars. The Life of Admiral Dewey,* copyright 1899.

MC KEE, Arnold
Artist, illustrator working primarily on the staff of *Life* magazine, of which he was a part for several years. McKee was active in the New York area from approximately 1905 through the teens.

MEIER, James E.
Contemporary advertising artist, illustrator, Meier has produced various works, such as menu art, from a period from approximately 1970 through the present.

MERRIMAN, Charles E.
A cartoonist whose work was used on the cover of the book, *Who's It In America,* in a color image of Uncle Sam.

MORGAN, Frederick
Artist, illustrator active in the Pennsylvania area from the late 1800s, Morgan was on the staff of the *Philadelphia Inquirer.*

MORRIS
Cartoonist living and working in the Tampa, FL, primarily for the *Tribune.* In 1929 his cartoons were reproduced in the "Review of Reviews."

MORRIS, Stuart
While on the staff of the *Post Intelligence* in Seattle, this artist, cartoonist created artwork in memorial to Teddy Roosevelt which appeared in papers across the nation.

MORRIS, T. L.
Artist, illustrator active in the New York area from approximately 1900 to 1925. As a cartoonist, Morris's work was utilized in the pages of *Life* magazine, as well as various other periodicals.

MUNSON, Floyd R.
Artist, illustrator who studied at the New York School of Art and Design 1937–1938. Work: Brown and Bigelow Calendar Company and Dow Publishing Company. Most noted for his pin-up art illustrations for calendar and playing cards. See plate 127.

MURPHY, Harry
Born: 1880 in CA. Contributor to the *Herald* and *Examiner.* Work: Hearst Papers, *New York Herald.*

NAST, Thomas (1840 – 1902)
Born: Landou, Bavaria. Died: Guayaquil, Ecuador. Residence: New York City. Studied: New York with T. Kaufmann, A. Frederics; National Academy of Design. At the age of 15, Nast furnished sketches for *Leslie's* of a prize fight in Canada. In England, he made sketches for the *New York Illustrated News.* Nast's Civil War pictures produced for *Harpers,* are among his most notable works. He was the first to introduce caricature work into America. He also painted in oil and watercolors. In 1902, Nast was appointed Consul-General to Ecuador. He created the Democratic Donkey and Republican Elephant symbols. In 1892 and 1893, he published *Nast's Weekly.* Folk etymology says that the term, "nasty" comes from his biting satirical caricatures. Work: Boston Museum of Fine Arts; Metropolitan Museum of Fine Arts. During the Civil War, Nast was so effective as a northern partisan that Lincoln called him, "Our best recruiting sergeant." In the realm of social subjects, he depicted family life and introduced the now accepted image of Santa Claus through hundreds of sympathetic cartoons. See plates 5 – 9, 551 – 561, 564 – 576, 578, 579, 581, 582, 588 – 593, 596 – 598.

NAUGHTON, C. F.
Cartoonist active in the Minnesota area from 1900 through 1930. While on the staff of the *Duluth Evening Herald,* one of his images was reproduced in *T. R. in Cartoon,* Saalfield Publishing Company.

NELAN, Charles (1854 – 1904)
Born: Akron, OH. Residence: New York City. Position: Staff, *New York Herald,* 1898. Studied: National Academy School. After one year, he earned the Elliot Medal there. In 1888, Nelan secured a position as cartoonist for the *Cleveland Press* and was soon picked up by the other papers of the Scripps-McRae League, thus becoming probably the first syndicated newspaper editorial cartoonist. In 1897, he was lured to the *New York Herald* where he gained greater fame because of a series of clever and sage commentson the Spanish-American War and America's Manifest Destiny. In 1899, Nelan was offered a huge contract by the *Philadelphia North American* to be its daily cartoonist. He remained there until his death at Clay Springs, Georgia.

NEWMAN, C. J. (Carl)
Painter living in Huntington Valley, PA, from his birth in 1858, also residing in Philadelphia. Newman was a member of the Society of Independent Artists and the Philadelphia Art Club. Exhibited: Pennsylvania Academy of Fine Arts, 1921. Work: Herron Art Institute, Indianapolis. See plate 341.

NUNEMAKER, A. W.
Artist and illustrator active between 1935 and 1955. Nunemaker produced numerous illustrations of military and political

subjects used for reproduction in poster form and in periodicals during World War II and the Korean War. See plate 645.

OLSON, Silas
Cartoonist, illustrator active in the Minneapolis, St. Paul area between 1930 and 1950 as a political cartoonist. Olson worked for the *Minneapolis Star and Tribune* newspaper. See plate 350.

O'MALLEY, M. Power (1880 – ca. 1930)
An American cartoonist born in Waterford, Ireland, O'Malley immigrated to America with his family at the age of six. Studying at the Artisian Institute in New York and the National Academy of Design, he won the Cannon Prize for drawing, the Baldwin Prize for etching, and other distinctions. After the turn of the century, *Life* became his primary outlet for pen-and-ink drawings, blossoming into full pages, center spreads, and covers into the 1920s. His style was realism and his themes often wistful, sentimental, and gently humorous. Studied: W. Ahirlaw; Henri; National Academy of Design. Exhibited: Aonach Sailteen, Dublin, 1924; San Antonio, Texas, 1927 (prize), 1929; California 1928 (metal).

OMISON, Walter
Working in the Missouri area, Omison created advertising art for the firm of Maas & Steffen, Inc. of St. Louis.

OPPER, Frederick Burr
Born: 1857 in Madison Lake County, OH. Residence New Rochelle, NY. On the art staff of Frank Leslie's weekly for three years, *Puck* for eighteen years, Opper severed connections with Puck to accept an offer from Hearst's *New York Journal* in May of 1899. Illustrator for Bill Nye, Mark Twain, Hobard (Dinkelspiel), Dunne (Dooley). See plates 416, 417, 427, 431, 440, 445, 454, 466, 473, 492, 493, 495, 496, 508, 510.

ORR, Carey (1890 – 1967)
Born in Ada, OK. Orr's career with the pen was inspired by a tramp cartoonist. While playing professional baseball, he earned the money to pursue cartooning and enrolled at the Chicago Academy of Fine Arts. Other instruction, which he valued highly, was through the W. L. Evans Cartoon Correspondence Course. In 1911, Orr joined the staff of Hearst's *Chicago Examiner,* the following year succeeding Charles Sykes on the *Nashville Tennessean,* where he attracted national attention. He was widely reprinted as the South's premier cartoonist. At the end of a two year contract renewal with the *Tennessean,* he accepted an offer from the *Chicago Tribune,* where he remained for 46 years. Beginning on March 5, 1932, Orr's cartoons often appeared on the front cover, nearly always in color. For years he taught cartooning at the Chicago Academy, putting an entire generation of successful cartoonists in his debt.

OSBORN, H. S.
Cartoonist, illustrator active in the Chicago area, Osborn contributed to the *Chicago Daily Tribune,* as well as to other publications.

PARRISH, Joseph
Cartoonist born in Summertown, TN, in 1905. In the early 1920s, Parrish began drawing political cartoons for the *Nashville Banner,* filling not only the professional shoes of earlier Nashville cartoonists Bill Sykes and Carey Orr, but their stylistic ones as well; his cartoons were filled with animation and relied on likenesses instead of caricature. Four years later, Parrish switched to the *Nashville Tennessean* where he stayed for another seven years. At the suggestion of Carey Orr, he moved to the *Chicago Tribune,* retiring in 1972, but continuing to draw his long-running Sunday feature, "Nature Notes" for the *Tribune.*

PARRISH, Maxfield Frederick (1870 – 1966)
Died: Plainfield, NH. Residence: Windsor, VT. Studied: His father, Stephen; Paris, 1884 –1886; Architects, Haverford College, 1888 –

1891; Pennsylvania Academy of the Fine Arts, 1891 – 1893; H. Pyle, at Drexel Institute. Member: Society of American Artists, 1897; Philadelphia Watercolor Club; Associate Member of the National Academy of Design, 1905; Full Member of the National Academy of Design, 1906; Cornish (N.H.) Colony from 1898 where he designed and built his home, "The Oaks." Exhibited: Paris Expo., 1900 (prize); Pan-Am. Expo. Buffalo, 1901 (medal); Philadelphia Watercolor Club, 1908 (prize); Architectural League of America, 1917 (gold). Important illustrator, best known for his unique style and for his "Maxfield Parrish blue," he mastered the mysterious effects of light and iridescent colors through a difficult glazing technique. Parrish always worked from photographs rather than live models. His most famous painting, "Daybreak," sold millions as a print. Maxfield Parrish was one of the better known professional artists during the first decades of this century. His many illustrations for children's books and various publications were executed in a wholly personal style that set his work apart from that of his contemporaries and brought a degree of public recognition seldom achieved by a living artist. The February 17, 1936, issue of *Time* reported, "As far as the sale of expensive color reproductions is concerned, the three most popular artists in the world are van Gogh, Cezanne, and Maxfield Parrish." See plate 600.

PAULL, Grace
Born: Cold Brook, NY. Residence: New York City; Cold Brook, NY. Studied: Pratt Institute of Art; Grand Central Art School; George Bridgmen; Alexander Archipenko. Exhibited: Pennsylvania Academy of Fine Art; Corcoran Gallery of Art; Munson-Williams-Proctor Institute. Author/Illustrator: *Raspberry Patch* and other juvenile books. Illustrator: *Peter by the Sea; Country Stop.* See plate 109.

PEASE, Lute (Lucius Curtis) (1869 – 1963)
Cartoonist, editor, and Pulitzer Prize winner born in Winnemucka, NV, Pease was graduated from the Franklin Academy in Malone, NY in 1887. In 1895 he was a reporter-artist for the *Portland Oregonian,* with more sketches demanded after he depicted a murder-suicide he witnessed. After being appointed by Teddy Roosevelt as U. S. Commissioner in northwest Alaska, the *Oregonian* again beckoned with an offer to become the paper's chief editorial cartoonist. For six years Pease was editor of the *Pacific Monthly,* raising circulation from 40,000 to 100,000. In 1912 the magazine sold and he traveled east, accepting a position as political cartoonist with the *Newark Evening News* where he remained until 1952. An accomplished painter, Pease wrote one book *Sourdough Bread* and drew a comic strip for the *News,* "Powder Pete." See plates 346 – 348.

PERRETT, Galen Joseph (1875 – 1949)
Born: Chicago, IL. Residence: Rockport, MA. Studied: Art Institute of Chicago; Art Students League; Academie Julian, Paris; National Academy, Munich, Germany; Colarossi Academy, Paris. Member: Salmagundi Club; North Shore Art Association; Rockport Art Association. Work: Newark Museum; Franklin (New Hampshire) Library. See plates 194, 195.

PETERSEN, H. A.
Cartoonist who contributed to *Judge,* as well as other publications, after the turn of the century.

PETRUCCELLI, Antonio
Designer/illustrator born in Fort Lee, NJ, in 1907, later residing in Mt. Tabro, NJ. Studied: M. M. White. Exhibited: Corona Mundi, New York, 1925 (prize), 1926 (prize); Art Alliance of America for International Press Exchange, Cologne, 1927 (prize); American Society of Control of Cancer, 1928 (prize); Johnson and Faulkner, New York, 1933 (prize); House Beautiful Cover Competition, 1928 (prize), 1929 (prize), 1931 (prize), 1933 (prize). Work: Mural decorator, Hotel Winslow, New York. Designer: Covers for *New Yorker, Collier's, Today,* and *Fortune* between 1932 and 1937. See plate 226.

PFEIFFER, E. H.
Illustrator primarily of sheet music, working in the New York area from approximately 1905 through 1935. See plates 380, 396, 401.

POY
English artist, illustrator working primarily in the London area, contributing to publications such as the *Evening News,* the *Weekly Dispatch,* and *Judy* around the turn of the century.

PRANG, Louis (1824 – 1909)
Born: Breslau, Germany. Residence: Boston, MA. Came to New York in 1850, settling in Boston. Died: Los Angeles, CA. Self-taught artist. After a partnership with J. Mayer, Prang opened his own lithographic firm in 1860, which became famous after the Civil War for its chromolithographic reproductions of famous paintings and his invention of the Christmas card in 1875. He also published popular drawing books. More than any other publisher, he realized his great ambition of spreading art appreciation before the American public. See plates 166, 168.

PUGHE, J. S. (1870 – 1909)
American cartoonist born in Dolgelly, Wales. During his short career he produced a large body of impressive work and influenced many of his contemporaries. His drawings, which began appearing in *Puck* just before the turn of the century, were striking in their freshness and vitality. His *Puck* cartoons were virtually all interior black and whites and, after 1900, were almost never political. See plates 444, 470, 501, 503, 504.

PYLE, Howard (1853 – 1911)
Born: Wilmington, DE. Died: Florence, Italy. Residence: Wilmington, DE/Chadds Ford. Studied: Philadelphia with Van der Weilen, 1869 – 1872. Member: National Academy of Design (Associate member), 1905; Full Member, National Academy of Design, 1907; Salmagundi Club, 1876; National Institute of Arts and Letters; Century; International Society of Sculptors, Painters & Gravers. Exhibited: Columbian Expo., Chicago, 1893 (medal); Pan-Am Expo., Buffalo, 1901 (gold medal); Paris Expo 1900 (medal). Author/Illustrator: 24 books Illustrator of over 100 books; every major magazine from 1876 on. Specialty: pen and ink drawings. Highly important and influential illustrator and teacher. Founder of the "Brandywine School" and is often referred to as, "The Father of American Illustration." Among his famous students were N. C. Wyeth and Maxfield Parrish. See plates 106, 107.

R., M. (RAMEREZ)
Contemporary, political cartoonist whose work has appeared in various periodicals, including an illustration of Uncle Sam with Lyndon Johnson entitled, "A One Man Band." See plate 689.

RAEMAEKERS, Louis (1869 – 1956)
Dutch editorial cartoonist born in Roermond, the Netherlands. After art study in Amsterdam, Brussels, and Paris, Raemaekers taught art at various Dutch schools during the 1890s. His earliest work was in the manner of the Swiss-born Parisian socialist artist, Steinlen. His personal style developed slowly while he worked for *Het Algemeen Handelsblad* in Amsterdam, blossoming at *De Telegraff.* The Dutch historian of humorous art, Cornelis Veth, asserts that Raemaeker attained the highest imaginative level of any Dutch cartoonist up to that time. Especially noteworthy were his caricatures of politicians collected in several volumes, including, "The Gentlemen in the Hauge," 1910. The Allied governments showered decorations on him and his war cartoons, which appeared at home between 1914 and 1917 and were extensively republished.

REBECHINI, Guido (1890 – 1962)
Born: Pietra Santa, Italy. Died: Chicago, IL. Son of sculptor, Pietro Rebechini, Guido studied sculpture in Rome as a pupil of Stago-Stagi, as well as of his father. He came to the United States in 1911 where he continued his studies at the Chicago School of Art while working and producing commercial sculpture for F. W. Eichorn as well as producing a variety of cemetery monuments and grave markers. In 1917 he was commissioned by F. W. Eichorn to produce a bronze, full-bodied, standing sculpture of Uncle Sam, which was also commercially cast in plaster to be used as an American flag holder for display purposes in storefront windows during World War I. Other noted works by Guido Rebechini are his life-size bronze sculpture of Thomas Edison, as well as a marble bust of Thomas Edison which was commercially cast in plaster as a production piece, and the life-size bronze monument of a World War I soldier, presently located in the gardens on the grounds of the Veterans Hospital in Chicago, IL. Rebechini is one of very few sculptors to have executed an academically noteworthy image of Uncle Sam in full dimension in bronze, as well as other mediums. See plate 351.

REEVES, Norman
Illustrator working and residing in the New York area from approximately 1925 through 1955. In May of 1935, Reeves' artwork of Uncle Sam on stilts was printed on the cover of Fortune magazine. See plate 605.

REHSE, George Washington (1868 – ca. 1930)
American cartoonist born in Hastings, MN. Educated: Minneapolis public schools and was self-taught in art, a profession he entered in 1895 when he joined the *Penny Press* as a staff artist. He remained in St. Paul and succeeded at the *Globe* and the *Pioneer Press* before joining Pulitzer's *New York Works* as a staff artist, assignment cartoonist, and editorial cartoonist. One of many cartoonists who filled in on the daily Metropolitan Movies panel before it became Denys Wortman's own.

REILLY, Paul (ca. 1880 – 1944)
Born Pittsburgh, PA. For years, one of the most published of the magazine cartoonists. Joined the staff of *Life* in 1913 and soon was appearing in *Puck* and *Judge,* as well. He never handled political subjects an, only during World War I, did he touch on international affairs. Generally, his subjects were domestic. Best at exasperated characters, usually men beset by bills, prohibition, or other annoyances. Eventually Reilly left cartooning to do portraits and landscape painting in Westport, CT.

RENESCH, E. G.
Artist, illustrator active in the early 1900s in the Chicago area. Renesch created numerous pieces of political art, primarily reproduced as posters. See plate 644.

REYNOLDS, E. S.
Cartoonist, illustrator active in the Washington State area from 1900 through approximately 1930. His work includes the *Tacoma Ledger,* as well as other publications of this time.

RICHARDS, Frederick Thompson (1864 – 1921)
Born: Philadelphia, PA. Studied: Pennsylvania Academy of Fine Arts with Eakins, E. B. Bensell; Art Students League. Member: Philadelphia Sketch Club; Players Club. Author: *Color Prints from Dickens, The Blot Book.* Positions: Staff of *Life,* starting 1888, cartoonist for the *New York Herald, Times, Philadelphia North American.*

ROCKWELL, Norman Percevel (1894 – 1978)
Born: New York City. Died: Stockbridge, MA. Residence: New Rochelle, NY; Arlington, VA; Stockbridge, MA. Studied: Chase School of Artists, Ca. 1908; National Academy of Design, ca. 1909; Art Students League with G. Bridgman, T. Fogarty, 1910. Frequently acclaimed as America's greatest illustrator, Rockwell created 322 covers for the *Saturday Evening Post* from 1916 through 1963. His work also appeared in Brown & Bigelow calendars from 1924 through 1976, as well as every major magazine. His illustrations for *Tom Sawyer* and *Huckleberry Finn* became classics. Rockwell's autobiography, *My Adventures as an Illustrator,* was copyrighted in 1960. The pictures of

Norman Rockwell were recognized and loved by almost everybody in America. The cover of the *Saturday Evening Post* was his showcase for over 40 years, giving him an audience larger than that of any other artist in history. Rockwell's personal contribution during World War II were his famous "Four Freedoms" posters, symbolizing for millions the war aims as described by President Franklin Roosevelt. His "Freedom of Speech" painting is in the collection of the Metropolitan Museum of Art. He painted Nassar of Egypt, Nehru of India, and Presidents Eisenhower, Kennedy, and Johnson. In 1957 the United States Chamber of Commerce in Washington cited him as a Great Living American, saying, "Through the magic of your talent, the folks next door — their gentle sorrows, their modest joys — have enriched our own lives and given us new insight into our countrymen." The Rockwell Museum has been established in Stockbridge, MA, where he maintained his studio. Housing a large collection of his original paintings, thousands of visitors continue to visit there each year. See plate 646.

ROGERS, Lou
Cartoonist, illustrator who produced numerous images for *Judge* magazine and other periodicals from approximately 1910 through 1940.

ROGERS, William Allen (1854 – 1931)
Born: Springfield, OH. Residence: Washington, D.C. Studied: Worcester Polytechnic Institute. Member: Society of Illustrators; Guild of Free-Lance Artists; Salmagundi Club, 1872 (founder). Work: on the staff of *Harper's Weekly, Harper's Magazine, Life, St. Nicholas, the Century, Washington Post,* and *New York Herald,* the latter for 19 years, following Thomas Nast. Author: *World Worth While, Danny's Partner, A Miracle Man, America's Black and White Book* — one of his two volumes of cartoons. Because of one of his anti-German war cartoons, Rogers was decorated as chevalier of the Legion of Honor in 1921. W. A. Rogers never graduated from the Worcester Polytechnic Institute; he taught himself art. His mother had some of his sketches published in a Dayton, Ohio, newspaper when he was 14, before he joined the staff of the experimental *New York Graphic,* assisting with news sketches and drawing cartoons in the company of later greats like C. J. Taylor, A. B. Frost, E. W. Kemble and Gray Parker. Rogers achieved great success, distinguished editors and art directors constantly published him or sought and reprinted his cartoons. See plates 430, 433, 488, 489.

RUSSELL
Artist, illustrator who worked with various periodicals from approximately 1890 through the early 1900s.

S., W. G.
Painter who was a member of the Washington Water Color Club.

SANDEN, Howard
Artist and illustrator born in St. Paul, MN, in 1903. Studied: Minneapolis School of Art 1923 – 1925. Did a variety of illustration art and cartoons for numerous regional and national magazines and newspapers. See plate 344.

SARNO, Anthony
Portrait and genre photographer who lived and worked in New York City out of his studio from 1915 – 1945. Member American Photographers Society, National Academy of Design.

SARKA, Charles Nicholas (1879 – 1960)
Sarka was one of the great contributors to American pen-and-ink technique, although he abandoned it for other media. He began drawing editorial cartoons in Chicago during the Spanish-American War, mostly dealing with local subjects. After moving to New York, Sarka bloomed. He started his career as an illustrator for *Cosmopolitan* and joined the staff of *Judge.* Although he did some lithographic color cartoons for that periodical, his best work was in the black-and-white mode. His art school was "To travel and paint; to paint and travel." This passion for painting led him to eventually abandon the pen for the water-

color brush. Before his death he became a life member of the American Watercolor Society. Exhibited: Architectural League of New York, 1913 (prize); St. Louis Pageant, 1914 (prize). See plates 523, 528, 536, 540.

SATTERFIELD
Cartoonist contributing work to various periodicals, including *Leslie's,* in the early part of the 1900s.

SAWLER, Bam
Contemporary artist. See plate 87.

SCHELL, Frank Cresson (1857 – 1942)
Illustrator born in Philadelphia, PA. Schell was a pupil of Thomas Eakins and Thomas P. Anshutz. Member: Artist' Aid Society; Fellowship, Pennsylvania Academy of Fine Arts; Philadelphia Art Alliance; Philadelphia Sketch Club.

SCHLAIKJER, J. W. (Jes Wilhelm)
Born: 1897. Lived in New York City. Studied: Ecole des Beaux-Arts, France; Art Institute of Chicago; Forsberg; Cornwell; Dunn; R. Henri. Member: National Academy of Design, 1932 (Associate) Artists Guild; Scandinavian-American Arts; Grand Central Art Gallery; Artists Fund Society. Exhibited: National Academy of Design, 1926 (prize), 1928 (prize), 1932 (prize). See plates 296, 622.

SCHRUPILE, J.
Active in the New York area around the turn of the century, Schrupile contributed to various periodicals including *Life* magazine.

SCOTT, Howard (1902 – 1983)
Resident of New York City and a member of the Society of Illustrators. Scott added a sparkling watercolor technique to his posters and an ability to obtain very realistic characterizations in a bold poster treatment. The moral of his 24 sheet poster designs had to be immediately clear to the highway driver. Long associated with Esso, Ford, Schlitz, Heinz, Servel, and other national products, Scott also designed magazine covers, including the *Saturday Evening Post.* Illustrator. See plate 294.

SEIBEL, Frederick Otto (1886 – 1969)
Born in Durhamville, NY. Seibel was educated in New York at the Art Students League from 1905 to 1907. Among his teachers were Kenyon Cox, Howard Pyle and Albert Sterner. Entering the art field in 1911, Seibel began a ten-year position as editorial cartoonist on the *Albany Knickerbocker-Press* in 1916 where he and his mascot (a bespectacled crow) attracted attention. In 1926, he moved to the *Richmond Times Dispatch,* remaining there until a year before his death. Member: Richmond Academy of Art. Exhibited: 200 cartoons, Virginia Museum of Fine Arts, 1944 (one-man).

SHAFER, Claude
Cartoonist born in L. Hocking, OH, in 1878. Staff of the *Cincinnati Times-Star,* Historical Society of Cincinnati.

SHIR, A. S.
Cartoonist working in the late 1800s and early 1900s. Shir contributed to various publications, including the reproduction of one of his cartoons on Teddy Roosevelt in *T. R. in Cartoon,* copyright 1910.

SHOEMAKER, Vaughn Richard
Born on the south side of Chicago in 1902, "Shoe" enrolled in the Chicago Academy of Fine Arts and accepted an office boy position at the *Chicago Daily News* in 1919. Within six month he was eased out of the Academy for lack of talent, but remained with the paper. In 1922 he was drafted to drew the day's editorial cartoon, continuing to do so for 30 years, winning two Pulitzers in that time. Seven years after leaving the Academy he returned as an instructor. In 1951, after moving to Carmel, CA, Shoemaker continued his daily cartoons to 100 clients by way of the Herald-Tribune Syndicate. Nine years later he also became

chief editorial cartoonist of Hearst's *Chicago American*. He was syndicated by National Newspaper Syndicate and the Chicago Tribune-New York Syndicate during his last active years. "Shoe" is reputed to have contributed the "Q" to John Q. Public and for years his "Common Man" was as recognizable as Uncle Sam. Occasionally drawing in a style of handsome realism, his cartoons were some of the most powerful statements in the history of the political cartoon. He won the Freedoms Foundation gold medals every year from 1949 to 1959, the National Headliners Award of 1945, and numerous National Safety Council awards. His work remains as some of the finest cartooning every produced in America.

SMITH, Dorman Henry (1892 – 1956)
Born: Steubenville, OH. Dorman Smith got his first artistic job drawing ads for the Jeffrey Manufacturing Company after taking the Landon correspondence course to cartooning. In 1919 he became an editorial cartoonist for the *Des Moines News* and, only two years later, became chief editorial cartoonist for the Newspaper Enterprise Association. Immediately, thereby, Smith was one of the most widely distributed of his profession in America. From 1927 to 1941 he drew for Hearst papers and for outlets in New York, Chicago, and San Francisco. Smith won awards for his watercolors, as well as for his cartoons. His books were largely instructional, including *101 Cartoons, Cartooning,* and *First Steps to a Cartoon Career.* Member: Bohemian Club, San Francisco; Marin County Artists Association, California.

SMITH, H. R.
Illustrator working primarily in the New York area in the early 1900s. See plates 400, 404.

SOREL, Edward (1929 – present)
Born in New York City, Ed Sorel attended Cooper Union, receiving his diploma in 1951, and accepting a position with *Esquire.* In 1953, along with two Cooper Union classmates, Milton Glaser and Seymour Chwast, he founded Push Pin Studio, an innovative enterprise that became highly influential in the commercial and graphic art worlds. In 1958, after making the decision to do freelance work, he progressed steadily during the 1960s and soon achieved a position in the first rank of political cartoonist-illustrators. Sorel contributes his political satire to various national publications and does a weekly panel for the *Village Voice.* Much of the best work from his later period has been collected in "Superpen," a Push Pin Studio retrospective, including a premiere viewing at the Graham Gallery in New York City, as well as the New School for Social Research in 1974. Sorel has received awards from the Society of Illustrators and the Art Directors Club of New York and was given the Augustus Saint-Gaudens medal by his alma mater. He is a member of the American Institute of Graphics Arts and the Alliance Graphique Internationale. A contributor to virtually every major American magazine, Edward Sorel is also the author of *How to be President, Moon Missing,* and *Making the World Safe for Hypocrisy.* See plates 682 – 688.

STANTON
Illustrator working in the New York area during the late 1800s and into the 1900s, Stanton produced work for various publications, including the *Syracuse Herald.*

STARMER
Research has uncovered no background information on this artist at this time. See plate 412.

STEELE, Albert Wilbur
Cartoonist born in 1862, in Malden, IL. Steele joined the staff of the *Denver Post* in 1897.

STROTHMANN, Fred (1879 – 1958)
Born: New York City. Studied: Carl Hecker Art School, New York; Berlin Royal Academy, Paris. Member: Society of Illustrators. Illustrated books by Mark Twain, Carolyn Wells, Ellis P. Butler, and Lucille Gulliver. Originally wanting to be a portrait painter, his natural inclinations gradually moved him to illustration with a comic slant. "It was at the suggestion of those whose portraits I tried to paint that I want in for funny pictures." A regular contributor to *Harper's Monthly, the Century,* Hearst's *International,* and other magazines, Strothmann also illustrated many books.

STUART, James R. (1890 – 1949)
Born: Madison, WI. Died: NY. Studied: Art Students League, New York 1913 – 1915. Worked in New York as illustrator and cover artist for numerous national periodicals between 1915 and 1940. See plates 215, 604, 648.

SULLIVAN, E. D.
Studied: Rockford College 1910 – 1912, and Chicago Art Institute 1912 – 1914. Lived and worked in Chicago, IL, as an illustrator until his death in 1937. See plate 377.

SYKES, C. H. Charles Henry
Cartoonist born in 1882, in Athens, GA, Charles ("Bill") Sykes was educated at the Drexel Institute, graduating in 1904, then freelancing as a cartoonist for two years. The *Philadelphia North American* was his first regular assignment, followed by stints on the *Williamsport News* (Pennsylvania) and the *Nashville Banner,* where he preceded Carey Orr as the city's star cartoonist. In 1911, he returned to Philadelphia to draw political and sports cartoons for the *Philadelphia Public Ledger,* becoming the *Evening Ledger's* first cartoonist after its reorganization in 1914. The papers only cartoonist, he retired when the publication went out of business in 1942, shortly before his death. As a regular editorial cartoonist for *Life* from 1922 to 1928, Sykes executed a weekly political drawing, full page and usually in wash. Upon the death of F. T. Richards (in 1921) he inherited the weekly and annual cartoon round-up of news subjects.

TALBURT, Harold M. (1895 – 1966)
Pulitzer Prize-winning cartoonist born in Toledo, OH, Talburt joined the staff of the *Toledo News-Bee* as a reporter in January of 1916. In 1921, when Negley Cochran went to Washington to set up Scripps-Howard's Washington bureau, he sent for Talburt. In 1922 he became Scripps-Howard's "Chief Washington Cartoonist." Talburt won his Pulitzer in 1933 and was president of the Gridiron Club in 1947. He retired in 1963.

TAYLOR, Charles Jay (1855 – 1929)
Born in New York City, Taylor was educated in the New York public school system and received art training at the National Academy; The Art Students League, and schools in London and Paris. Later in his career, he earned an LL.B. from Columbus (1874) and was given an honorary MA from Middlebury College (1911). Among the original staff artists on America's first illustrated daily, the *New York Graphic* (1876) and drew for the early issues of *Life* magazine, the first major black-and-white cartoon weekly. When he joined the staff of *Puck* in 1886, Taylor was already a veteran of wide fame and influence. He became a major fixture in *Puck.* At the turn of the century, he abandoned contract work to free-lance for *Life* and *Judge,* as well as *Punch* in England. His first book was, *The Taylor-Made Girl* (1888). Several more books followed. Exhibited: National Academy; The Society of American Artists; The Art Institute of Chicago; The Paris Salon; The Chicago World's Fair, and the Paris Expo. C. J. Taylor remains one of the greatest of America's unremembered cartoonists. See plates 428, 436, 439.

THIELE
Cartoonist primarily for the *Times-Mirror* in Warren, PA.

THOMPSON, Rodney
Born: 1878 in San Francisco, CA. Residence: New York City. Studied: Partington School of Illustrators. Member: Chicago Society of Etchers; Artists Guild.

THORNDIKE
Cartoonist living and working in the Philadelphia area in the early 1900s. Thorndike's work includes illustrations for the *Philadelphia Press,* as well as other publications of the time.

THULSTRUP, Thure (de Thulstrup) (1948 – 1930)
Born: Stockholm, Sweden. Residence: New York City. Studied: Paris, 1871, following service in the French Foreign Legion. Member: Century Club; Players Club; American Watercolor Society; Society of Illustrators; John Ericsson Society. Award: Swedish Knight, Order of Vasa. Exhibited: St. Louis Expo.; Pan-An. Expo., 1901. Specialty: military history. Staff artist on *Harper's,* the *New York Daily Graphic,* and *Leslie's.* In 1888, Thulstrup went to Russia to sketch the Kaiser of Germany on his visit to the Czar. He later produced some of the best known paintings of American colonial life. See plate 562.

TIGNER
Illustrator reproduced in the early 1900s, primarily on sheet music.

TRUMBULL, John
Artist, illustrator producing numerous illustration for *Life* magazine, as well as various other periodicals during a period from 1895 through 1925.

VAN LESHOUT, Alexander J. (1868 – 1930)
Born: Harvard, IL. Resided in Louisville, KY. Studied: Art Students League; Art Institute of Chicago; C. Beckwith; F. Freer; J. H. Vanderpoel; Holland; Paris. Member: Southern States Art League; Chicago Society of Etchers; Louisville Art Association. Position: Director, Louisville School of Artists; Conservatory of Music. See plate 340.

WALES, James Albert (1852 – 1886)
Cartoonist born in Clyde, OH, Wales moved to Toledo and Cincinnati where he decided to learn the art of woodcutting cartoons and illustrations. Eyestrain and the public's evident lack of interest in his prints prompted Wales to seek a career as a newspaper artist. Upon moving to Cleveland, he was hired by the *Leader.* In 1873, he accepted a position on *Leslie's Weekly* and *Wild Oats,* next to Fred Opper. When assembling an art staff, Joseph Keppler was impressed by Wales and hired him to draw for *Puck.* In 1875, Wales went to London where he drew for *Judy, Illustrated Sporting and Dramatic News,* and the *London Illustrated News.* By 1881 Wales sought to establish a rival to *Puck* and, gathering such veterans as Thomas Wroth, Frank Beard, and Frank Bellew, as well as newcomers Grant Hamilton and D. A. MacKellar, he founded *Judge.* Business and staff problems soon led him to sell his share of *Judge,* returning to *Puck.* Just a year later, a heart ailment felled him at the age of 34. His best remembered cartoon may be the "15-14-13 Puzzle" (1881). It was a classic cartoon and made Wales' career. See plates 414, 429, 512.

WALKER, Alanson Burton (1878 – 1947)
Born: Binghamton, NY. Educated: Buffalo Central High School, NY. Studied art and received an B. A. degree from the University of Rochester in 1897. Studied at the Art Students League. In 1901 Walker began contributing to magazines. For years his principal markets were *Life, Harper's,* and *Scribner's.* In the 1920s and 1930s, he contributed frequently to *Judge* and *Ballyhoo.* Member: Society of Illustrators. Illustrated book jackets for *Harper's,* Dodd Mead & Co., D. Appleton-Century, Payson & Clarke.

WALKER, Mort
Born: 1923. Studied: University of Missouri, B.A. Exhibited: Metropolitan Museum of Art, New York, 1952; Brussels World's Fair, 1964; Louvre, Paris, 1965; New York Worlds' Fair, 1967; Expo. Montreal, 1969. Awards: Reuben Award, 1954, and two Best Humor Strip Plaques, 1966 and 1969, National Cartoonists Society; Silver Lady, Banshees Society, 1955. Member: National Cartoonists Society (President, 1960); Newspaper Comics Council; Artists & Writers Associa-

tion. Publications: Editor, National Cartoonists Society Album, 1961, 1965, 1972; Author, *Mort, Land of Lost Things, Hi and Lois, Beetle Bailey.* See plate 246.

WALKER, Ryan (1870 – 1932)
Born: Springfield, KY. Received artistic training at the Art Students League. First professional work appeared in the *Kansas City Times* (1895 – 1898). Between 1898 and 1901, Walker was the chief cartoonist on the *St. Louis Republic.* In 1901, he drew for the *Boston Globe* for one year, at the same time, free-lancing to *Life, Judge,* the *Bookman* magazine, and the *Times* and *Mail Newspapers.* The International Syndicate of Baltimore distributed his political material between 1904 and 1911 and, until 1917, he featured Henry Dubb as a character representing the "Common Man." Walker was a prominent contributor to *Appeal to Reason* and the *Coming Nation,* as a political cartoonist on the *New York Call* (1916 – 1921). Between 1924 and 1929, he was the art director and rotogravure editor of the *New York Graphic.* Walker, after being a socialist for many years, became a communist and, while visiting Russia as the guest of the Soviet Government, died in the summer of 1932.

WALKER, William Henry (1871 – 1938)
Born: Pittston, PA. Walker studied at the University of Kentucky, the University of Rochester, and at the Art Students League. He began contributing to *Life* magazine in 1894 and, in 1898, joined the staff of Life as a personal favorite of editor J. A. Mitchell.
The brother of A. B. Walker, also on the *Life* staff, William was the magazine's major editorial cartoonist through the 1920s. Theodore Roosevelt was a favorite subject. In 1924, Walker retired from *Life* and became a landscape and portrait painter. See plates 256, 257, 335.

WALL, B.
Artist, illustrator whose work appeared on numerous postcards, as well as book illustrations and advertising art from 1900 through 1930. See plate 99.

WALLGREN
As a private with the United States Marine Corp stationed in France, Wallgren drew and wrote a cartoon strip for the *Stars and Stripes* newspaper, the official paper of the A. E. F. He also drew a regular cartoon titled, "Helpful Hints" for the same publication. Signing his work, "Wally," Wallgren was with the 5th regiment, contributing additional work to *Stars and Stripes* in the early twentieth century.

WARREN
Little is known regarding the background of this artist, other than the fact he was a contributor to the *New York Telegram* in the 1920s.

WESTERMAN, Harry James (1876 – 1945)
Born: Parkersburg, WV. Studied at the Columbus, OH, Art School, joining the art staff of the *Ohio State Journal* in 1897. From 1901 on, he cartooned exclusively, appearing in many periodicals besides the *State Journal.* His cartoons were syndicated by McClure, he drew the Dickenspiel strip (illustrated by Opper and Kemble), and was a major fixture on *Puck* in the mid 1910s. His books include *A Book of Cartoons* and *The Young Lady Across the Way.* Westerman drew most often with a pen and lightly shaded his cartoons on coarse paper. His work was pervaded by a warm good humor.

WHITE, Deke
While drawing cartoons for the *Daily Record* in Glasgow, Scotland, White's work was reproduced in the *Review of Reviews,* copyright 1929.

WILDER
Contributed cartoon work to *Life* magazine at the turn of the century.

WILLARD, Archibald M. (1836 – 1918)
Born: Cleveland, OH. A self-taught artist who in the 1850s and early

1860s painted trade signs, store fronts, wagons, and numerous pieces of furniture. During this period he began to do more serious illustration art under the commission of J. F. Ryder of Cleveland, OH, for whom he painted numerous paintings of children playing which were reproduced in lithography by J. F. Ryder. Eventually in 1875, Mr. Ryder had commissioned Archibald M. Willard to paint what became this artist's most famous work, being "Yankee Doodle," also known as "The Spirit of '76." This painting was reproduced as a stone lithograph and was sold by the thousands at the 1876 Centennial Exposition in Philadelphia. See plate 636.

WILLIAMS, Gaar B. (1880 – 1935)
Born: Richmond, IN. Residence: Glencoe, IL. Died: Chicago. Studied: Cincinnati Artists School; Art Institute of Chicago. Illustrator: *Indianapolis News,* 1919. Cartoon strips: "Just Plain Folks" for 14 years, distributed by the *Chicago Tribune;* New York News Syndicate.

WILLIAMS, Otey
Painter who resided in Philadelphia, PA. Contributor to the *Philadelphia Public Ledger.*

WIREMAN, K. R. (Katharine Richardson)
Residence: Germantown, PA. Wireman did cover illustration art for *Country Gentleman,* as well as numerous other publications between 1915 and 1925. She produced most of her work from a studio she maintained in Philadelphia.

WORTH, Thos. (1834 – 1917)
Born in New York City, Worth was an artist who was in on the birth of several important media and genres — and not just by chance. An art student at the Wells studio in New York, he later became the most prominent of Currier and Ives's humorous artists in the period of that lithographic firm's greatest popularity. He designed hundreds of prints (the lithographers always transferred then to stone), his most popular series being "Darktown." In the early 1870s Worth was the first major cartoonist to contribute regularly to the *New York Graphic,* America's first illustrated daily paper. Ten years later he was a main-stay of the new *Judge* magazine, also drawing for Truth a few years later. In the late 1890's he was one of the first artists to draw cartoons for William Randolph Hearst's *American Humorist* newspaper comic supplement. Later drawing for other papers and dabbling in the strip genre, Thomas Worth pioneered in many areas of cartooning. See Plate 570.

WRIGHT, Jud
Cartoonist from Los Angeles, CA.

WYETH, Newell Convers (1882 – 1945)
Residence: Chadds Ford, PA, Port Clyde, ME. Died: in a railroad accident near Chadds Ford. Studied: Mechanics Art School, Boston, 1899; Massachusetts Normal Art School with R. Andrew; Eric Pape School, Boston with G. L. Noyes, C. W. Reed; H. Pyle, 1902 – 1911. Member: Society of Illustrators, 1912; Wilmington Society of Fine Arts; Philadelphia Alliance; Chester Country Art Association; Full Member, National Academy of Design, 1941. Exhibited: Philadelphia Watercolor Club, 1910 (prize); Panama-Pacific Expo., San Francisco, 1915 (gold); Washington Society of Artists, 1931 (medal); Macbeth Gallery, New York, 1930 (one-man show). Work: murals, Capitol Missouri; Hotel Traymore, Atlantic City; Reading Museum of Fine Arts, various banks. One of Pyle's leading students, Wyeth produced more than 3,000 illustrations for hundreds of articles, numerous posters and more than 100 books. His best know book illustrations include, *Treasure Island, Kidnapped, Black Arrow,* all by Robert L. Stevenson; *Deerslayer, Last of the Mohicans, Robin Hood, Drums,* and *Robinson Crusoe.* After painting in oils for many years, Wyeth turned to the egg tempera medium and began to paint more for exhibitions. He encouraged an interest in the arts in his children. Daughters, Henriette and Caroline are both accomplished painters; son, Andrew, is famous as a painter. At the time of his death, N. C. Wyeth was one of America's best loved illustrators. See plate 677.

YOUNG, Crawford
Contributor to *Life* magazine, as well as various other periodicals from approximately 1912 through 1932.

Bibliography

Cartoon History of United States Foreign Police, A. New York: William Morrow and Company, 1975.

Fielding, Mantle. *Dictionary of American Painters, Sculptors and Engravers.* Green Farms, CT: Modern Books and Crafts, Inc.,1926, 1974.

Horwitz, Elinor Lander. *The Bird, the Banner and Uncle Sam: Images of America in Folk and Popular Art.* Philadelphia and New York: J. B. Lippincott Company, 1976.

Image of America in Caricature & Cartoon, The. Fort Worth, TX: Amon Carter Museum of Western Art.

Ludwig, Coy. *Maxfield Parrish.* New York: Watson-Guptill Publications, 1973.

Mallett, Daniel Trowbridge. *Mallett's Index of Artists.* New York: Peter Smith, 1935.

Mastai, Boleslaw and Marie-Louise D'otrange. *The Stars and the Stripes: The American Flags Art and as History from the Birth of the Republic to the Present.* New York: Alfred A Knopf, 1973.

Mott, Frank Luther. *A History of American Magazines.* Cambridge, Massachusetts: The Belknap Press of Harvard University Press, 1957.

Pitz, Henry C. *200 Years of American Illustration.* New York: Random House, 1977.

Reed, Walt and Roger. *The Illustrator in America, 1880 – 1980: A Century of Illustration.* New York: Madison Square Press, Inc., 1984.

Roering, Fred and Joyce Herndon. *Collector's Encyclopedia of Cookie Jars, Book II.* Paducah, KY: Collector Books, 1994.

Samuels, Peggy and Harold. *Samuels' Encyclopedia of Artists of the American West.* Castle, Inc., 1985.

Who Was Who In American Art. Madison, CT: Sound View Press, 1985.

Who's Who in American Art. New York and London: Jaques Cattell Press, 1973.

World Encyclopedia of Cartoons, The. New York and London: Chelsea House Publishers, 1980.

Uncle Sam. Who Is He? Directed by Ray W. Steele, 1981.

About The Author

Gerald Czulewicz began collecting and researching art as a teenager in Erie, Pennsylvania, his hometown. His interest in rare American books and documents led to his lifelong fascination with Americana, particularly the image of Uncle Sam. His fascination with this national symbol led him to seek out the works of numerous American illustrators, especially the key Uncle Sam artists, Thomas Nast and James Montgomery Flagg, from whose estates he acquired numerous original drawings, watercolors, documents, and photographs. The Uncle Sam costumes used by models for both Nast and Flagg are among the many unique and fascinating artifacts which he has acquired in decades of researching and pursuing obscure leads in order to compile his collection. With over 4,000 objects, Mr. Czulewicz's collection of Uncle Sam art and objects is the largest of its kind in the world.

Professionally, Mr. Czulewicz has been actively involved as a dealer and appraiser of nineteenth and early twentieth century American works of art, working on a regular basis with major American museums, historical societies, corporate collections as well as in the private sector, for the past 25 years. During this time, he passionately pursued his interests as an American art historian and lecturer for the National Endowment for the Arts. He was regional director of the International Society of Appraisers and is actively involved as a board member of the Shakespeare Globe Center in London, England; The Roger Pruess Art Museum of Waterville, Minnesota; and The Rainbow Children's Museum, Inc., Judy Garland's Birthplace at Grand Rapids, Minnesota; and is a member of numerous organizations, including the National Arts Club of New York; the American Art Appraisers Association; the C.M. Russell Museum in Great Falls, Montana; and the Chelsea Club and Sloan Club in London, England. He has been actively involved for the past eight years in Washington DC as a sponsor member of the Decorative Arts Committees of both the U. S. Department of State and Blair House in Washington DC and in 1991 was officially recognized as Philanthropist to the Arts for his numerous contributions to the national collection through his involvement with the diplomatic reception rooms of the U.S. Department of State and Blair House. Gerald, and his wife, Barbara Jean reside in Minnesota, where they continue to pursue their interests in art, music, and American antiques, as Gerald applies himself toward his long-awaited career as an artist and song writer.

Books on Collectibles

This is only a partial listing of the books on antiques that are available from Collector Books. All books are well illustrated and contain current values. Most of the following books are available from your local bookseller, antique dealer, or public library. If you are unable to locate certain titles in your area, you may order by mail from COLLECTOR BOOKS, P.O. Box 3009, Paducah, KY 42002-3009. Customers with Visa or MasterCard may phone in orders from 7:00–4:00 CST, Monday–Friday, Toll Free 1-800-626-5420. Add $2.00 for postage for the first book ordered and $0.30 for each additional book. Include item number, title, and price when ordering. Allow 14 to 21 days for delivery.

DOLLS, FIGURES & TEDDY BEARS

2382	**Advertising Dolls**, Identification & Values, Robison & Sellers	$9.95
2079	**Barbie** Doll Fashions, Volume I, Eames	$24.95
3957	**Barbie** Exclusives, Rana	$18.95
3310	**Black Dolls**, 1820–1991, Perkins	$17.95
3873	**Black Dolls**, Book II, Perkins	$17.95
3810	**Chatty Cathy** Dolls, Lewis	$15.95
2021	Collector's **Male Action Figures**, Manos	$14.95
1529	Collector's Encyclopedia of **Barbie** Dolls, DeWein	$19.95
3727	Collector's Guide to **Ideal Dolls**, Izen	$18.95
3728	Collector's Guide to Miniature **Teddy Bears**, Powell	$17.95
4506	**Dolls in Uniform**, Bourgeois	$18.95
3967	Collector's Guide to **Trolls**, Peterson	$19.95
1067	**Madame Alexander** Dolls, Smith	$19.95
3971	**Madame Alexander** Dolls Price Guide #20, Smith	$9.95
2185	**Modern Collector's** Dolls I, Smith	$17.95
2186	**Modern Collector's** Dolls II, Smith	$17.95
2187	**Modern Collector's** Dolls III, Smith	$17.95
2188	**Modern Collector's** Dolls IV, Smith	$17.95
2189	**Modern Collector's** Dolls V, Smith	$17.95
3733	**Modern Collector's** Dolls, Sixth Series, Smith	$24.95
3991	**Modern Collector's** Dolls, Seventh Series, Smith	$24.95
3472	**Modern Collector's** Dolls Update, Smith	$9.95
3972	Patricia Smith's **Doll Values**, Antique to Modern, 11th Edition	$12.95
3826	Story of **Barbie**, Westenhouser	$19.95
1513	**Teddy Bears & Steiff** Animals, Mandel	$9.95
1817	**Teddy Bears & Steiff** Animals, 2nd Series, Mandel	$19.95
2084	**Teddy Bears, Annalee's & Steiff** Animals, 3rd Series, Mandel	$19.95
1808	**Wonder of Barbie**, Manos	$9.95
1430	**World of Barbie** Dolls, Manos	$9.95

TOYS, MARBLES & CHRISTMAS COLLECTIBLES

3427	**Advertising Character** Collectibles, Dotz	$17.95
2333	Antique & Collector's **Marbles**, 3rd Ed., Grist	$9.95
3827	Antique & Collector's **Toys**, 1870–1950, Longest	$24.95
3956	Baby Boomer **Games**, Identification & Value Guide, Polizzi	$24.95
1514	Character **Toys** & Collectibles, Longest	$19.95
1750	Character **Toys** & Collector's, 2nd Series, Longest	$19.95
3717	**Christmas** Collectibles, 2nd Edition, Whitmyer	$24.95
1752	**Christmas** Ornaments, Lights & Decorations, Johnson	$19.95
3874	Collectible Coca-Cola Toy **Trucks**, deCourtivron	$24.95
2338	Collector's Encyclopedia of **Disneyana**, Longest, Stern	$24.95
2151	Collector's Guide to **Tootsietoys**, Richter	$16.95
3436	Grist's Big Book of **Marbles**	$19.95
3970	Grist's Machine-Made & Contemporary **Marbles**, 2nd Ed.	$9.95
3732	**Matchbox®** Toys, 1948 to 1993, Johnson	$18.95
3823	**Mego** Toys, An Illustrated Value Guide, Chrouch	15.95
1540	**Modern Toys** 1930–1980, Baker	$19.95
3888	**Motorcycle** Toys, Antique & Contemporary, Gentry/Downs	$18.95
3891	Schroeder's Collectible **Toys**, Antique to Modern Price Guide	$17.95
1886	Stern's Guide to **Disney** Collectibles	$14.95
2139	Stern's Guide to **Disney** Collectibles, 2nd Series	$14.95
3975	Stern's Guide to **Disney** Collectibles, 3rd Series	$18.95
2028	**Toys**, Antique & Collectible, Longest	$14.95
3975	**Zany Characters** of the Ad World, Lamphier	$16.95

JEWELRY, HATPINS, WATCHES & PURSES

1712	Antique & Collector's **Thimbles** & Accessories, Mathis	$19.95
1748	Antique **Purses**, Revised Second Ed., Holiner	$19.95
1278	Art Nouveau & Art Deco **Jewelry**, Baker	$9.95
3875	Collecting Antique **Stickpins**, Kerins	$16.95
3722	Collector's Ency. of **Compacts, Carryalls & Face Powder Boxes**, Mueller	$24.95
3992	Complete Price Guide to **Watches**, #15, Shugart	$21.95
1716	Fifty Years of Collector's **Fashion Jewelry**, 1925-1975, Baker	$19.95
1424	**Hatpins** & Hatpin Holders, Baker	$9.95
1181	100 Years of Collectible **Jewelry**, Baker	$9.95
2348	20th Century Fashionable Plastic **Jewelry**, Baker	$19.95
3830	Vintage **Vanity Bags & Purses**, Gerson	$24.95

FURNITURE

1457	American **Oak** Furniture, McNerney	$9.95
3716	American **Oak** Furniture, Book II, McNerney	$12.95
1118	Antique **Oak** Furniture, Hill	$7.95
2132	Collector's Encyclopedia of **American** Furniture, Vol. I, Swedberg	$24.95
2271	Collector's Encyclopedia of **American** Furniture, Vol. II, Swedberg	$24.95
3720	Collector's Encyclopedia of **American** Furniture, Vol. III, Swedberg	$24.95
1437	Collector's Guide to **Country** Furniture, Raycraft	$9.95
3878	Collector's Guide to **Oak** Furniture, George	$12.95
1755	Furniture of the **Depression Era**, Swedberg	$19.95
3906	**Heywood-Wakefield** Modern Furniture, Rouland	$18.95
1965	**Pine** Furniture, Our American Heritage, McNerney	$14.95
1885	**Victorian** Furniture, Our American Heritage, McNerney	$9.95
3829	**Victorian** Furniture, Our American Heritage, Book II, McNerney	$9.95
3869	**Victorian** Furniture books, 2 volume set, McNerney	$19.90

INDIANS, GUNS, KNIVES, TOOLS, PRIMITIVES

1868	Antique **Tools**, Our American Heritage, McNerney	$9.95
2015	Archaic **Indian** Points & Knives, Edler	$14.95
1426	**Arrowheads** & Projectile Points, Hothem	$7.95
1668	**Flint Blades** & Projectile Points of the North American Indian, Tully	$24.95
2279	**Indian** Artifacts of the Midwest, Hothem	$14.95
3885	**Indian** Artifacts of the Midwest, Book II, Hothem	$16.95
1964	**Indian** Axes & Related Stone Artifacts, Hothem	$14.95
2023	**Keen Kutter** Collectibles, Heuring	$14.95
3887	Modern **Guns**, Identification & Values, 10th Ed., Quertermous	$12.95
2164	**Primitives**, Our American Heritage, McNerney	$9.95
1759	**Primitives**, Our American Heritage, Series II, McNerney	$14.95
3325	Standard **Knife** Collector's Guide, 2nd Ed., Ritchie & Stewart	$12.95

PAPER COLLECTIBLES & BOOKS

1441	Collector's Guide to **Post Cards**, Wood	$9.95
2081	Guide to Collecting **Cookbooks**, Allen	$14.95
3969	Huxford's **Old Book** Value Guide, 7th Ed.	$19.95
3821	Huxford's **Paperback** Value Guide	$19.95
2080	Price Guide to **Cookbooks** & Recipe Leaflets, Dickinson	$9.95
2346	**Sheet Music** Reference & Price Guide, Pafik & Guiheen	$18.95

OTHER COLLECTIBLES

2280	Advertising **Playing Cards**, Grist	$16.95
2269	Antique **Brass & Copper** Collectibles, Gaston	$16.95
1880	Antique **Iron**, McNerney	$9.95
3872	Antique **Tins**, Dodge	$24.95
1714	**Black** Collectibles, Gibbs	$19.95
1128	**Bottle** Pricing Guide, 3rd Ed., Cleveland	$7.95
3959	**Cereal Box** Bonanza, The 1950's, Bruce	$19.95
3718	Collector's **Aluminum**, Grist	$16.95
3445	Collectible **Cats**, An Identification & Value Guide, Fyke	$18.95
1634	Collector's Ency. of Figural & Novelty **Salt & Pepper Shakers**, Davern	$19.95
2020	Collector's Ency. of Figural & Novelty **Salt & Pepper Shakers**, Vol. II, Davern	$19.95
2018	Collector's Encyclopedia of **Granite Ware**, Greguire	$24.95
3430	Collector's Encyclopedia of **Granite Ware**, Book II, Greguire	$24.95
3879	Collector's Guide to Antique **Radios**, 3rd Ed., Bunis	$18.95
1916	Collector's Guide to **Art Deco**, Gaston	$14.95
3880	Collector's Guide to **Cigarette Lighters**, Flanagan	$17.95
1537	Collector's Guide to **Country Baskets**, Raycraft	$9.95
3966	Collector's Guide to **Inkwells**, Identification & Values, Badders	$18.95
3881	Collector's Guide to **Novelty Radios**, Bunis/Breed	$18.95
3729	Collector's Guide to **Snow Domes**, Guarnaccia	$18.95
3730	Collector's Guide to **Transistor Radios**, Bunis	$15.95
2276	**Decoys**, Kangas	$24.95
1629	**Doorstops**, Identification & Values, Bertoia	$9.95
3968	**Fishing Lure** Collectibles, Murphy/Edmisten	$24.95
3817	**Flea Market Trader**, 9th Ed., Huxford	$12.95
3819	**General Store** Collectibles, Wilson	$24.95
2215	Goldstein's **Coca-Cola** Collectibles	$16.95
3884	Huxford's Collector's **Advertising**, 2nd Ed.	$24.95
2216	**Kitchen Antiques**, 1790–1940, McNerney	$14.95
1782	1,000 **Fruit Jars**, 5th Edition, Schroeder	$5.95
3321	Ornamental & Figural **Nutcrackers**, Rittenhouse	$16.95
2026	**Railroad** Collectibles, 4th Ed., Baker	$14.95
1632	**Salt & Pepper Shakers**, Guarnaccia	$9.95
1888	**Salt & Pepper Shakers** II, Identification & Value Guide, Book II, Guarnaccia	$14.95
2220	**Salt & Pepper Shakers** III, Guarnaccia	$14.95
3443	**Salt & Pepper Shakers** IV, Guarnaccia	$18.95
2096	**Silverplated Flatware**, Revised 4th Edition, Hagan	$14.95
1922	Standard **Old Bottle** Price Guide, Sellari	$14.95
3892	**Toy & Miniature Sewing Machines**, Thomas	$18.95
3828	Value Guide to **Advertising Memorabilia**, Summers	$18.95
3977	Value Guide to **Gas Station** Memorabilia	$24.95
3444	**Wanted to Buy**, 5th Edition	$9.95

Schroeder's
ANTIQUES
Price Guide

. . . is the #1 best-selling antiques & collectibles value guide on the market today, and here's why . . .

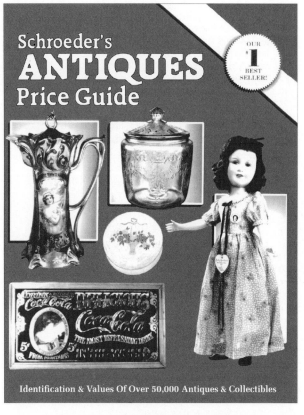

Schroeder's
ANTIQUES
Price Guide

OUR #1 BEST SELLER!

Identification & Values Of Over 50,000 Antiques & Collectibles

8½ x 11, 608 Pages, $14.95

• *More than 300 advisors, well-known dealers, and top-notch collectors work together with our editors to bring you accurate information regarding pricing and identification.*

• *More than 45,000 items in almost 500 categories are listed along with hundreds of sharp original photos that illustrate not only the rare and unusual, but the common, popular collectibles as well.*

• *Each large close-up shot shows important details clearly. Every subject is represented with histories and background information, a feature not found in any of our competitors' publications.*

• *Our editors keep abreast of newly developing trends, often adding several new categories a year as the need arises.*

If it merits the interest of today's collector, you'll find it in *Schroeder's*. And you can feel confident that the information we publish is up to date and accurate. Our advisors thoroughly check each category to spot inconsistencies, listings that may not be entirely reflective of market dealings, and lines too vague to be of merit. Only the best of the lot remains for publication.

Without doubt, you'll find
SCHROEDER'S ANTIQUES PRICE GUIDE
the only one to buy for
reliable information and values.

COLLECTOR BOOKS
A Division of Schroeder Publishing Co., Inc.